Mass Unemployment and the State

Mass Unemployment and the State

Johannes Lindvall

OXFORD
UNIVERSITY PRESS

OXFORD

UNIVERSITY PRESS

Great Clarendon Street, Oxford OX2 6DP

Oxford University Press is a department of the University of Oxford.
It furthers the University's objective of excellence in research, scholarship,
and education by publishing worldwide in

Oxford New York

Auckland Cape Town Dar es Salaam Hong Kong Karachi
Kuala Lumpur Madrid Melbourne Mexico City Nairobi
New Delhi Shanghai Taipei Toronto

With offices in

Argentina Austria Brazil Chile Czech Republic France Greece
Guatemala Hungary Italy Japan Poland Portugal Singapore
South Korea Switzerland Thailand Turkey Ukraine Vietnam

Oxford is a registered trade mark of Oxford University Press
in the UK and in certain other countries

Published in the United States
by Oxford University Press Inc., New York

British Library Cataloguing in Publication Data

Data available

Library of Congress Cataloging in Publication Data

Data available

Typeset by SPI Publisher Services, Pondicherry, India
Printed in Great Britain
on acid-free paper by
MPG Books Group, Bodmin and King's Lynn

ISBN 978–0–19–959064–3

1 3 5 7 9 10 8 6 4 2

Preface

Ever since the mid-1970s, the problem of unemployment has defined politics in Western Europe, but European governments have chosen different policy responses. On the basis of an investigation of policymaking in Austria, Denmark, the Netherlands, and Sweden, this book argues that the variation in economic and labor market policies across countries and over time is, at least partly, a result of developments in domestic politics. Low unemployment was the linchpin of political arrangements in West European states in the first decades after the Second World War. When mass unemployment became a threat once more in the 1970s, Austria and Sweden, where the postwar political order remained intact, therefore responded more forcefully than Denmark and the Netherlands, where political arrangements were already changing. This set these four countries on different paths, with enduring political, economic, and social consequences.

Austria, Denmark, the Netherlands, and Sweden have all been celebrated as employment miracles, but for different reasons, and at different points in time. Austria was renowned for its economic performance in the 1970s, when the *Financial Times* and the *International Herald Tribune* praised the policies of its social democratic government. Sweden's time came in the mid-1980s, when its social democratic government appeared to have found an alternative to the harsh policies of the new right. In 1987, for instance, the *Economist* wrote that the Swedish economy worked "like a dream." By the 1990s, the Dutch labor market model received a lot of attention, and the President of the United States, Bill Clinton, said that the Netherlands put "the 'third way' into practice before anyone else." In the 2000s, international observers—and the European Commission—celebrated Denmark's model of "flexicurity," which promised to meet the requirements of a postindustrial economy while preserving the solidarity of the welfare state. This book describes the political circumstances and considerations that shaped and motivated these different attempts to deal with the problem of unemployment.

At the time of writing, in 2010, the topic of unemployment has acquired an urgency that I did not expect when I began this project. When the financial crisis that began in 2007 generated a full-blown macroeconomic crisis in the autumn of 2008, unemployment rose markedly in most industrialized democracies. The main reason why we should care about this is that unemployment is a "major source of human misery," as Richard Layard, Stephen Nickell, and Richard Jackman put it in their famous book *Unemployment*. But students and scholars of government and politics have additional reasons. Unemployment has important political consequences, and political circumstances matter greatly to the policies governments use to address this economic and social problem. An analysis of the politics of unemployment from the 1970s onward may help us to better understand present and future economic crises, and their effects.

Many scholars have helped me with this project. Christian Huber, Malte Ibsen, and Gabriëlle Krapels provided excellent research assistance. Herbert Obinger, Thomas Paster, Otto Penz, and Martin Pletersek were kind enough to answer all my questions about Austria. Balder Asmussen, Lotte Jensen, Lars Bo Kaspersen, Christoffer Green-Pedersen, Martin Marcussen, and Ulrich Schmidt-Hansen helped me to understand the Danish case better. Karen Anderson, Uwe Becker, Anton Hemerijck, Corina Hendriks, Rick van der Ploug, Jelle Visser, and Steven Wolinetz were kind enough to share some of their knowledge of the Netherlands. Jenny Andersson, Hans Bergström, Kristina Boréus, Johan Davidsson, Marie Demker, Björn Elmbrant, the late Nils Elvander, Tomas Englund, Jakob Gustavsson, Jörgen Hermansson, Christine Ingebritsen, Lars Jonung, Peeter-Jaan Kask, Jessica Lindvert, Ulf P. Lundgren, Ulf Olsson, Bo Sandelin, Helena Stensöta, Urban Strandberg, Mats Svegfors, Torsten Svensson, Torsten Sverenius, Åsa Vifell, and Per-Ola Öberg have told me many things that I did not know about my own country, Sweden. I owe general intellectual debts to Nancy Bermeo, Pablo Beramendi, Mark Blyth, Jonas Hinnfors, Peter Katzenstein, Desmond King, Jonas Pontusson, Bo Rothstein, David Rueda, Martin Seeleib-Kaiser, David Soskice, Sven Steinmo, Peter Swenson, and Timo Weishaupt. Four anonymous reviewers for Oxford University Press offered detailed advice on how to improve the manuscript.

My work on economic policy, labor market policy, and the politics of unemployment has been carried out at three academic institutions. It began with a dissertation on Swedish macroeconomic policy, written at the Department of Political Science in Gothenburg in 1998–2004. My subsequent research on Austria, Denmark, and the Netherlands commenced while I worked as a research fellow in the research project *Smallcons*, also in Gothenburg, in 2004–5, and continued while I was a STINT fellow at the European University Institute in Florence in 2006. The final version of the book was written in 2007–10, when I was the Samuel Finer Post-Doctoral Fellow in Comparative Government at the Department of Politics and International Relations, Oxford University, and a Fellow of Lincoln College, Oxford.

I gratefully acknowledge financial support from the Bank of Sweden Tercentenary Foundation (which funded the program *The Fall of the Strong State*), the European Union Fifth Framework Programme (which funded the program *Smallcons*), the Fulbright Foundation, the Swedish Foundation for International Cooperation in Research and Higher Education, the Royal Swedish Academy of Sciences, the Royal Society of Arts and Sciences, Helge Ax:son Johnsons stiftelse, Knut och Alice Wallenbergs stiftelse, Wilhelm och Martina Lundgrens stiftelse, Harald och Louise Ekmans stiftelse, Stiftelsen Siamon, Paul och Marie Berghaus donationsfond, Göteborgs universitets jubileumsfond, Kungliga och Hvitfeltska stiftelsen, and the Zilkha Fund at Lincoln College, Oxford.

Some of the ideas and results that I present in the book have previously been presented in "The Politics of Purpose" (*Comparative Politics* 38:3, 2006; reprinted with permission), "Sweden: The Fall of the Strong State" (*Scandinavian Political Studies* 29:1, 2006; with Bo Rothstein), "Party Competition and the Resilience of Corporatism" (*Government and Opposition* 44:2, 2009; with Mette Anthonsen), and "The Real but Limited Influence of Experts" by Johannes Lindvall (*World Politics* 61:4, October 2009 Copyright © 2009 Trustees of Princeton University; reprinted with the permission of Cambridge University Press).

This book owes a great deal to the generosity of the present and former government ministers, central bank governors, civil servants, and economic experts who let me interview them about their experiences of economic policymaking and labor market policymaking. All those I have interviewed are listed in Appendix B. It goes without saying that the interviewees are not responsible for any errors on my part. Three of the interviewees are no longer alive: the Danish politician Anders Andersen and the Swedish politician Jan Bergqvist died in 2006, and the Danish politician Svend Auken died in 2009. They were different in many ways, but they were equally kind and patient with me when I sought their help with this project.

My mother, Ingrid, gave me some German lessons. Carl Dahlström, colleague and friend, read the manuscript in its entirety. So did my father, Lars, and my wife, Johanna. Our two young sons, Otto and Ingemar, would also have been happy to help, I think, if they had known how to read. Their time will come; I suspect that they will soon know more than their father about a great many things.

Contents

Contents

List of Figures

List of Tables

Abbreviations

ALMPs	Active labor market policies
AMS (Austria)	*Arbeitsmarktservice* (the Austrian public employment service)
AMS (Sweden)	*Arbetsmarknadsstyrelsen* (the Swedish public employment service)
ARP	*Anti-Revolutionaire Partij* (a Dutch Protestant Christian democratic party)
BGBl	*Bundesgesetzblatt für die Republik Österreich*
BZÖ	*Bündnis Zukunft Österreich* (an Austrian far-right party)
c	*Centerpartiet* (the Centre Party, a Swedish center-right party)
CD	*Centrumdemokraterne* (the Center Democrats, a Danish centrist party)
CDA	*Christen Democratisch Appèl* (a Dutch Christian democratic party)
CPB	*Centraal Planbureau* (The Netherlands bureau for economic policy analysis)
CU	*ChristenUnie* (a Dutch Christian party)
D66	*Democraten 66* (Democrats 66, a Dutch social liberal party)
DF	*Dansk Folkeparti* (the Danish People's Party, a far-right party)
EC	The European Community
EMU	The Economic and Monetary Union
EU	The European Union
FNV	*Federatie Nederlandse Vakbeweging* (a Dutch trade union federation)

fp	*Folkpartiet liberalerna*, until 1990 *Folkpartiet* (a Swedish liberal party)
FPÖ	*Freiheitliche Partei Österreichs* (an Austrian far-right party, formerly liberal)
GDP	gross domestic product
ILO	The International Labour Organization
IMF	The International Monetary Fund
kd, kds	*Kristdemokraterna*, 1987–1996 *Kristdemokratiska samhällspartiet*, until 1987 *Kristen Demokratisk Samling* (a Swedish Christian democratic party)
KF	*Det Konservative Folkeparti* (a Danish conservative party)
KrF	*Kristeligt Folkeparti* (a Danish Christian democratic party)
KVP	*Katholieke Volkspartij* (a Dutch Catholic Christian democratic party)
LO (Denmark)	*Landsorganisationen i Danmark* (The Danish Confederation of Trade Unions)
LO (Sweden)	*Landsorganisationen i Sverige* (The Swedish Trade Union Confederation)
LPF	*Lijst Pim Fortuyn* (a Dutch far-right party)
m	*Moderata samlingspartiet* (a Swedish conservative party)
NVV	*Nederlands Verbond van Vakverenigingen* (a Dutch social democratic trade union; merged with a Catholic trade union in 1976 to form the FNV)
nyd	*Ny Demokrati* (a Swedish far-right party)
OECD	The Organisation for Economic Co-operation and Development
ÖGB	*Österreichischer Gewerkschaftsbund* (the Austrian Trade Union Federation)
OPEC	The Organization of Petroleum Exporting Countries
ÖVP	*Österreichische Volkspartei* (an Austrian Christian democratic party)
PPR	*Politieke Partij Radikalen* (a Dutch left-wing party)
PvdA	*Partij van de Arbeid* (a Dutch social democratic party)

RV   *Det Radikale Venstre* (a Danish social liberal party)

s, SAP *Sveriges socialdemokratiska arbetareparti* (a Swedish social democratic party)

S   *Socialdemokratiet* (a Danish social democratic party)

SAF   *Svenska arbetsgivareföreningen* (the Swedish Employers' Confederation)

SER   *Sociaal Economische Raad* (the Social and Economic Council, a Dutch corporatist institution)

SPÖ   *Sozialdemokratische Partei Österreichs*, until 1991 *Sozialistische Partei Österreichs* (an Austrian social democratic party)

v, vpk *Vänsterpartiet*, until 1990 *Vänsterpartiet kommunisterna*, until 1967 *Sveriges kommunistiska parti* (a Swedish left-wing party, formerly communist)

V   *Venstre* (a Danish liberal party)

VVD   *Volkspartij voor Vrijheid en Democratie* (a Dutch conservative-liberal party)

WKÖ   *Wirtschaftskammer Österreichs* (the Austrian Chamber of Commerce)

WRR   *Wetenschappelijke Raad voor het Regeringsbeleid* (the Scientific Council for Government Policy, a Dutch government agency)

1

The Unemployment Problem in Europe

In the 1970s and 1980s, mass unemployment returned to Western Europe. Its return was unexpected, for in the 1950s and 1960s unemployment was widely regarded as a thing of the past, associated with the social and political evils of the interwar years. Politicians and economists were confident that modern techniques of economic management would enable rich, democratic states to maintain low levels of unemployment. The state should ensure that there were enough jobs, and it had the means to do so—that was the dominant thinking a generation ago.

Ever since the 1970s, the problem of unemployment has been one of the most salient political issues in Europe. This book is concerned with what European politicians have done about unemployment and what unemployment has done to European politics from the early 1970s to the mid-2000s. Drawing on official documents, archives, and more than eighty interviews with policymakers, the book examines political responses to rising unemployment in four states whose policies and experiences were surprisingly different: Austria, Denmark, the Netherlands, and Sweden.

The first question that I seek to answer is why these four states responded differently to the *threat* of unemployment in the 1970s and 1980s. Whereas Danish and Dutch governments believed themselves unable to prevent an increase in unemployment early on, in the mid-1970s, Austria and Sweden were among the last European states to change the main objective of economic policy from full employment to low inflation and balanced budgets. The second question is why these four states adjusted differently to the *fact* of unemployment in the 1990s and 2000s. Denmark and the Netherlands have become famous for a series of labor market and social policy reforms that were designed to reduce unemployment and increase employment, creating a model of labor market policy that is now known as "flexicurity." In Austria and Sweden, labor market reforms have been more cautious, and in many cases adopted to cut costs, not to increase employment.

Unemployment returned at a time of major political changes in European democracies. Most importantly, the 1970s and 1980s was a period when the *postwar settlement*—the uncommonly stable political order that had characterized the 1950s and 1960s—unraveled in many European countries. But domestic political arrangements were more stable in some countries than others. When the European economy went into recession in the mid-1970s, they were still intact in Austria and Sweden, but not in Denmark and the Netherlands. This mattered greatly to the subsequent development of economic policies and labor market policies in these four countries. It mattered to economic policies in the 1970s and 1980s since governments in Austria and Sweden used economic policy as an outer line of defense to protect their political models, unlike governments in Denmark and the Netherlands, where political arrangements had already changed. It mattered to labor market policies in the 1990s and 2000s since governments in Denmark and the Netherlands, where postwar political models had now been reformed and renegotiated, were prepared to develop and implement new labor market policies, especially since the long period of high unemployment rates in the 1970s and 1980s had changed the beliefs and work preferences of the main political parties and interest organizations.

This book makes two contributions to the literature. First, and most importantly, it demonstrates that the politics of unemployment can only be understood against the background of profound political changes in European states. Contemporary research in political economy is dominated by structural–institutional approaches to politics, and hence by explanatory models that explain policy changes with reference to underlying social and economic factors, not to developments within the political domain itself. This book brings politics back in. The belief that governments were able to solve the problem of unemployment was a core element in the set of norms that defined West European politics in the first decades after the Second World War. This meant that the threat of unemployment was more than a policy challenge—it was a *political* challenge, threatening to undermine a certain way of doing politics.

Second, this book presents an analysis of economic policymaking and labor market policymaking over a period of more than three decades, from the early 1970s to the mid-2000s. With a few important exceptions (notably the contributions to Scharpf and Schmidt 2000), economic policy and labor market policy have been studied by different scholars, who have based their analyses on different theoretical assumptions. Many previous studies have therefore had limited scope, dealing either with the period when governments responded to the *threat* of unemployment (i.e., to the shocks of the 1970s and 1980s) or with the period when governments adjusted to the *fact* of unemployment (the 1990s and 2000s). This book is concerned with both.

My argument contradicts, in important ways, previous research on economic policies and labor market reforms in Europe. The dominant explanation of the variation in economic policy priorities in the 1970s and 1980s is concerned with labor market institutions and the relationship between governments and central banks. I argue, however, that what distinguished Austria and Sweden from Denmark and the Netherlands was not primarily their institutional capacity; it was the fact that political elites in these two countries assumed that established institutions must be preserved. The dominant explanation of the variation in labor market reform intensity in the 1990s and 2000s is that politicians in some countries have developed reform discourses, convincing voters of the necessity of change, whereas politicians in other countries have not. The weakness of this argument is that the ability of politicians to develop reform discourses remains unexplained. This book will show that political circumstances in Denmark and the Netherlands in the 1990s were conducive to large-scale labor market reforms, given their prior history of mass unemployment and political change.

Research Design

Figure 1.1 describes the mean unemployment rate in the thirteen European countries that have been democracies continuously since the end of the Second World War (excluding countries with fewer than 1 million inhabitants): Austria, Belgium, Denmark, Finland, France, Germany, Ireland, Italy, the Netherlands, Norway, Sweden, Switzerland, and the United Kingdom. In the 1960s and early 1970s, average unemployment in this group of countries was low (approximately 2 percent of the labor force), but the economic downturns of the mid-1970s, early 1980s, and early 1990s all led to lasting increases in unemployment rates.

Although all European democracies have experienced increasing unemployment since the early 1970s, the experiences of individual countries have been far from uniform. Two cross-country differences are particularly

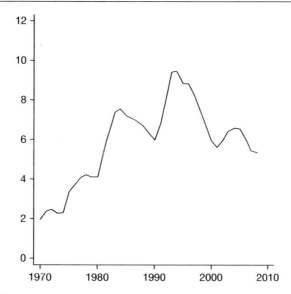

Figure 1.1 The return of mass unemployment in Europe

Data source: OECD (2009*a*). The line represents the mean unemployment rate in the thirteen European countries that have been democracies since the Second World War, excluding countries with a population of less than 1 million.

striking. First, in the 1970s and 1980s, unemployment increased sooner and more steeply in some countries than others. Second, in the 1990s, some countries that had long suffered from high unemployment achieved significant reductions, while others did not. Although unemployment is not just a function of public policy, but also of factors that governments cannot control, it seems clear that at least some of the cross-country variation in unemployment rates can be attributed to political institutions and the policy choices of governments (Bean 1994, Nickell 1997, and Blanchard 2006 provide comprehensive surveys of the rich literature on European unemployment in economics). An analysis of political circumstances helps to explain why countries made different policy choices in these two crucial periods.

When unemployment became a threat once more in the 1970s, some countries used the instruments of macroeconomic policy to ensure that domestic economic activity was high enough to sustain more or less full employment. Austria and Sweden—and also Norway—pursued employment-oriented macroeconomic policies well into the 1980s, much longer than other European countries, such as Denmark and the Netherlands, which changed the primary objective of economic policy from full employment to low inflation and balanced budgets already in the mid-1970s. Later on, when mass unemployment had become a fact of life in many European societies, governments started to treat unemployment as a microeconomic problem, reforming their labor market policies in order to ensure that the unemployed were looking for jobs, well-trained, and matched with employers willing to hire them. Here, Denmark and the Netherlands have belonged to the most reform-intensive countries in Europe—in the 1990s, they undertook comprehensive labor market and social policy reforms that were explicitly designed to increase employment and reduce unemployment.

The question why Austria, Denmark, the Netherlands, and Sweden pursued different economic and labor market policies in the 1970s, 1980s, 1990s, and 2000s is not merely of academic interest. Figure 1.2—which compares unemployment in these four countries to the mean rate of unemployment that was reported in Figure 1.1—suggests that their policy choices had important consequences for unemployment. In the beginning of the 1970s, all four countries had unemployment rates of 1–2 percent of the labor force. During most of the 1970s, 1980s, and 1990s, however, their experiences were different. In Denmark and the Netherlands, the increase in unemployment in the mid-1970s was early and steep, and they experienced another jump in unemployment in the early 1980s. In the late 1990s, however, Denmark and the Netherlands achieved unemployment rates of 3–5 percent once more, as a result of the Danish and Dutch "miracles" (Visser and Hemerijck 1997; Schwartz 2001). In Austria and Sweden, unemployment started to increase much later—in the mid-1980s in Austria, and only in the early 1990s in Sweden. Since that time, unemployment appears to have become stuck at a higher level in these two countries. In fact, from the late 1990s to the late 2000s, according to data from the Organisation for Economic Co-operation and Development (OECD), Denmark and the Netherlands had lower unemployment rates than Austria and Sweden.

Although their policies and labor market outcomes have varied, Austria, Denmark, the Netherlands, and Sweden are in many ways quite similar, which makes the fact that they responded differently to the unemployment problem especially intriguing. All four countries are relatively small: in late 2009, the smallest, Denmark, had approximately 5.5 million inhabitants whereas the largest, the Netherlands, had a population of around 16.7 million (the population figures are from the CIA's *World Factbook*; in 2009, according to the same source, the Austrian population

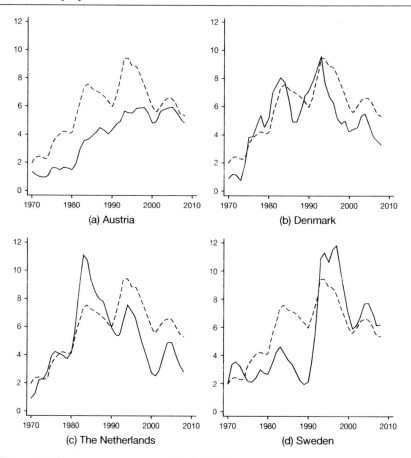

Figure 1.2 Open unemployment, 1970–2008

Data source: OECD (2009a). The dotted line represents the mean unemployment rate in the thirteen European countries that have been democracies since the Second World War, excluding countries with a population of less than 1 million. Unemployment can be measured in different ways, and cross-country comparisons should be interpreted with some caution— not least because national unemployment statistics often differ slightly from those published by international organizations such as the EU, the ILO, and the OECD (used here).

was approximately 8.2 million and the Swedish just over 9 million). Their basic political institutions are also relatively similar: they are parliamentary democracies with proportional electoral systems and more or less unitary state structures (Austria is formally semi-presidential and federal, but it is in practice a parliamentary country with most policy competencies concentrated in the central government; see Müller 2003, 122). Austria and the Netherlands have bicameral parliaments, whereas Denmark and Sweden have both been unicameral in the period considered in this book, but the Austrian and Dutch upper houses—the *Bundesrat* and the *Eerste Kamer der Staten-Generaal*—are relatively powerless (the Huber et al. 2004 dataset categorizes the Austrian constitution as "very weak bicameralism" and the Dutch as "weak bicameralism").

The Austrian, Danish, Dutch, and Swedish welfare states all belong to the most generous in the world (Huber and Stephens 2001, 88–90; Pontusson 2005, 144–6), and for most of the postwar period, their political systems have been characterized by what Peter Katzenstein (1985*b*) has called "democratic corporatism," a mode of policymaking that aims for smooth adjustment to international economic developments by means of negotiations between governments and powerful interest organizations. Scholars of the welfare state sometimes categorize Austria and the Netherlands as conservative welfare states and Denmark and Sweden as social democratic (Esping-Andersen 1990), but in terms of economic and labor market policy, as I will show, Austria and Sweden have in many ways had more in common with each other than with either of the two other countries, and vice versa (for similar reasons, Katzenstein's distinction between "liberal" and "social" corporatism fails to explain why these countries have responded differently to the problem of unemployment: Katzenstein categorizes the Netherlands as liberal, Austria and Denmark as social, and Sweden as a mixture of the two).

Finally, as Figure 1.3 shows, Austria, Denmark, the Netherlands, and Sweden are all open economies, and increasingly so (the trade-to-GDP ratio in Austria, Denmark, and Sweden has increased from 35–50 percent to approximately 100 percent since the 1970s; in the Netherlands, it has increased from 50–60 to 140 percent in the same period). This matters greatly to economic and labor market policymaking, for economic interdependence makes domestic macroeconomic management more involved, since expansionary policies will not only lead to increased demand for domestic products but also for imported goods, and vice versa (Cooper 1968). Moreover, as Peter Katzenstein (1985*b*) has argued, openness increases the demands on a country's capacity for continuous social and labor market policy adjustment.

Governments, political parties, and interest organizations in Austria, Denmark, the Netherlands, and Sweden assigned a high priority to the goal of full employment in the first postwar decades, and all four countries have ratified the International Labour Organization's Convention on Employment Policy (ILO Convention 122, 1964), which requires them to "declare and pursue, as a major goal, an active policy designed to promote full, productive and freely chosen employment." In 1965, Sweden became

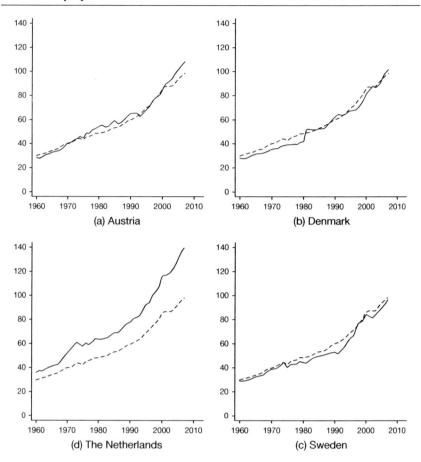

Figure 1.3 Economic openness, 1970–2007

Data source: Heston, Summers, and Aten (2009). The openness of the economy is calculated according to the formula (imports + exports)/GDP. The dotted line represents mean level of economic openness in the thirteen European countries that have been democracies since the Second World War, excluding countries with a population of less than 1 million.

the first country in the world to ratify this convention (Lindvert 2006, 43). The Netherlands ratified it in 1967, Denmark in 1970, and Austria in 1972.

The commitment to full employment was expressed in different ways in domestic politics. In Austria, both of the two major parties in the postwar Second Republic (the Christian democratic ÖVP, *Österreichische Volkspartei*, and the socialist SPÖ, *Sozialistische Partei Österreichs*) emphasized the fight against unemployment early on, as did the social partners, which was probably due to the damaging effects of unemployment in Austria's First Republic (Tálos 1987, 91 dates the institutionalization of the full employment objective to the second half of the 1950s, soon after Austria regained full independence in 1955). In Denmark, the social democratic postwar program—*The Future Denmark (Fremtidens Danmark)*—was based on a vision of full employment, and although some aspects of this program were politically controversial, its emphasis on full employment was not (Pekkarinen 1989, 339; Asmussen 2004, 133–5). In the Netherlands, the goal of full employment was included in the list of policy objectives that the main Dutch corporatist body, the Social and Economic Council, formulated in the early 1950s—a list of priorities that was later adopted by the government as official policy. Moreover, the goal of full employment is enshrined in the Dutch constitution (Andeweg and Irwin 2009, 215–16; on the status of employment objectives in the first decade after the war, see also Jones 2008, 99–100). Finally, in Sweden, as in Denmark, full employment was the central theme of the social democratic postwar program, and the goal of full employment was recognized as paramount by all Swedish parties after the Second World War (Lewin 1967, 222).

In spite of all these similarities, governments in Copenhagen, The Hague, Stockholm, and Vienna responded differently to the threat of unemployment in the 1970s and 1980s, and to the fact of unemployment in the 1990s and 2000s. That is the puzzle at the heart of this book.

The Argument in Brief

This book is concerned with macroeconomic policy and labor market policy. The main macroeconomic instruments are fiscal policy (taxation and spending), monetary policy (interest rates and money supply), and exchange rate policy (the choice of currency regime and, with a fixed rate, the price of the currency). Labor market policy also has three elements: employment protection legislation, income support for the unemployed, and active labor market policies (supply-side measures intended to enhance the skills and employability of workers and improve labor market matching; see Rueda 2006, 385). For reasons that I explain in Chapter 4, I concentrate on unemployment benefits and active labor market policies, and how they are combined.

The first research question is why governments in Austria and Sweden changed the main objective of economic policy from full employment to low inflation and balanced budgets some ten to fifteen years later than Denmark and the Netherlands. My answer is that as long as political arrangements were stable in the two former countries, their governments used economic policies to maintain full employment, in an attempt to avoid reforming other policies, changing their political models. In the 1970s and early 1980s, Austria and Sweden remained highly integrated states in the sense that governments were expected to defend existing political arrangements, individual policies were seen as elements in a coherent whole, and there were institutional and political mechanisms that allowed political agents to coordinate policies across policy domains. In Denmark and the Netherlands, the postwar political settlement was already destabilized by the early 1970s—their party systems had fragmented, coalitions were unstable, corporatist institutions were deadlocked, and new, divisive conflicts had emerged over the purpose of political authority.

The fact that the postwar settlement was disintegrating in Denmark and the Netherlands but not in Austria and Sweden before the economic crisis of the 1970s began was partly a result of historical circumstances (new political cleavages manifested themselves sooner in the Danish and Dutch societies). But it was also a result of the fact that the Austrian and Swedish postwar models were more strongly integrated than the Danish and Dutch political systems, making them more resilient. As Anton Hemerijck and Martin Schludi (2000, 136) have noted, the Swedish political model of the 1960s and 1970s was a particularly "tightly coupled" and "interdependent" state, and I will argue that domestic political arrangements in Austria's Second Republic had similar characteristics (although the Austrian and Swedish political models were organized and sustained in different ways).

The second research question is why governments in Denmark and the Netherlands implemented comprehensive labor market and social policy reforms in the 1990s, whereas governments in Austria and Sweden were more cautious. My answer is that political circumstances continued to shape government responses to the unemployment problem. Political circumstances mattered *indirectly* since the persistence of high unemployment from the late 1970s onward persuaded political parties and interest organizations in Denmark and the Netherlands that reform was necessary. Political circumstances also mattered *directly* since the Danish and Dutch labor market reforms in the 1990s were based on a new understanding between political parties and interest organizations, dating back to the 1980s.

The Indirect Effects of Employment and Unemployment

According to the International Labour Organization, the unemployed are working-age individuals who are without work, currently available for work, and actively seeking work (ILO 1982, §10). The unemployment rate is defined as the percentage of the labor force that is unemployed (where the labor force consists of all individuals who are available for work). The employment rate is the percentage of the working-age population (normally defined as the age span 15–64) that is either in paid employment or self-employed (ILO 1982, §9). Individuals who are neither unemployed nor employed are counted as "inactive" and hence not included in the labor force (ILO 1982, §11).

The direct social and individual costs of unemployment are large. For society, unemployment represents a waste of human capital. For the individual, it is associated with low income, low levels of life satisfaction, and sometimes even a breakdown of personality, as Marie Jahoda and Paul Lazarsfeld documented in their vivid study of an Austrian industrial town in the 1930s, *Die Arbeitslosen von Marienthal* (Jahoda, Lazarsfeld, and Zeisel 1972 [1933]). Recent scholarship has shown that unemployment is one of the life events that reduce individual happiness the most (Layard, Nickell, and Jackman 2005, xxxix–xl), which is probably a result of the fact that paid employment imposes a certain regularity on life, stimulates the mind, and offers opportunities for social interaction (Kenworthy, forthcoming).

What mattered most to the politics of unemployment in Western Europe in the first postwar decades, however, were arguably the indirect, political consequences of full employment. I believe that this has not been fully recognized in the scholarly literature, and that many studies of economic policymaking and labor market reform have underestimated the role of politics since they have relied on the simplifying assumption that governments are chiefly concerned with the direct economic effects of economic and labor market policies. If one allows for the possibility that politicians are not only—or even primarily—concerned with the direct economic and social effects of the policies they make, but also with their indirect political effects, it becomes easier to explain two important features of economic and social policymaking in European countries from the 1970s onward.

First, economic policy shifts are often correlated with changes in other policy areas. This would not be surprising if there were a strong functional relationship between these other policy areas and economic policy, but I will provide several examples where changes in economic policy were associated with policy shifts in areas that are quite remote from economic policy. In Sweden, for example, the transition to economic policies oriented toward low inflation and balanced budgets took place around 1990, a period of big changes in Swedish public policy—not just in areas closely related to economic policy, but also in areas such as education and housing (see Chapter 3).

Second, economic and labor market policy shifts often occur in the wake of changes in the political system, such as the rise of new parties or a change in the norms that govern the interaction within and between political elites. If politicians were mainly concerned with social and economic outcomes as such, it is not clear why this pattern would emerge. This is a central theme of Chapters 2 and 3, where I show that changes in economic policies were not only correlated with changes in industrial relations systems—which has already been well documented—but also with changes in party systems and, more broadly, with changes in the norms that constitute national political cultures. In Chapter 4, I also show that the labor market policy changes that occurred in Denmark and the Netherlands from the late 1980s onward required the establishment of new political arrangements in these two countries after the upheavals of the 1970s and early 1980s, which again testifies to how developments within the political system shape the policy choices of governments.

Several case studies of Austria, Denmark, the Netherlands, and Sweden have already suggested that political conflicts over economic and labor market policy have centered around the indirect effects of these policies. For example, Peter Katzenstein's work on Austria in the early 1980s was based on the premise that Austrian politicians were concerned with their political room for maneuver, not with economic performance as such.

What interests me and, I think, what interests the Austrians are the secondary consequences of policy on the future range of political choice that the country has. These secondary consequences are shaped greatly by the character of Austria's domestic political arrangements. (Katzenstein 1982, 151)

Experts on Sweden have made similar observations. As Helen Ginsburg put it in a study of employment policies, also from the early 1980s,

[F]ull employment is not viewed solely in economic terms. Equally significant is its linkage to other important aspects of Swedish society. Full employment is the linchpin of Sweden's comprehensive social-welfare policy, is essential to LO's [the main trade union confederation's] wage policy, and is considered the practical means of breathing life into a widely shared egalitarian philosophy. (Ginsburg 1983, 122)

Case studies of macroeconomic policymaking in the Netherlands and Denmark in the 1970s and 1980s, on the other hand, have emphasized the decline of established political models in these two countries. For example, Erik Jones's book on economic policy in Belgium and the Netherlands (2008) shows that Dutch economic policymaking in the 1970s and 1980s was influenced by the transition from consociationalism to more majoritarian political practices, and Hemerijck, Unger, and Visser (2000, 253) have argued that the "internal cohesion" in Austria in the 1970s and 1980s was different from Dutch politics, "where the postwar consensus had in fact ended and was to be renegotiated within and between the different segments of society." Concerning the Danish case, one of the main conclusions of Balder Asmussen's comprehensive study of Danish economic policy and labor market policy since the 1970s is that the leading politicians of the 1970s and 1980s were not primarily interested in economic policy as such—they were concerned with the political strategies that a change in economic policies would prevent them from pursuing, or enable them to pursue (Asmussen 2007, 190). More-over, in a comparison of Denmark and Sweden, Benner and Vad (2000, 454–5) note that the policy differences between these two countries in the 1980s and 1990s can be explained by the fact that in Sweden, "golden age institutions and functions were maintained, while in Denmark the traditional institutional boundaries were broken down as new functions emerged."

The argument of this book is consistent with, and builds on, these observations. In my view, the Austrian experience, the Danish experience, the Dutch experience, and the Swedish experience are all parts of a wider European story about the end of the postwar political settlement and the consequences of this event for economic policy and labor market reform in the late twentieth and early twenty-first centuries.

The idea that the state might be able to solve the unemployment problem was a revolution in political affairs in the 1930s and 1940s. When it became clear that the Second World War would bring full employment to the advanced, industrialized economies in Western Europe and North America, two social scientists, writing independently of each other, predicted that full employment would have profound effects on postwar politics. In his essay "Political Aspects of Full Employment," which was published in the *Political Quarterly* in 1943, Michal Kalecki argued that full employment would increase the power of the working class, which, he believed, would either lead to the downfall of capitalism or to the creation of new social and political institutions (Kalecki 1943, 331). The following year, in 1944, Elmer Eric Schattschneider published his paper "Party Government and Employment Policy" in the *American Political Science Review*. "What people do about the government depends on what they think the government is able to do," Schattschneider noted. The solution to the unemployment problem was therefore "almost certain to have a great impact on the political behavior of millions of people." Eventually, Schattschneider predicted, "the political system will be made to work in ways in which it has never worked before" (Schattschneider 1944, 1148).

Both of these arguments proved remarkably prescient. As Michal Kalecki had predicted, the postwar full employment society did require new social and political institutions. Through these institutions, the political agents of the working class—social democratic parties and trade unions—were included in new political bargains throughout Western Europe (in some countries, this process had started earlier, but mainly where governments had begun to address the unemployment problem early on, such as in 1930s Sweden). As Schattschneider had predicted, the political consequences of full employment were not limited to an increase in the power of the working class—the scope of government expanded more generally, as political agents across the political spectrum grew accustomed to a more active and interventionist state.

In Western Europe, the mechanisms that Michal Kalecki and E. E. Schattschneider identified led to the institutionalization of a political order that can be called the *postwar settlement*. This term has often been used to denote specific bargains between labor and business, but I am using it here in a broader sense, referring to a set of formal and informal institutional arrangements that shaped the political system as a whole. There were important cross-national differences, which I will come back to later, but across Western Europe, the postwar nation state rested, as Alan Milward puts it, on a wider "political consensus" than interwar politics, involving groups that had not previously been well represented politically: workers, farmers, and "a diffuse alliance of lower and middle income beneficiaries of the welfare state" (Milward 1992, 27). The wider consensus was based on certain core policies, including agricultural subsidies, welfare state programs, and employment policies (Milward 1992, 27–42). On an abstract level, these political arrangements were the West European version of what Michael Mann (2004, 2) has called the dominant political idea of the twentieth century: the notion that the state has a moral purpose to improve society (see also Finer 1997, vol. III, 1479, and Berman 2006).

The emergence of macroeconomic policy as a new policy domain in the 1930s and its institutionalization after the Second World War was an important condition for the "consensus" that Milward identifies, since it allowed politicians to overcome the divisive conflicts between protectionism, socialist planning, and laissez-faire liberalism that had characterized the decades before the war (Hall 1989, 366–8; Hirschman 1989, 355–6; see also Gourevitch 1986, 228). In that sense, macroeconomic policy was not merely a set of instruments that governments could use to manage the economy: the shared belief that the government could influence economic activity—and therefore also unemployment—was an important condition for the stability of the postwar settlement as a whole. This, I argue, is why low unemployment remained the overriding objective of economic policy as long as the postwar settlement was intact. When the institutions and norms that constituted the postwar settlement changed, however—and they did everywhere, sooner or later—low unemployment became one policy objective among many: governments still cared about unemployment, but now they did so because of its direct economic and social effects, not because of its indirect, political effects. It therefore became possible to weigh low unemployment against other objectives.

My argument is related to Anton Hemerijck's and Martin Schludi's conjecture that third-order policy changes (see below) tend to result in widespread institutional reform (Hemerijck and Schludi 2000, 134), but I turn this argument on its head: in my view, major policy changes are only possible if established norms and institutions are first undermined. My argument also has a lot in common with Margaret Weir's work on employment policy in the United States, which demonstrates that institutions and historical experience can create "boundaries" of policy innovation, so that "some questions are asked and others are left unspoken, some issues are defined as problems amenable to public action and others are regarded as natural or inevitable phenomena, and some lines of action are embarked upon with little controversy while others are not even broached" (Weir 1992, 163). However, in my analysis such norms do not emerge *within* policy areas; instead, norms concern the way in which different institutions and policies should interact.

Finally, my argument draws on Göran Therborn's idea that full employment was preserved (longer) in countries that had institutionalized a commitment to full employment before the economic crisis of the 1970s began (Therborn 1986). However, the premise of Therborn's argument was that an institutionalized commitment to full employment provided some states with the *capacity* to pursue full employment policies. My interpretation is different. In my view, some governments were more *eager* to defend full employment, since the political models of their countries depended on it.

Political Arrangements

Institutional explanations of political decision-making are normally concerned with the effects of enduring features of political systems, such as constitutional rules and political cultures. The subject matter of this book requires a different approach. In the period covered in this study—the early 1970s to the mid-2000s—European countries simultaneously experienced profound political and economic changes, and I wish to show whether the timing and character of these changes mattered to the choices that governments made. The focus on institutional change rather than stability makes my argument less generalizable than other institutional accounts of policymaking, for to the extent that scholars of comparative politics can make lawlike generalizations—which is itself debatable—they can do so because political behavior tends to acquire a certain regularity when the same set of institutions is in place for long periods of time.

Austria, Denmark, the Netherlands, and Sweden are fairly similar constitutionally. However, scholars of comparative politics have long concerned themselves with other layers of political systems. For example, in his *Patterns of Democracy* (1999), Arend Lijphart investigates not only formal political institutions but also the "practices" of democracy, and in his earlier book, *The Politics of Accommodation* (1968), Lijphart developed a detailed analysis of the norms that governed party politics in the Netherlands, as Gerhard Lehmbruch (1967) did for the Austrian and Swiss political systems. Peter Katzenstein, whose *Small States in World Markets* remains an important source of inspiration for students of the "small" European countries, defines "democratic corporatism" as a combination of (*a*) centralized and concentrated interest groups, (*b*) voluntary and informal coordination of conflicting objectives through political bargains, and (c) an ideology of social partnership (Katzenstein 1985b, 87–93). In other words, his analysis is concerned with the main actors in the political system, the institutions in which they operate, and the norms that govern their interaction. So is my own analysis of political arrangements in Austria, Denmark, the Netherlands, and Sweden, which concentrates on two subsystems—the party system and the system of interest organizations—and the way in which they influence each other.

The term "party system" is often used loosely to refer to the parties in a particular country (as in "the Dutch party system"). However, as Luciano Bardi and Peter Mair have pointed out (2008, 152), a "system" is more than the sum of its parts, and in a stricter sense, the term "party system" refers to the nature of the interaction between political parties. The simplest way to characterize party systems is to count the number of parties, and almost all classifications begin with some sort of numerical criterion (Ware 1996, Chapter 5)—not least since many scholars of party systems believe that the number of parties influences the character of political competition in predictable ways (see especially Sartori 1976). When I discuss the development of party systems in Austria, Denmark, the Netherlands, and Sweden in Chapters 2 through 4, I am concerned with the (effective) number of parties, but not only that: since postwar political arrangements depended on the political competition between stable sets of parties that represented relatively specific interests, I also seek to identify discontinuities in the *composition* of party systems by noting when new types of parties became represented. Finally, I seek to identify changes in the character of partisan competition, particularly when it comes to coalitions and government formation (Mair 1996).

For a long period after the Second World War, party competition in Austria, Denmark, the Netherlands, and Sweden involved the same political parties. Table 1.1—which lists the parties that were represented in the Austrian, Danish, Dutch, and Swedish parliaments in the 1950s—illustrates this important point. Across these four countries, only one party won representation for the first time in the 1950s: the Dutch Pacifist Socialist Party, a minor left-wing party that was represented in the lower house of the Dutch parliament from 1959 to 1989 (when it merged with several other left-wing parties). As I show in Chapters 2 and 3, from the 1960s onward, things were different: these stable patterns of political competition came to an end in Denmark and the Netherlands in the late 1960s and early 1970s, and in Austria and Sweden in the late 1980s and early 1990s.

Table 1.1 Political parties in the 1950s

Country	Parties
Austria	The Christian Democrats (*Österreichische Volkspartei*)
	The Communist Party (*Kommunistische Partei Österreichs*, lost representation in 1959)
	The Freedom Party (*Freiheitliche Partei Österreichs*, liberal)
	The Social Democrats (*Sozialistische Partei Österreichs*)
Denmark	The Communist Party (*Danmarks Kommunistiske Parti*)
	The Conservatives (*Det Konservative Folkeparti*)
	The Justice Party (*Retsforbundet*, a single tax party)
	The Liberal Party (*Venstre*)
	The Social Democrats (*Socialdemokraterne*)
	The Social Liberal Party (*Det Radikale Venstre*)
The Netherlands	The Anti-Revolutionary Party (*Anti-Revolutionaire Partij*, Christian democratic, protestant)
	The Catholic People's Party (*Katholieke Volkspartij*, Christian democratic, catholic)
	The Christian Historical Union (*Christelijk Historische Unie*, Christian democratic, protestant)
	The Communist Party (*Communistische Partij Nederland*)
	The Labor Party (*Partij van de Arbeid*, social democratic)
	The Liberal Party (*Volkspartij voor Vrijheid en Democratie*, conservative-liberal)
	The Pacifist Socialist Party (*Pacifistisch Socialistische Partij*, represented in parliament from 1959)
	The Political Reformed Party *Staatkundig Gereformeerde Partij* (Christian democratic, protestant)
Sweden	The Communist Party (*Sveriges kommunistiska parti*)
	The Conservative Party (*Högerpartiet*)
	The Farmers' Party/Centre Party (*Bondeförbundet/Centerpartiet*, center-right, agrarian)
	The Liberal Party (*Folkpartiet*)
	The Social Democrats (*Sveriges socialdemokratiska arbetareparti*)

Note: All parties represented in parliament are listed, excluding parties that never held more than one or two seats, and not counting the representatives of the Faroe Islands and Greenland in the Danish parliament.

Although four parties were represented in the Austrian *Nationalrat* for most of the 1950s, the Communist Party was rapidly losing influence and relevance, and as a result of the Hungarian crisis in 1956, the communists lost their remaining seats in 1959 (Jelavich 1987, 270–3). Between 1959 and 1986, only three political parties were represented in the Austrian parliament: the Christian Democrats (*Österreichische Volkspartei*), the Social Democrats (*Sozialistische Partei Österreichs*, renamed *Sozialdemokratische Partei Österreichs* in 1991), and the Freedom Party (*Freiheitliche Partei Öster-reichs*), a small liberal party with roots in German nationalism (which changed into a far-right party in the mid-1980s). The Christian Democrats and the Social Democrats were clearly dominant, ruling the country as a Grand Coalition until 1966 and establishing an unusually consensus-oriented political model.

In the 1950s and 1960s, Denmark and Sweden were both representative of the "Nordic five party model" (Demker 2006): they had large social democratic parties and small communist or left socialist parties on the left and agrarian, liberal, and conservative parties on the right. The main Danish parties were the Conservatives (*Det Konservative Folkeparti*), the Social Democrats (*Socialdemokraterne*), the Liberal Party (*Venstre*), and the Social Liberal Party (*Det Radikale Venstre*). The two latter parties originally represented agrarian interests (*Det Radikale Venstre* split from *Venstre* in the early twentieth century). The Social Democrats were the strongest individual party, but they were counterbalanced more effectively than the Swedish Social Democrats by the mobilization of commercial and agrarian interests in the Conservative Party and the Liberal Party (Pekkarinen 1989, 338–9). In Sweden, the same five parties were represented in parliament from the 1910s to the late 1980s: the Communist Party (*Sveriges kommunistiska parti*, renamed *Vänsterpartiet kommunisterna* in 1967 and *Vänsterpartiet* in 1990), the Social Democrats (*Socialdemokratiska arbetarepartiet*), the Liberal Party (*Folkpartiet*), the agrarian Farmers' Party (*Bondeförbundet*, renamed *Centerpartiet* in 1957), and the conservative Right Party (*Högerpartiet*, renamed *Moderata samlingspartiet* in 1969). With the exception of 1951–7, when the Social Democrats were in coalition with the Farmers' Party, Sweden was ruled by single-party social democratic governments from 1945 to 1976 (the social democrat Tage Erlander was prime minister for most of this period, from 1946 to 1969).

As Arend Lijphart showed in his classic study of politics in the Netherlands (1968, Chapter 2), Dutch politics in the 1940s, 1950s, and most of the 1960s was dominated by five political parties, which represented the four main social "pillars" in Dutch society. The Catholics were represented by the Catholic People's Party (*Katholieke Volkspartij*); the Calvinists were represented by the Anti-Revolutionary Party (*Anti-Revolutionaire Partij*) and the Christian Historical Union (*Christelijk Historische Unie*); the socialists were represented by the Labor Party (*Partij van de Arbeid*); and the liberals were represented by the People's Party for Freedom and Democracy (*Volkspartij voor Vrijheid en Democratie*). There were other, smaller parties in the Dutch parliament—as in the Danish—but they did not matter much to political competition at this time.

The term "corporatism" has several different meanings (for good overviews, see Molina and Rhodes 2002, Baccaro 2003, and Kenworthy

2003). On the one hand, the term refers to a particular system of industrial relations, consisting of monopolistic, centralized interest organizations, often combined with centralized wage bargaining institutions (Schmitter 1974, 13). On the other hand, it refers to a method of policymaking: a set of procedures whereby governments negotiate or consult with interest organizations before making important political decisions (Lehmbruch 1977, 94). It is essential to distinguish between these two concepts of corporatism, for as the recent literature has shown (see the articles cited above), countries are often corporatist in one dimension but not in the other. My argument is concerned with policymaking, and especially the ability and willingness of political agents to coordinate policymaking across policy areas, so I use the term "corporatism" in the second sense, referring to a method of political decision-making.

In Austria, Denmark, the Netherlands, and Sweden, policymaking in the politically stable 1950s and 1960s was a matter of bargaining and negotiations between the state and the main interest organizations—not only labor market organizations, but also organizations for farmers and other interest groups. The nature of the relationship between the state and interest organizations varied between countries—and across policy areas within countries—but as Colin Crouch's detailed historical analysis has shown, Austria, Denmark, the Netherlands, and Sweden all had high levels of institutionalized political cooperation between governments and interest organizations compared to most other European countries. By 1950, interest organizations in the Scandinavian countries had already begun to participate in national-level policymaking and administration. Such a system was also beginning to emerge in Austria, and Crouch notes that there was a "new orientation" in Dutch politics in the first years after the Second World War, a period that saw the creation of the two main Dutch corporatist institutions: the bipartite Labor Foundation (*Stichting van de Arbeid*) and the tripartite Social and Economic Council (*Sociaal Economische Raad*, SER) (Crouch 1993, 178–9). By the early 1960s, these institutional networks had "thickened" in all four countries. This is especially true for Austria, Denmark, and Sweden, where unions and employer organizations had become "deeply engaged," not only in wage formation but also in national-level policymaking, particularly in the labor market domain (the main Austrian corporatist institution, the parity commission for prices and wages, *Paritätische Kommission für Preis- und Lohnfragen*, was set up in the mid-1950s). But it is also true for the Netherlands, even if Crouch notes that Dutch interest organizations were concerned with a "somewhat narrower range of issues" and depended more on the government than interest organizations in the three other countries (Crouch 1993, 205–6).

In addition to identifying the most important discontinuities in party systems and corporatist institutions, with respect to the actors and the way they interacted, Chapter 3 seeks to identify discontinuities in the political cultures, or norms, that dominated politics in the two countries where postwar arrangements were most durable: Austria and Sweden. The main challenge for any study of norms is to avoid confusing them with the outcomes they are supposed to explain (see Jon Elster's comments on this problem in Swedberg 1990, 245–6). The reason why this is so difficult is that norms are not directly observable, which means that it is necessary to study them via an analysis of the actions they bring about (Eckstein 1988, 32). In order not to confuse cause and effect, I examine policy changes in areas other than economic and labor market policy. As I will show, economic policy changes tend to follow in the wake of policy shifts in other areas (which are sometimes only loosely connected to the problem of unemployment). This suggests that significant changes in economic policy priorities are more likely to occur in periods when norms concerning the purpose of political authority are changing.

Models of Politics

The arguments that I present in this book depend on certain theoretical assumptions. Most importantly, the idea that institutions and norms defined the options that policymakers considered in the 1970s, 1980s, 1990s, and 2000s assumes that political agents are not fully informed and strategic. Policymaking is a *rational* process in the sense that politicians and other powerful agents choose the policies they think are best, given their preferences and the information that is available to them (Elster 1986, 12–16), but political rationality is *bounded* in the sense that "choice takes place in an environment of 'givens'—premises that are accepted by the subject as bases for his choice; and behavior is adaptive only within the limits set by these 'givens'" (Simon 1947, 79). That is, policymaking rests on certain premises that are taken for granted and do not normally enter the strategic calculations of politicians and other agents. The main reason is that policymaking involves radical uncertainty, so decision-makers cannot process all relevant information; they must construct simplified "models" of the real situations they find themselves in (Simon 1957, 199).

In a world organized around the principle of the sovereign state, such "mental models" (Denzau and North 1994) are arguably defined by, and originate in, the development of domestic political arrangements over time. The political settlements that were established in Western European countries in the aftermath of the Second World War simplified and structured politics in the sense that they institutionalized certain norms regarding the purpose of political authority. As Peter Hall (1997, 194) has put it, norms specify "a repertoire of strategies for action or commonly accepted ideas about how one can behave that influence behavior, not by prescribing or proscribing particular acts but by providing the basic templates through which the world and its possibilities are construed." Policymakers often exclude certain policies and political strategies without question, since these policies and strategies do not fit with prevailing norms. This constraint is particularly relevant to big political decisions such as a change in the objectives of economic or labor market policy. These are not just big decisions because they have far-reaching and unpredictable consequences; they are also transformative in the sense that they are likely to change the beliefs and preferences of the actors themselves, who would thus be unable to evaluate their consequences even if they could predict them (Ullmann-Margalit 1986, 442; see also Elster 1986, 19–20, and 1990, 40).

To see why big policy decisions are associated with radical uncertainty, consider the distinction between the settings of policy instruments, the policy instruments themselves, and the policy objectives. Suppose the government has decided to make low unemployment the primary objective of economic policy. Assume that to attain that objective, the government may use either fiscal policy or monetary policy. Suppose the government decides that fiscal policy is the most appropriate instrument. The next step is to decide the settings of that instrument: the size of the budget deficit (or surplus) and the structure of taxation and spending. Given the distinction between objectives, instruments, and settings, it is possible to make a further distinction between three kinds of policy changes. First-order changes occur frequently, whenever the interest rate or the budget deficit, or the settings of any other monetary or fiscal instrument, are changed. Second-order changes occur more rarely, when one set of instruments replaces another. Finally, third-order policy changes take place when not only settings and instruments change, but also the entire hierarchy of policy objectives (the distinction between first-, second-, and third-order changes was introduced in Hall 1993, 278–9).

When politicians consider first-order changes, the objectives and instruments of policy are given, so policymakers and other agents are likely to have relatively stable sets of preferences and beliefs. Policymakers are clear about what is in their interest, and act to secure outcomes that they think are best for them and their constituencies, given present constraints and opportunities: that is, they strive to fulfill ideological aims and succeed in elections (Alvarez, Garrett, and Lange 1991, 540). Since first-order policy decisions are outcomes of conflicts and bargains between well-defined coalitions of actors, I call the first model of policymaking *the politics of bargaining*. This is a model where policies are determined by economic circumstances, parties, and elections—the standard variables of comparative politics.

When politicians consider second-order policy changes, the objectives of policy are still given, but second-order changes include the use of new policy instruments, so policymakers face a different kind of uncertainty. Actors find it difficult to make informed choices, since they do not know the probability that different outcomes will occur. As Hugh Heclo has put it, politics is often about "collectively wondering what to do" (Heclo 1974, 305), and this is especially the case when politicians consider second-order changes. For this reason, *experts* become influential in the political process (Lindvall 2009). Policymakers who rule complex societies always rely on expertise, but experts are only agents of change in particular circumstances. I therefore refer to the second model of policymaking as *the politics of expertise.*

When politicians consider third-order changes, the judgments they must make are not limited to predicting the immediate effects of policy changes. Since policies are often nested, a decision to change policy objectives in one area tends to have important implications for other policy areas. The politics of third-order changes is all about such indirect effects. In normal times, when actors conform to a given set of norms that simplify decision situations and coordinate social expectations, third-order changes are therefore not considered at all. When they do consider third-order policy changes, politicians do not primarily ask what alternatives are in their interest; they ask what their interest is in the first place—should old norms and practices be abandoned, and if so, by what new norms might they be replaced? I refer to this third model of policymaking as *the politics of purpose*, since it involves the purpose of political authority.

In Ann Swidler's phrase, political norms can be described as "the authorized beliefs of a society about itself." In every polity, Swidler writes, there are "constitutive rules" that "establish a public model of collective life," which is "the shared 'default option' for collective action in periods of uncertainty" (Swidler 2001, 212–13). Postwar political arrangements in Western Europe constituted a model of collective life that structured policymaking over a period of several decades.

Alternative Explanations

In addition to developing the argument that I have introduced in this chapter, Chapters 2 through 4 discuss a number of alternative explanations for the macroeconomic policies and labor market policies of Austrian, Danish, Dutch, and Swedish governments in the period from the early 1970s to the mid-2000s. In order to explain where my argument complements previous scholarship and where I mean to suggest new explanations for the policy choices of governments, I summarize the most important alternative explanations, and my responses to them, in this section. The alternative explanations fall into five broad categories: arguments about the *economic circumstances* that countries have found themselves in, arguments concerning the *institutional capacity* of governments, arguments about the policy preferences of *political parties*, arguments about the role of *European integration* (and the economic and political influence of larger European states, particularly Germany), and, finally, arguments that emphasize the effects of *ideas* on policy.

Economic Circumstances

When politicians explain their policies, they often claim that they have merely done what was necessary to do in response to pressing economic circumstances. Many scholars have also explained policy shifts in this manner, arguing that the choices of governments should primarily be seen as reactions to economic events. For example, with respect to economic policy, scholars such as Jonathon Moses (1994) and Paulette Kurzer (1993) have argued that the integration of international financial markets has constrained governments, complicating the pursuit of certain domestic economic objectives (notably full employment).

The literature on Austria, Denmark, the Netherlands, and Sweden has identified other, more specific economic problems that allegedly persuaded—or even forced—governments to give up their attempts to maintain full employment by means of economic policy in the 1970s and 1980s. Interestingly, however, governments justified these policy changes by referring to a different economic problem in each country. In Austria, governments in the mid-1980s said that budget consolidation was of paramount importance because of the mounting government debt. In Denmark, governments in the mid-1970s referred to the country's endemic current account deficit. In the Netherlands, governments in the mid-1970s were mainly concerned with the increase in labor costs and public spending in the late 1960s and early 1970s. In Sweden, finally, governments in the early 1990s said that a change in policy was necessary because of the high level of inflation in Sweden in the late 1980s and the first years of the 1990s.

These problems were real: public debt had increased in Austria; Denmark had a history of current account deficits; public spending was increasing in the Netherlands; and inflation was high in Sweden in the overheating economy of the late 1980s and early 1990s. But when other countries confronted the same problems, they did not always respond in the same manner. For example, when Austria's current account deficit increased in the 1970s, the Austrian government's response was not primarily fiscal restraint—as in Denmark—but more targeted efforts to reduce imports and increase exports. And when the budget deficit and the deficit in the current account increased in Sweden in the early 1980s, Swedish governments did not give up on full employment, which is what governments did in Denmark and the Netherlands in the mid-1970s; instead, two successive Swedish governments devalued the currency (by 10 and 16 percent) in order to increase foreign demand for Swedish export goods.

I do not argue that countries could have gone on pursuing full employment-oriented economic policies forever—it seems clear that both economic and institutional changes have made the pursuit of such policies more involved, at least in the form that they were pursued in the past (for an overview, see Iversen and Soskice 2006). But economic problems can be interpreted and addressed in different ways—depending, I will argue, on political circumstances. Similarly, although the labor market policy changes that have occurred in many European countries in the 1990s and 2000s can be seen as the result of a different form of economic pressure— the experience of high and persistent unemployment—governments have responded to this problem in different ways, and politics explains how and why (see Chapter 4).

The economic explanations that I have mentioned in this section are discussed and evaluated in more detail and depth in Chapters 2 through 4.

Institutional Capacity

The most influential explanations for the divergence of economic policies in the 1970s and 1980s are concerned with institutional capacity.
Several prominent scholars of European politics, notably Fritz Scharpf
(1991, 2000) and Torben Iversen (1999), have argued that cross-country
economic policy differences can be explained with reference to the interaction of governments, labor market organizations, and central banks.
The institutions that govern this interaction, it is argued, determine the
ability of governments to use economic policies to pursue objectives such
as low unemployment and low inflation (at least their ability to pursue
these objectives simultaneously).

With regard to the role of central banks, the argument is that independent central banks tend to give priority to low inflation rather than
low unemployment, which does not only mean that governments are
restricted to nonmonetary instruments; it also means that any attempt
to maintain high levels of economic activity through fiscal policy may
be offset by restrictive monetary measures. With regard to the role of
labor market organizations, the argument is that employment-oriented
economic policies require voluntary wage restraint (in order to contain
inflation) and that this is only possible in countries with centralized or
otherwise highly coordinated wage bargaining systems (for clear sum-
maries of these two ideas, see Scharpf 1991, Chapters 9–10, and Iversen
1999).

These institutional factors have clearly mattered to the policies of
European governments, but the following two observations, to which
I return in Chapters 2 and 3, suggest that the relationship between
institutions and policy choices is more complicated than it seems: first,
the relationship between governments and central banks is not only
defined by formal and enduring institutional rules but also by political
circumstances; second, even wage bargaining systems that were formally
centralized and coordinated were unable to deliver wage moderation
in the high inflation environment of the 1970s and 1980s, and where
they did, as in Austria, wage-setters depended on a number of political
mechanisms beyond the wage bargaining system as such.

Today, most central banks in Europe are independent in the sense
that governments cannot exert direct control over monetary policy. In
the 1970s and 1980s, there was more variation between countries. Most
scholars agree that the West German *Bundesbank* was the most independent central bank in Europe, and that the Bank of England was least

independent (before the new Labour government introduced central bank independence in 1997). The countries featured in this book were somewhere in between: the *Österreichische Nationalbank*, *Danmarks Nationalbank*, *De Nederlandsche Bank*, and *Sveriges Riksbank* did not enjoy the kind of independence that Germany's *Bundesbank* enjoyed, nor were they as politicized as the Bank of England.

There is some evidence that the Danish and the Dutch central banks were more independent than the Austrian and the Swedish central banks in the 1970s and 1980s, which might explain why Danish and Dutch governments changed the objective of economic policy from low unemployment to low inflation and balanced budgets sooner than governments in Austria and Sweden. However, the ranking of these four countries is not consistent across the indicators of central bank independence that are included in Armingeon et al.'s *Comparative Politics Data Set* (2009): the Swedish *Riksbank* ranked as the least independent of the four on most indicators until the late 1990s, when it became independent, but according to Cukierman's widely used measure of central bank independence, Austria's *Nationalbank* was actually more independent than the Danish and Dutch central banks.

In Chapters 2 and 3, where I examine the interaction of central banks and governments in Austria, Denmark, the Netherlands, and Sweden, I argue that the relationships between politicians and central bankers were defined more by political and historical circumstances than by formal institutional rules. *De jure*, governments and parliaments had authority over monetary policy in all four countries. *De facto*, central banks were more independent in Denmark and the Netherlands. But this was a result of the fact that Danish and Dutch governments gave central banks considerable room for maneuver since they had no well-defined agenda in monetary policy in the 1970s (unlike governments in Austria and Sweden, who expected central banks to contribute to the government's efforts to maintain full employment). Across Europe, there has been a shift in the locus of authority in economic policy from general government offices to central banks and finance ministries, but this shift was not an exogenous factor that shaped the institutional capacity of governments; it was one element in a wide set of political changes in European states from the 1970s to the 1990s.

Many scholars attribute the economic policies and employment strategies of European countries to the institutional capacity for coordination among labor market actors. In countries such as Austria and Sweden, it is argued, wage bargaining was centralized and coordinated, which meant that unions, firms, and governments could cooperate, allowing for an economic strategy that put employment first without risking inflation— something that governments in countries with weaker labor market institutions could not do. In order to evaluate this argument, it is helpful to examine how the centralization and coordination of wage bargaining in the four countries have changed over time. Based on a comprehensive survey of different measures, Lane Kenworthy (2001b, 93–4) recommends one measure of centralization (which has been developed by Iversen 1999) and one measure of coordination (his own). Figures 1.4 and 1.5, which compare Austria, Denmark, the Netherlands, and Sweden to the average levels of centralization and coordination in a larger sample of European democracies, are based on variants of these two measures. Figure 1.4 describes the *centralization* of wage bargaining in the four countries from 1960 to 2007, using data compiled by Jelle Visser (2009) on the basis of Iversen's definition of centralization. Figure 1.5 describes the *coordination* of wage bargaining in the four countries from 1960 to 2007, again using data compiled by Jelle Visser (2009), but this time guided by a methodology proposed by Kenworthy (2001a).

As Figure 1.4 shows, Austria's wage bargaining system has always been much more centralized than wage bargaining arrangements in the three other countries. Even if the level of centralization declined somewhat in the early to mid-1980s, the Austrian wage bargaining system remains more centralized than the highest levels of centralization in the other three countries in the 1960s and 1970s (with the exception of Dutch wage bargaining in the early 1960s). Among the three other countries, Figure 1.4 shows that the level of wage bargaining centralization had declined in Denmark and the Netherlands before the early 1970s—the period that concerns me in Chapter 2—but remained relatively stable in Sweden until the early 1980s.

As Figure 1.5 shows, all four countries have moved from fully coordinated bargaining (5 represents national-level bargaining) to some lower level of coordination. The Netherlands changed first—the national-level bargaining system was destabilized already in the early 1960s. Then, for a period of some twenty years, the level of coordination changed frequently, until a new stable system of coordinated industry-level bargaining was introduced with the Wassenaar Agreement in 1982 (see Chapter 3). In the three other countries, the early 1980s was a watershed: Denmark moved to a lower level of coordination around 1980. So did Austria and Sweden one or two years later.

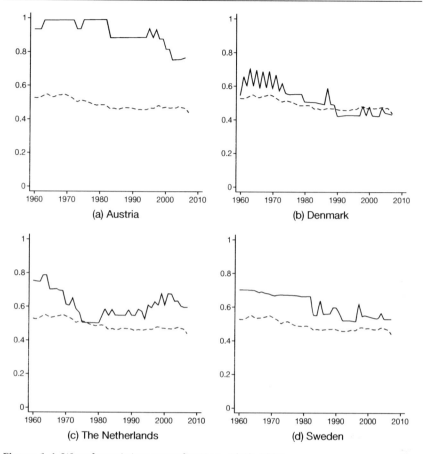

Figure 1.4 Wage bargaining centralization, 1960–2007

Data source: Visser (2009). Visser's centralization measure is a summary measure of the centralization and coordination of union wage bargaining, similar, but not identical, to the measure proposed in Iversen (1999). The dotted line represents the mean level of centralization in the thirteen European countries that have been democracies since the Second World War, excluding countries with a population of less than 1 million.

Given that Denmark and the Netherlands changed their economic policies already in the mid-1970s, the data in Figure 1.4 are consistent with the explanation that wage bargaining centralization increases the ability of governments to pursue employment-oriented economic policies, since wage bargaining centralization declined in both countries in the 1960s and early 1970s. In Chapter 3, I will argue, however, that whereas wage bargaining institutions appear to have played a major role in

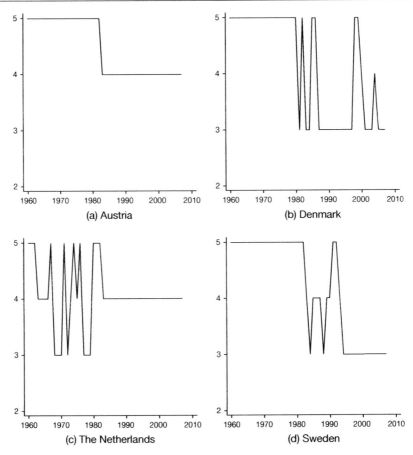

Figure 1.5 Wage bargaining coordination, 1960–2007

Data source: Visser (2009). Visser's coordination measure is a five-point classification, similar, but not identical, to the measure proposed in Kenworthy (2001*a*): (1) Fragmented bargaining, mostly at company level. (2) Mixed industry- and firm-level bargaining. (3) Industry-level bargaining. (4) Mixed industry- and economy-wide bargaining. (5) Economy-wide bargaining.

Austria—where interest organizations cooperated closely with the government in order to reduce the current account deficit in the second half of the 1970s—an examination of the Swedish case reveals that the centralized wage bargaining system did not deliver wage moderation in the 1970s: Swedish governments had to resort to a series of currency devaluations in order to maintain competitiveness. This suggests that wage bargaining institutions cannot fully explain the variation in economic policies in the period after the first oil crisis.

Party Politics

Many scholars have argued that political parties have different preferences over economic policy since left parties care more about unemployment and right parties care more about inflation (Hibbs 1977; for a recent literature review, see Franzese 2002). As Göran Therborn (1986, 96–7) has noted, however, the party composition of governments does not appear to have mattered much to the timing of economic policy shifts in the 1970s and 1980s. In fact, Chapters 2 and 3 will show that in Austria, Denmark, the Netherlands, and Sweden, the transition from employment-oriented economic policies to budget balance- and low inflation-oriented economic policies began under social democratic prime ministers and finance ministers: Anker Jørgensen's social democratic minority government in Denmark in the mid-1970s, Joop den Uyl's center-left coalition government in the Netherlands (also in the mid-1970s), Fred Sinowatz's and Franz Vranitzky's social democratic-led coalition governments in Austria in the mid-1980s, and Ingvar Carlsson's social democratic minority government in Sweden in the early 1990s (a complete list of post-1973 governments can be found in Appendix A).

When it comes to labor market policy, which is the topic of Chapter 4, many scholars also believe that the party composition of governments matters greatly to which policies are chosen. Concerning unemployment insurance, the generally accepted view is that a history of center-left government tends to be associated with more generous unemployment insurance (Korpi and Palme 2003; Allan and Scruggs 2004). Concerning active labor market policies, some authors, notably David Rueda (2006), have argued that social democratic parties are no more likely than other parties to increase spending on such programs, whereas Huo, Nelson, and Stephens (2008) do identify an effect of the party composition of governments. As I show in Chapter 4, electoral politics mattered to some elements of labor market policymaking in Austria, Denmark, the Netherlands, and Sweden in the 1980s, 1990s, and 2000s, but many cross-country policy differences cannot be explained by such party-political differences.

None of this is to say party politics is irrelevant. In Chapter 2, for example, I will show that the party composition of governments had important effects on the character of fiscal policy measures in the 1970s, when policymakers in all countries still worked under the assumption that fiscal policy could be used to control the level of activity in the economy. Moreover, in Chapter 4, I will show that party politics mattered greatly to the mix of labor market programs that countries adopted in the 1990s and 2000s. These observations suggest that the party composition of governments influences policy changes within policy regimes, but it does not determine the timing or character of regime changes.

The European Dimension

One important difference between Austria, Denmark, the Netherlands, and Sweden is that they joined the European Union (previously the European Community) at different points in time: the Netherlands was a founding member, Denmark joined in 1973, and Austria and Sweden joined in 1995. This is unlikely to have mattered to the development of labor market policies, since the European Union's involvement in member state labor market policies did not begin in earnest until the mid-1990s, when all four countries were already members (see Chapter 4). However, it is important to consider the possibility that membership in the European Community—and economic and geographical proximity to West Germany—might have shaped the economic policies of Danish and Dutch governments in the 1970s and 1980s. It is also important to consider the possibility that the prospect of membership in the European Community may have contributed to Austrian and Swedish economic policy changes in the late 1980s and early 1990s.

For reasons that I explain in more detail in Chapters 2 and 3, however, domestic political circumstances mattered more in both cases. European exchange rate cooperation in the 1970s, when Danish and Dutch governments changed their economic policies, was more informal than it would later become, and not all member states participated. If Danish and Dutch policymakers had found the constraints unacceptable, they would have been able to opt out, as Sweden did when it left the "Snake" system of exchange rate cooperation in 1977. Moreover, the Austrian government decided to peg its currency, the *schilling*, to the West German *mark* soon after the breakdown of the Bretton Woods system in 1971–3, and it is hard to see why Austria should be less dependent on the German economy than Denmark and the Netherlands. In Chapter 3, I show that economic policy changes in Austria and Sweden in the 1980s and 1990s were motivated by domestic concerns—the decision to apply for membership the European Community was at least partly a *result* of underlying political changes that also led to changes in economic policy, not a *cause* of these changes.

Ideas and Discourse

The 1970s and 1980s, when most European governments changed their economic policies, giving higher priority to low inflation and balanced budgets, was a period of idea-changes among academic economists and in international economic organizations. A broadly Keynesian approach was replaced by monetarist and neoclassical ideas. This has led many scholars—such as Kathleen McNamara (1998), Martin Marcussen (2000), and Mark Blyth (2002)—to argue that the shift from employment-oriented macroeconomic management to austere fiscal policies and low-inflation-oriented monetary policies in the 1980s and 1990s was a result of the decline of Keynesianism and the emergence of competing approaches to macroeconomics. One could make a similar argument concerning labor market policies, for as Blanchard (2006) has documented, economic ideas and political agendas have developed in tandem in Europe since the 1980s in this policy domain.

As Chapters 2 and 3 will show, however, in the cases of Austria, Denmark, the Netherlands, and Sweden, changes in the objectives of economic policy have not resulted from the decline of Keynesianism and the emergence of competing approaches to macroeconomics (for a more detailed analysis of ideas and economic policies in Austria, Denmark, and Sweden, see Lindvall 2009). As I will show in Chapter 2, politicians in Austria and Denmark stopped using macroeconomic policy to preserve full employment while Keynesian ideas were still strong. In Sweden, the reverse was true, for the change in the objectives of economic policy occurred at a point in time when neoclassical ideas had become highly influential.

Many scholars of social policy and labor market reforms have argued that the ability of governments to convince the electorate of the need for change is an essential part of the explanation for the variation in reforms across countries. For example, Robert Cox (2001) has argued that reforms are only possible when governments are able to formulate a persuasive reform "discourse." In a similar vein, Vivien Schmidt (2002, 169) has claimed that governments must create a "consensus for change," enabling the public to "change its perceptions of self-interest and [accept] new institutional practices." According to this literature, the key political problem in the politics of reform is not the institutional capacity of governments, but whether governments manage to establish a consensus on the need for change.

The question, however, is why some governments successfully establish such discourses but not others. In Chapter 4, I will demonstrate that while efforts of persuasion have mattered to the politics of reform, it is necessary to take a longer historical view in order to understand why they do not always work. The fact that Denmark and the Netherlands had lived with high unemployment since the 1970s and renegotiated their domestic political arrangements in the 1980s were both essential to the politics of reform in the 1990s. In Austria and Sweden, governments did not push for wide-ranging social and labor market policies, at least not before the late 2000s. This is probably a result of the late onset of high unemployment in these two countries, and the fact that political arrangements, while weakened, had not been thoroughly reformed (however, the Austrian and Swedish cases were in many ways rather different, as I show in Chapter 4).

Notes on Method

The premise of this book is that it is possible to learn about the conditions of economic and labor market policymaking by following four similar countries over a long period of time, observing how governments and political actors have responded to sequences of political and economic events. Like all methods, this method has its limitations. The fact that Austria, Denmark, the Netherlands, and Sweden are fairly similar makes it easier to identify the factors that mattered to choices governments made, but it also complicates the generalization of the results since there is no way to determine empirically whether the causal relationships that this book identifies depend on specific circumstances in relatively small European countries with strong social democratic parties and a history of corporatism. The trade-off between identification and generalization is characteristic of small-n comparative research. For the purposes of this study, which sets out to examine the interaction of economic and political change since the 1970s, I give priority to the former.

The empirical analysis is primarily based on official documents, most importantly the government's or the finance ministry's annual or biannual economic policy statements. In the Austrian case, my main source is the finance minister's annual budget speech (or *Budgetrede*). In the Danish case, my main source is the finance ministry's annual review of economic policy (*Budgetredegørelsen*, or *Finansredegørelsen*), which includes reprints of interparty agreements on economic policy (important in Denmark, since almost all governments are minority governments). My main source on Dutch economic policy is the government's budget memorandum, which is the finance minister's annual speech on the budget, or *Miljoe-nennota* (held in September each year). In the Swedish case, my main source is the fiscal plan (*Finansplanen*), the government's own account of its economic policies, which is published twice per year—a new fiscal plan is included in each budget bill and in each revised budget bill. All quotes from non-English sources, including secondary sources, have been translated by the author.

Since official documents are often vague, having to please many audiences at once, the empirical analysis is also based on interviews with former prime ministers, ministers of finance, senior civil servants, and central bank governors. Interviews are sometimes unreliable—our memories can fail us in many different ways—but they are useful as complements to other sources, aiding the interpretation of the evidence. All the interviewees are listed in Appendix B. The interviews took place over a period of almost a decade, from December 2000 to February 2010. Most of the Swedish interviews were made in October–November 2001 and in the spring of 2002. The Danish interviews took place in the spring and summer of 2005. Most of the Austrian and Dutch interviews were made in 2006 and 2007, a few in 2010. All quotes from the interviews have been sent to the interviewees for approval. In a few cases, the interviewees requested minor changes, but none of those changes altered the meaning of the quotes substantially. The language of the quotes has been edited slightly. All quotes in Danish and Swedish have been translated to English by the author. The original versions of these quotes are available from the author on request.

The first two empirical chapters are concerned with third-order changes in economic policymaking in Austria, Denmark, the Netherlands, and Sweden in the 1970s and 1980s, when full employment (which was the primary objective of economic policy in the first decades after the war) was gradually given lower priority than low inflation and balanced budgets (which are the primary objectives at present). For each of the four countries, Chapters 2 and 3 seek to identify the point in time when neither of the main macroeconomic instruments—fiscal, monetary, and exchange rate policy—was assigned to reduction of unemployment or the maintenance of full employment.

There are two things to note about the definition of "objectives" that is implicit in the last paragraph. First, objectives are conceptually distinct from outcomes. If unemployment is high, one cannot infer that low unemployment is not an objective of government policy (and vice versa; if unemployment is low, that does not necessarily mean that full employment is a prioritized political objective). Second, and more importantly, objectives are specific to policy domains, which means that they are distinct from the government's *general* preferences over different states of the world. It is entirely possible for a government to have a strong preference for low unemployment without making it an objective of economic policy (the government may believe, for example, that economic policy does not influence the level of unemployment). Clearly, then, objectives are difficult to observe: they cannot be inferred from outcomes, nor from the government's overall ideological orientation. Fortunately, governments tend to provide relatively precise descriptions of how they use the macroeconomic policy instruments they have at their disposal. The empirical sections below will start from these declarations, but they will also use other sources of evidence, including interviews, to evaluate the primary sources.

Few governments say that they do not care about employment. When they change policies, they claim, instead, that their policies will contribute to an optimal level of employment in the long run even if they are associated with high unemployment in the short run. What characterized the first decades after the Second World War, however, was that governments took it upon themselves to *guarantee* a low level of unemployment. Nowadays, many governments try to facilitate increased employment through labor market reforms, but low unemployment is one objective among many. From a political point of view, this is a big difference, and the change from one to the other is associated with the deeper political change described in this book. Governments used to maintain low unemployment in order to preserve domestic political arrangements; now they sometimes change domestic political arrangements in order to reduce unemployment.

Chapter 4 is concerned with third-order policy changes of a different kind, since it tries to establish whether governments have introduced employment objectives in their social and labor market policies (or placed more emphasis on such objectives), by increasing the incentives for the unemployed to look for jobs, helping to improve their chances of finding one, or both. The methodological problem here is similar to the problems that I deal with in Chapters 2 and 3: it is always difficult to draw conclusions about the priorities of governments on the basis of how they describe and justify their policies. However, unemployment compensation arrangements are defined by legal rules, and active labor market policy spending is controlled directly by the government, which means that it is possible to develop a relatively precise account of how such policies change, and how they vary between countries.

2

The Threat of Unemployment

In the early 1970s, the advanced economies in Western Europe were confronted with a number of problems that threatened to undermine the economic and institutional structures that provided for growth, prosperity, and high employment in the 1950s and 1960s. Internationally, the two most important challenges were the breakdown of the Bretton Woods system of exchange rate cooperation in 1971–3 and the first oil crisis in the autumn of 1973. Domestically, a more subtle and creeping change was occurring, although its significance was not well understood at the time: a fall in the rate of productivity growth in the late 1960s and early 1970s (Glyn 2006, 8–13). The supply shocks, the instability in international financial affairs, and the declining productivity growth complicated economic policymaking and required difficult adjustments in domestic economies, especially a reduction of real labor costs, in order to avoid macroeconomic imbalances (Calmfors 1990, 11–12; Blanchard 2006, 13–19).

At a meeting in Kuwait on October, 17–18 1973, the Arab oil-producing states declared that they would make monthly 5 percent reductions in oil production in order to put pressure on governments that supported Israel in its war with Egypt and Syria. On November 4, an immediate 25 percent cut was announced. This prompted oil-exporting countries in general, represented by OPEC (the Organization of Petroleum Exporting Countries), to raise oil prices, which increased by several hundred percent. The economic effects of these events, which are known as the first oil crisis, have sometimes been exaggerated (Marglin 1990, 23), but it still makes sense to start the analysis in the autumn of 1973. First, it seems clear that the oil crisis contributed to intensified distributional conflicts and rising inflation and unemployment in Western democracies. Second, and more importantly, it proved to be a political turning point, for it made politicians and their economic advisers aware that unemployment had once more become a serious threat, after a long period of postwar reconstruction and growth. This chapter investigates how governments in Austria, Denmark, the Netherlands, and Sweden responded to the threat of unemployment from the autumn of 1973—when the first oil shock occurred—until they decided to give priority to objectives other than full employment some time in the 1970s (Denmark and the Netherlands), 1980s (Austria), or early 1990s (Sweden).

When the economic crisis began in the mid-1970s, social democratic parties were in power in many of the smaller European countries. In Austria, the first socialist one-party government ever was formed in 1970, and the Social Democrats stayed in power until 2000, albeit in coalition with the liberal Freedom Party or the Christian Democrats from 1983 onward. In Denmark, the Social Democrats were in power from 1971 to 1973 and again—after a brief liberal interlude—from 1975 to 1982. In the Netherlands, a progressive social democrat-led coalition governed from 1973 to 1977 (when a Christian democratic–liberal coalition took over). In Sweden, finally, all prime ministers had been social democrats ever since the 1930s, and although the long era of social democratic hegemony was coming to an end—the parliament was hung in 1973–6 and the center-right were in power from 1976 to 1982—the Social Democrats were the dominant party for most of the 1970s. With the exception of Austria, however, where the Social Democrats controlled an absolute majority of the seats in parliament, the *Nationalrat*, from 1971 to 1983, the 1970s were also a period of weak and unstable governments, who found it difficult to build support for consistent economic policies.

At first, Austria, Denmark, the Netherlands, and Sweden all responded to the threat of unemployment by means of expansionary fiscal programs that were intended to support domestic demand and counteract the contractionary effects of the oil price increases. This macroeconomic response to the crisis was encouraged by international economic organizations. By the end of 1973, the OECD Secretariat was arguing that the oil crisis could be expected to result in a global increase in savings, since oil-producing countries would not spend all their oil revenues immediately, so oil-consuming countries should pursue expansionary fiscal policies. An OECD memorandum issued in December 1973 noted that if governments wished to "take explicit policy action to offset the oil price rise and its subsequent effects," the most straightforward method was to "neutralize it by an equivalent reduction in taxation" (OECD 1973, 10). Austria, Denmark, the Netherlands, and Sweden all followed this advice—reducing taxes or increasing spending, or both.

After one or two years, however, important differences emerged between these four countries. In Austria and Sweden, governments launched ambitious fiscal policy programs that lasted into the 1980s, and in the Swedish case, governments followed up these programs with a series of devaluations that supported employment for much of the 1980s. In Denmark and the Netherlands, in contrast, attempts to use macroeconomic policy to keep unemployment low were short-lived and subject to political controversy. Gradually, Danish and Dutch governments began to put other macroeconomic goals first. The 1970s and early 1980s were characterized by inconsistent economic policies and policymaking stalemates, as finance ministries and central banks sought more autonomy while other actors inside and outside government argued that the large spending cuts and incomes policy measures that finance ministries and monetary authorities favored would be socially, economically, and politically unacceptable.

In order to explain the end of employment-oriented economic policies in Denmark and the Netherlands in the second half of the 1970s and the long struggle to maintain full employment in Austria and Sweden, it is helpful to examine the state of domestic political arrangements in these four countries at the time of the oil crisis. I will show that the Danish and the Dutch political systems were already in a state of transition by the early 1970s. In party politics as well as industrial relations, the stability that had characterized the postwar years was over, for new parties had entered parliament, the relationship between unions and employer organizations had become strained, and the relative ideological consensus that characterized the 1950s and 1960s had given way to significant political conflicts. The highly integrated political models in Austria and Sweden, on the other hand, remained intact. This meant that giving up on full employment was simply not seen as an option before the mid- to late 1980s. In Austria, the Social Democrats had won an absolute majority in 1971, and were set on proving their governing capacity by using Austria's strong social partnership institutions to achieve social reform and economic progress. In Sweden, a long period of social democratic government was drawing to a close, but the Social Democrats had managed to impose their "image of society" (Castles 1978) so strongly on Swedish public life that even the center-right parties, in government from 1976 to 1982, sought to preserve the Swedish model.

Denmark

The year of the oil crisis, 1973, was also a year of major political changes in Denmark. In January, the country joined the European Community, and in December, five new parties won representation in the Danish parliament, *Folketinget*, increasing the number of parliamentary parties from five to ten. A decade of uncertain and unstable political conditions ensued. After the 1973 election, the social democratic minority government that had been in power since 1971 was replaced by a small Liberal single-party government, which held power for a year and a half, from the autumn of 1973 to the spring of 1975. Since the effects of the oil crisis were not felt immediately—the economy was booming in the first half of 1974 (Nannestad 1991, 142–7)—the first steps to counter the recession were taken under the Liberal government.

Economic Policies in the 1970s

After the summer of 1974, the Liberal government proposed and implemented an income tax cut that amounted to seven billion Danish *kroner* in reduced revenues, a large sum at the time. This policy had the support of all major political parties (the Social Democrats abstained from voting), the only exception being the right-wing populist Progress Party (*Frem-skridtspartiet*), which had won 28 of the 175 seats in *Folketinget* in the election of 1973, and wanted an even larger tax cut. Although the government probably had ideological and tactical motives as well (Asmussen 2007, 46), the stated aim of the tax cut was to increase private demand in order to support economic activity and maintain low unemployment (Budgetdepartementet 1974, 12–13, 16). According to Anders Andersen, who was finance minister in 1973–5, the goal was to stabilize the economy: "By reducing [taxes], we hoped to increase economic activity, which would compensate for the problems that followed from the oil price increases," Mr Andersen said in an interview with the author shortly before his death in 2006 (interview with Anders Andersen, Grenå, June 20, 2005).

When the Social Democrats returned to power in 1975, they implemented further stimulus measures. Most importantly, the new government, which was supported by the Social Liberals in *Det Radikale Venstre* and three other centrist parties, implemented a temporary reduction of the sales tax from 15 to 9.25 percent. The aim was to support domestic economic activity and prevent unemployment from increasing further

(Budgetdepartementet 1975, 8–10, Appendix 16). Anker Jørgensen, the social democratic prime minister in 1975–1982, explains the temporary tax cut in the following way: "We did it because we wanted to make sure no one would be able to say about us that we didn't do all we could to reduce unemployment" (interview with Anker Jørgensen, Copenhagen, August 25, 2005).

Thus in the first two years after the oil crisis, two different Danish minority governments—supported by different combinations of opposition parties—pursued expansionary fiscal policies in order to mitigate the effects of the oil crisis. But already at this time, there were indications that the goal of full employment did not have the same status in Denmark as it had in Austria and Sweden, whose policies I account for later in this chapter. In 1974, Erik Hoffmeyer, the governor of the Danish central bank—*Nationalbanken*—said openly that in his view, fiscal policy could not be used to preserve employment, and two years later, he said publicly that since the large European states had chosen low inflation over low unemployment, Denmark had to follow (Hoffmeyer 1993, 70–4). In Austria and Sweden, such statements from a central bank governor would have been inconceivable in the 1970s. Austria's *Nationalbank* and Sweden's *Riksbank* were expected to contribute to the government's main political effort, which was to fight unemployment.

Erik Hoffmeyer explains today that by the late 1960s, he had come to the conclusion that the central bank must give priority to exchange rate stability. In the 1950s and 1960s, economic policies in Denmark, as in other countries, had been coordinated between the government, the central bank, the trade unions, and the employer organizations, and in this coordination process, employment considerations had top priority. But by the late 1960s, he says, the fiscal authorities and the wage-setters no longer "played along." The bank therefore had to change its policies, and "a stable exchange rate policy became the number one priority." he did not regard employment considerations as irrelevant, and the central bank supported and participated in the temporary expansionary program that the social democratic government launched in 1975–6. But employment no longer came first. In these circumstances, he thought it best to "say openly that we could not pursue autonomous employment policies." He does not believe that this statement was controversial at the time (interview with Erik Hoffmeyer, Copenhagen, March 17, 2005).

By 1976, the government had come to share the central bank's pessimism concerning the room for maneuver in fiscal policy, and most attempts to use generally expansionary macroeconomic policies to shield

Denmark from the international recession were given up. The main reason was that Denmark had a large deficit in its current account—imports exceeded exports—and this was regarded as an unacceptable state of affairs. In August 1976, the Social Democrats reached an agreement with the Social Liberal Party (*Det Radikale Venstre*) and two other centrist parties about a new program of more restrictive fiscal policies. In a joint statement, the four parties said that although the expansionary policies had achieved some good results, the current account deficit had increased too much in the first half of 1976, so it had become necessary to change policies, creating a program of long-term economic stabilization (Budgetdepartementet 1976, 43*–4*). As for employment, no immediate reduction was envisioned. According to the finance ministry's annual economic report, the government's aim was to "secure the basis for the reestablishment of full employment" within a few years (Budgetdepartementet 1976, 9).

The decision to withdraw fiscal stimulus measures in 1976 was not prompted by the failure of expansionary programs to reduce unemployment. Knud Heinesen (2006, 259–61), who was Denmark's finance minister from 1975 to 1979, writes in his memoirs that the fiscal policies had a positive effect on employment. He attributes the tightening of fiscal policy in 1976 entirely to the rising current account deficit. According to data from the OECD (2009a), the Danish unemployment rate increased from less than 1 percent in 1973 to 1.7 percent in 1974 and 3.9 percent in 1975, but there was no further increase between 1975 and 1976, which might reasonably have been interpreted as evidence that the stimulus measures had the intended effect on unemployment (after the withdrawal of the stimulus measures, unemployment kept increasing: it reached 4.7 percent in 1977 and 5.4 percent in 1978). The view at the time, judging both from domestic sources and the OECD's economic surveys of Denmark, was that more expansionary policies would have been desirable, if only the balance of payments situation had allowed for such policies.

Experts on Danish economic policy disagree on the timing of the shift in macroeconomic policy objectives from low unemployment to external (trade) balance, budget balance, and low inflation. Nannestad and Green-Pedersen (2000, 11) attribute this policy shift to the center-right government that came into power in 1982 (see Chapter 3). Asmussen (2007), on the other hand, dates the "third-order" policy change in Danish economic policy to the late 1980s, well into the center-right government's term in office, whereas the former central bank governor Erik Hoffmeyer says that "the choice between stability and employment" was made in late 1979, when the social democratic government began a process of real wage adjustment, and was consolidated in 1986, when the center-right government tightened fiscal policy in order to finally eliminate the current account deficit (interview with Erik Hoffmeyer, Copenhagen, March 17, 2005). There are arguments for all these views. But when you compare Denmark to countries such as Austria and Sweden, it seems clear that there was a marked difference in policy priorities already in 1976.

It would be an exaggeration, however, to claim that the government gave up all attempts to use economic policy to reduce unemployment as early as the mid-1970s. In the late 1970s and early 1980s, the government sought to keep overall economic policy tight, in order to reduce private demand and bring down the current account deficit, while at the same time trying to promote employment through public investments and changes in the composition of public spending. The mix of restrictive fiscal policies and selective employment measures was a source of increasing controversy between the finance ministry, which emphasized budget balance and balance on the current account, and the ministry of labor, which emphasized employment goals (Asmussen 2007, 56–7, 70–2). Beginning in 1977, the government presented parallel economic policy strategies, in the sense that the restrictive budgetary policy was complemented with "employment plans," which were administered by the ministry of labor (Budgetdepartementet 1977, 80*, 83*). Henrik Hassenkam— a former civil servant in the ministry of labor—says that over time, the employment plans "got so large that in the final years [before the Social Democrats lost power in 1982], you could almost speak of an alternative budget." He explains that all ministries submitted proposals on how to use these funds, and then the ministry of labor selected proposals with high expected employment effects. The aim was to make public spending "as employment-intensive as possible" (interview with Henrik Hassenkam, Copenhagen, March 14, 2005).

The future social democratic party chairman Svend Auken, who became minister of labor in 1977, was close to the prime minister, and close to the leadership of the main trade union confederation LO (*Landsorganisationen i Danmark*). In an interview with the author, Mr Auken said that although he was convinced that generally expansionary measures such as the liberal government's tax cut in 1974 and the temporary cut in consumption taxes in 1975–6 were ineffective, he believed that a "combination of active labor market policy and an active economic policy" was still feasible (interview with Svend Auken, Copenhagen, June 21, 2005). The two social democratic finance ministers in the late 1970s and early 1980s, on the other hand, believed that they were being prevented from dealing effectively with other pressing economic problems. Knud Heinesen, finance minister in 1975–9, describes Svend Auken's attitude to economic policy as reckless (*letsindig*; interview with Knud Heinesen, Copenhagen, March 25, 2005), and his successor Svend Jakobsen, who was appointed finance minister in 1979, disagreed with what he took to be Mr Auken's view that unemployment should be reduced "at any cost," since it is "pointless to maintain a slightly higher level of employment now if there is a boomerang effect, leading to even more unemployment in the future" (interview with Svend Jakobsen, Taastrup, March 15, 2005). In Mr Auken's view, however, the finance ministry "had no answers—they did not know what to do" (interview with Svend Auken, Copenhagen, June 21, 2005).

These conflicts within the government meant that for a few years in the late 1970s—after the withdrawal of general stimulus measures in 1976—the Danish government's economic policies were not quite what the finance ministry wanted, nor quite what the ministry of labor wanted. The finance ministry pressed for more budget cuts and efforts to control wage inflation, which was regarded as a major threat to economic stability from the mid-1970s onward, just as in the three other countries. The ministry of labor sought to do more about unemployment and wished to avoid a clash with the trade unions.

In 1978, in an attempt to secure support for austerity measures (but perhaps also in an attempt to divide the right (see Asmussen 2007, 60–5), the Social Democrats formed a coalition government with their main ideological opponents, the Liberal Party *Venstre*. The minister of finance, Knud Heinesen, who proposed this unusual coalition, says that his intention was to get more support "for a tougher, more restrictive economic policy, and above all incomes policies" (interview with Knud Heinesen, Copenhagen, March 18, 2005). This political experiment was discontinued after only a year, however, since the two parties could not overcome their political differences and mutual distrust. When the coalition government broke down, Mr Heinesen resigned. In a television interview following his resignation, he famously said that the Danish economy was heading for the "abyss."

After the breakdown of the short-lived coalition with the Liberal Party, the Social Democrats negotiated a new economic program with the Social Liberal Party, *Det Radikale Venstre*. In late 1979, the two parties agreed on a so-called Comprehensive Solution (*Helhedsløsningen*), which provided for restrictive fiscal policies, incomes policies, and a 5 percent devaluation of the Danish currency, the *krone* (Asmussen 2007, 74). The program was first developed by a small group of policymakers and functionaries within the labor movement, including the new finance minister, Svend Jakobsen, the minister of labor, Svend Auken, and two economists from the trade union confederation LO: Holger Jensen and Poul Nyrup Rasmussen (the latter would later serve as prime minister in 1993–2001).

The main aim was to reduce the current account deficit, which was an important concern for Danish policymakers, as it had been for many years. Tight fiscal policies, lower wage increases, and a reduction of real wages, through the devaluation, were all expected to contribute to this goal. Judging from the finance ministry's budget report in April 1980, the objective of lowering unemployment was now postponed further into the future: the aim of economic policy, according to the finance ministry, was to "guarantee a reduction of the current account deficit in order to achieve a situation *in the second half of the 1980s* where the current account is in balance and there is a basis for a reduction in unemployment" (Budgetdepartementet 1980, 47, my italics).

LO's most important demand in the negotiations was legislation on "economic democracy" (*økonomisk demokrati*), an idea that LO had first introduced in the early 1970s. Economic democracy involved the creation of a central, union-controlled fund that would be able to accumulate and invest a large proportion of private sector profits, increasing the economic power of the trade unions (Anthonsen, Lindvall, and Schmidt Hansen 2009, Section 4). In return for supporting the government's economic program, LO expected that the government would finally implement economic democracy reforms. In the subsequent negotiations with the Social Liberal Party, however, the Social Democrats failed to get support for this part of the agreement. This had important consequences for the relationship between Danish LO and the Danish Social Democrats. Svend Jakobsen, finance minister from 1979 to 1981, recalls that the LO chairman, Thomas Nielsen, "became very, very angry with the government and said some very ugly things about us. This damaged the relationship between the party and the trade union movement, and those wounds have never been healed."

Following the adoption of the new economic policy package in 1979, the government pursued a policy of devaluations, tight fiscal policies, and more restrictive incomes policies. The consequence was that real wages decreased in Denmark, which improved the competitiveness of Danish firms in international markets and arguably created the conditions for a future economic recovery. The conflicts within the government remained, however, and policies were not entirely consistent even after 1979. As I show below, the government's exchange rate policies were somewhat indecisive, and in 1981 the finance minister felt compelled to make the budget more expansive "in a few selected areas," as Svend Jakobsen puts it (interview with Svend Jakobsen, Taastrup, March 15, 2005), although the main policy was one of fiscal restraint.

In 1982, the social democratic government resigned, having failed to win support in parliament for a new economic policy package, and a center-right government was formed. As I show in Chapter 3, the new government made some important policy changes that the Social Democrats had been unwilling to make—freezing the indexation of wages and committing to a fixed exchange rate policy—but in terms of the trade-off between full employment and other economic policy goals, a gradual change in priorities had already taken place in the late 1970s and the beginning of the 1980s.

Danish Choices

The most common explanation for the economic policy choices of Danish governments in the 1970s and 1980s is that Denmark's endemic current account deficit made more expansionary policies impossible. In certain periods, the government sought to increase domestic economic activity by means of fiscal policy measures, but these policies were soon reversed when the deficit on the current account increased. Unlike in Austria and Sweden, where full employment had top priority throughout the 1970s, these concerns with external stability came to dominate economic policy in Denmark early on. Full employment became a medium-term or even long-term target rather than a short-term imperative.

Since there was so little room for maneuver in fiscal policy, the government's main economic advisers—the "Wise Men," three economics professors appointed by the government—suggested as early as 1974 that a policy of currency devaluations was one possible way to improve competitiveness (Det økonomiske Råd 1974, 15–55). Otherwise, Denmark's history of balance of payments difficulties made it difficult to counteract the employment effects of diminished foreign demand with expansionary policies (although the Wise Men still recommended expansionary policies—combined with incomes policies since it was "impossible for the state to guarantee employment without regard to the development of real wage costs"). At least in principle, larger devaluations would have encouraged exports and discouraged imports, reducing the current account deficit (and thereby creating more room for maneuver in economic policy). "Fiscal policy could only influence domestic demand," notes the economist and former social democratic politician Bent Rold Andersen. "We still had a big deficit on the current account, and it would keep growing unless we did something else. So the devaluation option was discussed all the time" (interview with Bent Rold Andersen, Næstved, March 16, 2005).

Danish governments did make a series of currency devaluations in the late 1970s and early 1980s, but the devaluations were not large enough to make a real difference to unemployment, and except for the devaluation in 1979, they were all associated with adjustments within the European exchange rate system, the "Snake" (for a history of European currency cooperation, see McNamara 1998). In Sweden, by contrast, the government decided to leave the "Snake" and made much larger devaluations—the Swedish *krona* was devalued by 10 percent in both 1977 and 1981, and by another 16 percent in 1982. Some Danish politicians—such as Ivar Nørgaard, the minister for economic affairs—were in favor of a more active exchange rate policy (Hoffmeyer 1993, 93), as were some leading civil servants in the Finance Ministry (Asmussen 2007, 77), but these ideas were never put into practice, although further devaluations of the *krone* was a real possibility until a new center-right government was formed in 1982. Knud Heinesen, who was finance minister in 1975–9 and 1981–2, claims that the economic program that the Social Democrats tried to get support for in 1982 "does not make sense unless you take a very important assumption into account: a big strategic devaluation" (interview with Knud Heinesen, Copenhagen, March 18, 2005).

The primary reason why Denmark did not opt for larger devaluations was that Denmark's European partners would not allow it. In February, 1982, the minister of economic affairs, Ivar Nørgaard, sought a big devaluation, but failed to secure the approval of the other Snake countries (Asmussen 2007, 84, 95). Theoretically, Denmark could have left the Snake—as Sweden did in 1977, and as even the Danish Council of Economic Advisers suggested in 1982 (Det økonomiske Råd 1982, 57)—but no Danish politician appears to have taken that option seriously. The failure to get European approval for a new devaluation in 1982 made a big impression, also within the social democratic party. Mogens Lykketoft—a government minister in 1981–2 who would go on to become finance minister in 1993–2000 and social democratic party leader in 2002–5—says that for many leading social democrats, this event was important since it convinced them that the devaluation instrument was no longer available (interview with Mogens Lykketoft, Copenhagen, March 14, 2005).

But there were also domestic political reasons for the reluctance of Danish governments to devalue, which brings us to some important features of Denmark's political arrangements in the 1970s and early 1980s. As several earlier studies have pointed out, the political turmoil in Denmark in the 1970s complicated economic policymaking (see, e.g., Nannestad 1991, 139), and one tool that was particularly difficult to use effectively was the devaluation instrument. "The reason that we didn't do more," Bent Rold Andersen explains, "was that the political composition of *Folketinget* [the Danish parliament] did not allow for sufficiently strong follow-up legislation. If the government devalued, it would be very tempting for the opposition to oppose and stop such legislation, forcing the government to resign" (interview with Bent Rold Andersen, Næstved, March 16, 2005).

It was particularly difficult to find support for a tight fiscal policy (which is necessary for a devaluation to have the desired effects), since wages and social benefits in Denmark were index-linked to inflation. Any attempt to ensure that real wages remained low after a devaluation required the parliament to cancel indexation, which was politically difficult, especially for the Social Democrats. The possibility of further devaluations was discussed from time to time within government circles, according to Svend Jakobsen, finance minister in 1979–81, but "there was fairly broad agreement that we would not be able to adopt the follow-up legislation that was necessary to realize all the gains from such a devaluation."

In sum, Danish governments in the 1970s did some things to keep unemployment low, but the objective of lowering unemployment was given gradually lower priority from the mid-1970s onward. By the early 1980s, the Social Democrats had resigned themselves to policies that gave priority to balance on the current account, hoping that Denmark would be able to return to full employment after a relatively long period of economic adjustment. But some influential politicians wanted to do more to reduce unemployment, and consequently economic policymaking was characterized by conflicts within the government, and between the government and the trade union movement.

At the center of this conflict was the prime minister, Anker Jørgensen. In an interview with the author, Mr Jørgensen reflected that the government's economic advisers just told the government what it could *not* do; they offered no acceptable positive alternatives:

What did they want to do instead? That was always the problem, because that was to reduce the size of the public sector, and that is what we did not want to do, not even those who said that we had to. ... Those were areas where sick people, weak people, could really suffer (interview with Anker Jørgensen, Copenhagen, August 25, 2005).

The Danish Social Democrats found no way out of this impasse when they were in government in the 1970s and early 1980s. The reason, I suggest, was that the new and uncertain political situation that emerged after the "landslide election" in 1973 complicated the pursuit of consistent economic policies, as did the deadlock within corporatist institutions and the conflicts between the government and the trade unions. An analysis of Danish politics from the mid-1970s to the early 1980s illustrates the consequences of a breakdown in established political arrangements.

The Netherlands

In the period from the mid-1970s to the early 1980s, there were important similarities between the Netherlands and Denmark, even if the balance of political power was slightly different. Just like Danish governments, Dutch governments were characterized by internal differences and conflicts over economic policy, and there were powerful conflicts between governments and interest organizations. The background was that the old Dutch political model of the 1950s and 1960s had changed profoundly in the years immediately preceding the first oil crisis. Later on, I will describe the Austrian and Swedish cases, and the comparison will demonstrate the difference that the character and stability of political arrangements made for economic policy in the 1970s and early 1980s.

From 1973 to 1977, the government of the Netherlands consisted of a coalition between the social democratic party PvdA (*Partij van de Arbeid*), the Christian democratic parties KVP (*Katholieke Volkspartij*, a Catholic party) and ARP (*Anti-Revolutionaire Partij*, a Protestant party), the progressive liberal D66 (*Democraten 66*), and the left-wing Christian party PPR (*Politieke Partij Radikalen*). The agenda of the new center-left government is commonly described as radical, and this is reflected in economic policy documents from the mid-1970s. "The government is of the opinion that structural changes are necessary in our society," said the new finance minister, Wim Duisenberg, when he presented the government's first budget in the autumn of 1973. Duisenberg (who would later become the first governor of the European Central Bank) added that the government would give priority to "the improvement of the quality of life and the maintenance and improvement of living, housing, and working conditions" (Ministerie van Financiën 1974, 3).

In the economic domain, however, the government was, at least initially, quite conservative. Already before the oil crisis, the government took some measures to "secure an early drop in the now high level of unemployment," but it did so "without going so far as to endanger the programme designed to bring about an appreciable reduction in the rate of price increases" (Ministerie van Financiën 1973, 67). Before the oil crisis, while unemployment rates were still relatively low, inflation was seen as the main economic problem in the Netherlands, also on the left.

Economic Policies in the 1970s

After the oil crisis, the government responded with moderately expansionary fiscal programs in an attempt to maintain low unemployment. The government argued that the Netherlands could afford such a policy. "With her strong external position—partly, though not entirely, due to her resources of natural gas—the Netherlands is one of the few industrialised countries which can and must permit herself a policy of compensatory growth in spending," the government said, adding that such a policy was also "necessitated" by the rise in unemployment in the Dutch economy. The expansionary economic policies were also used to further other political aims, such as the expansion of the public sector and the redistribution of income (Ministerie van Financiën 1974, 3).

The absence of external constraints due to increasing revenue from natural gas permitted expansionary economic policies, or so it was thought at the time. Later on, many Dutch politicians and economists came to the conclusion that the access to natural gas reserves contributed to a "Dutch disease" since it created the illusion that the Netherlands could avoid dealing with underlying economic problems. But this would only become a more generally accepted view later on.

Within a year after the launch of the new expansionary programs, fiscal policies changed once more (Toirkens 1988, 32–52). A "1 percent policy" was applied to government spending: the size of the public sector was not allowed to grow by more than 1 percent of GDP per year (Ministerie van Financiën 1975, 3). Some expansionary policies remained, but they were now mainly motivated by the perceived need to facilitate corporatist bargains over wages, which was increasingly regarded as the main economic problem (wage restraint has always been a core element of Dutch economic strategy). The government sought to "make a contribution toward moderating the trend of labor costs" by means of tax cuts and spending increases that would compensate wage earners for exercising wage restraint (Ministerie van Financiën 1976, 4, 33).

Just as in Denmark, the decision to withdraw some fiscal stimulus measures in 1975–6 does not appear to have been prompted by the failure of expansionary programs to achieve their intended aims. According to OECD data, the Dutch unemployment rate increased from 2.3 percent in 1973 to 2.8 percent in 1974 and 3.9 percent in 1975 (OECD 2009a). This was a significant increase, by the standards of that time, but not obviously evidence that expansionary programs were ineffective (the unemployment rate remained approximately 4 percent for the remainder of the 1970s). The view of many international observers at the time, judging from the annual OECD Economic Surveys of the Netherlands, was that the Dutch government should pursue *more* expansionary policies—only in 1980 did the OECD Secretariat agree with the Dutch government that economic policy should be directed toward medium-term fiscal goals rather than immediate economic needs (OECD, *Economic Survey: The Netherlands* 1980, 57–61). As late as 1979, the OECD insisted that the Dutch government should pursue more expansionary fiscal policies, even if the Dutch government believed, by then, that policies had been *too* expansionary for a period of several years (OECD, *Economic Survey: The Netherlands* 1980, 41).

The center-left government's "1 percent policy" can be seen as the first attempt of economic policymakers within the Finance Ministry and the central bank to impose some constraints on government policy, limiting the rise in public spending (as many authors have noted, and as my interviews confirm, the link between Dutch finance ministers and the Dutch central bank is strong). The tension between fiscal and monetary authorities on the one hand and other political agents on the other hand would be an important theme of Dutch economic policy for several years. There was no consensus on the new approach. The prime minister and the minister of social affairs were less skeptical of expansionary policies than the finance minister was. As in Denmark, the result was a standoff between different groups of politicians and civil servants within the political system.

The active use of fiscal policy to reduce unemployment was not abandoned completely, then, but a reorientation of economic policy began already in the mid-1970s. "If the international economic situation deteriorated to such an extent, the Netherlands alone could not possibly compensate for that," says Hans Margés, an economic adviser in the prime minister's office:

Some people in the cabinet—the prime minister himself, but also, very strongly, the minister of social affairs, who had to deal with trade unions and so on—felt that it should be given a try. The minister of finance, on the other hand, said that this was not the way to solve the problem: what we should do was to try to limit the growth of government expenditure, the tax burden, and the [social insurance] premiums, because it was becoming a cycle. (interview with Hans Margés, The Hague, March 22, 2006)

In the course of the 1970s and early 1980s, the Dutch government and central bank introduced a hard currency policy (as I show below, the Austrian monetary authorities followed a similar course in this period). The hard currency policy was implemented gradually during the 1970s, as the Dutch *guilder* increasingly followed the West German *mark*, if not perfectly, then at least more closely than most other European currencies. The last two (minor) devaluations against the *mark* would occur in 1979 and 1983. There were two reasons for linking the *guilder* to the *mark* (which was done explicitly from 1983 onward). First, Germany was and is economically important for the Netherlands. Second, this policy was a way to enforce price stability through the creation of an external constraint on policy, a strategy supported by both the central bank and the Finance Ministry (Szász 1999, 196, 210–11).

André Szász, a long-time member of the Dutch central bank's executive board, says that the hard currency policy was an attempt to strengthen the position of the finance minister. "The finance ministers were helped *vis-à-vis* the spending departments. You can argue that the central bank was their only real ally," he said in an interview with the author (telephone interview with André Szász, 18 April 2006). The prime minister, Joop Den Uyl, had a different view, according to Mr Szász: "Den Uyl was by temperament and education a Keynesian, and for that reason he had instinctive difficulties with constraints. He felt that monetary policy should be a part of the general policy of government. This was not the feeling of Duisenberg, and there was always this difference between the two." But the hard currency policy was supported by the Finance Ministry and the central bank, and prevailed.

Although the social democratic party PvdA increased its vote share in the next election, which was held in 1977, Joop Den Uyl's center-left government was replaced by a center-right coalition, led by the Christian democrat Dries Van Agt. The new government emphasized the need for fiscal consolidation and a reduction of labor costs. The finance minister said in his first budget speech in 1978 that a "major aspect" of the government's medium-term fiscal policy—detailed in the fiscal consolidation program *Blueprint for 1981*—was "to moderate the growth in labor costs in real terms," and to improve the budget balance. At this stage, however, the government still considered a large deficit "permissible," because of the expected effect on employment (Ministerie van Financiën 1978, 7). In other words, the government had not yet completed the transition from the employment-oriented, active fiscal policy that had been pursued in the mid-1970s to policies based on low inflation and balanced budgets, which were the main objectives from the early 1980s onward.

Frans Andriessen, who was finance minister in 1977–80, says that he saw some room for using macroeconomic policy to fight unemployment, but he was concerned that such efforts would lead to ever-increasing public spending: "the problem was that they wanted these programs to be structural, permanent measures, and I was not prepared to accept that. I was prepared to have incidental measures, of a conjunctural nature" (interview with Frans Andriessen, The Hague, March 22, 2006). For Mr Andriessen, rising debt and high wages were the main problems in the Netherlands. With regard to the unemployment problem, Andriessen was in favor of structural changes such as a decoupling of social security and wages (i.e., an end to indexation). But at this stage, there was no support for such ideas within the government, nor within Mr Andriessen's own Christian democratic party.

Economic policy during the Van Agt governments in 1977–82 was characterized by significant conflicts within the government, between the ministry of finance and the ministry of social affairs. Frans Andriessen wished to implement a mandatory wage freeze and pursue more restrictive fiscal policies, whereas other members of the government—notably the minister of social affairs, Wil Albeda—were concerned that austere economic policies would slow down the economy, and wished to maintain a working relationship with the trade unions (Toirkens 1988, 53–85; Snels 1999, 113–15). To some extent, this conflict was one of economic philosophies. "Already in the beginning," Wil Albeda says, "there was a difference between my own Keynesianism and the ideas of the minister of finance, Frans Andriessen, who rejected Keynes" (telephone interview with Wil Albeda, April 21, 2006). But it was also, and perhaps more importantly, a clash of political styles. The minister of social affairs, Mr Albeda, wanted to work within the boundaries of the established Dutch negotiation system, engaging with the unions and avoiding drastic political measures such as wage freezes and large spending cuts. Frans Andriessen, on the other hand, appears to have believed that if radical measures were required to improve the public finances and limit wage increases, such measures had to be taken even if they led to political conflicts.

The consolidation program *Blueprint for 1981*—which contained approximately 10 billion *guilders* worth of cuts in public expenditure and social security—was adopted after long negotiations, and in spite of strong opposition from the trade unions (Hemerijck 1992, 303). After this, however, it proved difficult to reach agreement on further austerity measures, although the finance minister believed that such measures were necessary. In February 1980, Mr Andriessen resigned as a result of his frustration with the government's policies: "I made concessions time and again, to find solutions," Mr Andriessen says today. "I came to a point where I couldn't continue without giving up my basic approach" (interview with Frans Andriessen, The Hague, March 22, 2006). It is noteworthy that one Danish and one Dutch finance minister—the social democrat Knud Heinesen in Denmark and the Christian democrat Frans Andriessen in the Netherlands—resigned over economic policy disagreements at approximately the same time, in late 1979 and early 1980 (October 1979 in Mr Heinesen's case; February 1980 in Mr Andriessen's).

Economic policies continued to change after Frans Andriessen's resignation. There was no mention of further expansionary measures in Mr Andriessen's last budget, the budget for 1980, and in subsequent budgets such measures were explicitly rejected. The government declared openly that in the short and medium term, increased employment would have to be given lower priority than other political objectives. It had become necessary to concentrate on the stabilization of public finances and the reduction of labor costs.

Whilst in the past the economic prospects allowed a number of objectives of economic policy to be pursued in concert, it is now no longer possible simultaneously to reduce unemployment, improve the profitability and competitive position of industry, continue to provide public services at the same level and maintain purchasing power. To put it another way: the pursuit of one objective can jeopardise the prospects of achieving one or more of the other objectives. (Ministerie van Financiën 1980, 33)

Therefore, a "genuine change for the better" would take time, requiring "radical and painful remedies." After the second oil crisis, it is clear that full employment was no longer one of the primary operative targets of Dutch economic policy, and the government declared that there would be no increase in spending to compensate for the fall in demand in the recession. Wil Albeda, the minister of social affairs, who had previously resisted austere fiscal policies and wage policies, says that he changed his mind about economic policy around 1979–80. "The big change of opinion was in 1979," Mr Albeda recalls. "We had a discussion with the Secretariat of the OECD that made a lot of impression on everybody. We all had the feeling that the matter had changed" (telephone interview with Wil Albeda, April 21, 2006). In 1982, a new center-right government, headed by the Christian democrat Ruud Lubbers, embarked on a program of budget consolidation—much like Poul Schlüter's center-right government in Denmark, which had been formed less than two months earlier. I will account for the policies of these governments in Chapter 3.

Dutch Choices

In the aftermath of the first oil crisis, in the mid-1970s, the Dutch center-left government pursued expansionary fiscal policies, which were intended to prevent unemployment increasing. As in Denmark, however, this policy was given up quite soon, and in the remainder of the 1970s, governments sought to pursue mixed goals, combining a policy of overall fiscal restraint with fiscal policy measures that were intended to support domestic demand and facilitate moderate wage agreements. Gradually, economic policy was reoriented, and fiscal consolidation and attempts to control real wage growth took precedence over low unemployment. As Hans Margés—an economic adviser to Joop Den Uyl and Dries Van Agt—puts it, "The ministry of finance played an ever more prominent and even dominant role. That is a clear conclusion, I think, that you can draw from that period" (interview with Hans Margés, The Hague, March 22, 2006).

There were important disagreements and conflicts over economic policy within the center-left government that was in power in 1973–7 and, even more so, within Dries Van Agt's center-right government, in power from 1977 to 1981. For the Van Agt government, the political situation was particularly difficult since the senior partner in the coalition, the Christian democratic party CDA, was the product of a recent merger of the three main Dutch Christian democratic parties (two Protestant, one

Catholic). The desire to keep the new party together sometimes took precedence over the coherence of government policy. Ruud Lubbers—the parliamentary leader of CDA in the late 1970s and early 1980s and prime minister in 1982–94—says that his "first priority was to realize CDA," and he suggests that the interest of maintaining party unity "was a reason why we were not so focused on financial and economic issues" (interview with Ruud Lubbers, Rotterdam, March 21, 2006).

The formation of the CDA was a response to the political changes that had reshaped Dutch politics in the late 1960s and early 1970s, and the fact that the formation of CDA complicated economic policymaking in the late 1970s and early 1980s is one of several pieces of evidence that political instability and uncertainty explains many of the choices that Dutch governments made in this period.

The main difference between Denmark and the Netherlands was that the Netherlands opted for a hard currency policy sooner, and only used the devaluation instrument for minor adjustments in 1979 and 1983 (see Chapter 3). One reason why devaluations were never seriously considered was the large extent of wage indexation in the Netherlands at this time (OECD 1988, 93); price increases on imported goods would have had an immediate effect on wages, offsetting the impact of the devaluation. But it should also be noted that the Dutch natural gas resources provided for a positive current account balance for most of the 1970s and 1980s, which meant that Dutch monetary authorities could preserve external balance without any devaluations.

Accounts of the Dutch unemployment crisis in the 1970s and early 1980s have focused either on intra-party strife and political stalemates, or on the failure of interest group concertation, which precluded comprehensive wage agreements in the period from 1970 to 1982 (Hemerijck 1992, 289). Both these conflicts were clearly important, but they were in themselves a consequence of the fact that the Dutch political model of the 1940s, 1950s, and early 1960s was crumbling. As a result, full employment was not the main priority of the finance ministry and the central bank (who both focused on low inflation and balanced budgets) nor the focus of the ministry of social affairs and the trade unions (who were more concerned with social benefits and wages). As Erik Jones (2008, 139) notes,

[A] change in social values complicated relations between elites by causing some to pursue more competitive behavior as others remained committed to consensus building. While elites debated how they should relate with each other and with society, they found little opportunity to forge agreements on what to do about the economy.

This is why the legacy of the progressive Den Uyl government was not effective policies against unemployment but egalitarian policies for income redistribution and new social programs (Snels 1999, 136), and this is why the Van Agt government's term in office was a period of strong conflicts within the government.

Austria

So far, I have discussed two countries whose governments decided that they were unable to prevent an increase in unemployment already in the mid-1970s, and who experienced a further, large increase in unemployment around 1980. I have suggested, and I argue further below, that this was at least partly a result of political uncertainty and instability. Austria, by contrast, is the clearest example of how a stable political system and tightly coupled institutions could increase a government's willingness and ability to pursue employment-oriented macroeconomic policies in the adverse economic circumstances of the 1970s. The Austrian economic policy strategy—which was based on an "unconventional assignment of instruments to goals"—was highly dependent on Austria's political arrangements.

Ever since the aftermath of the Second World War and the formation of the Second Republic (Austria gained full independence when the State Treaty was signed by the allied powers in 1955), the Austrians had constructed an elaborate, integrated political model, built on principles of power sharing and social partnership (*Sozialpartnerschaft*; for a detailed account of Austria's "social corporatism," see Katzenstein 1984). At the time of the first oil crisis, Austria was ruled by a social democratic single-party government that had been in power since 1970. From 1971 to 1983, the Social Democrats controlled an absolute majority of the seats in the lower chamber of the Austrian parliament, the *Nationalrat*. The federal chancellor, Bruno Kreisky, had been elected party leader at the 1967 party congress, where the Social Democrats had moved toward the center, attempting to win the support of growing constituencies of white-collar workers and professionals (Jelavich 1987, 298, 302).

There can be no doubt that full employment was the primary goal of economic policy in what the Austrians call the "Kreisky Era" (1970–83). Each year, the finance minister's annual economic policy declarations placed the objectives of *Vollbeschäftigung* (full employment) and *Arbeitsplatzsicherung* (job protection) first on the government's list of priorities (see, e.g., Österreichischer Nationalrat, October 22, 1974, 11450–5; November 12, 1975, 157; October 21, 1976, 3154). An often cited ideological expression of the government's commitment to full employment is Bruno Kreisky's dictum that he lost more sleep over one unemployed person than over a million Austrian *schilling* in government debt (Pick 2000, 141).

According to Hannes Androsch, who was finance minister in 1970–81, there were both economic and political reasons for the government's belief that it was necessary to maintain full employment. The economic crisis of the 1930s was still in living memory, and the civil war and 1938 *Anschluss* were widely regarded as indirect results of the employment crisis during the Great Depression.

We were fully aware that economic mismanagement and economic failure would have severe social consequences; but even worse, could lead to terrible political consequences. That was our mindset. Keeping unemployment as low as possible was, undoubtedly, our primary objective. (interview with Hannes Androsch, Vienna, November 22, 2007)

There is a lot of evidence that the memory of the Great Depression had a direct impact on the Austrian approach to the problem of unemployment in the 1970s and early 1980s (for the testimony of the chancellor himself, see Kreisky 1989). But the memory of the 1930s also mattered indirectly, since the political institutions of the Second Republic were designed to manage economic and social conflicts, avoiding the ideological and political polarization that had destroyed the First Republic before the war.

Economic Policies in the 1970s

Austria was affected later by the economic downturn after the oil crisis than most other European countries, but toward the end of 1974, it became clear that economic activity was slowing down, and Austria had negative growth in 1975. The social democratic government responded with highly expansionary fiscal policy measures that were intended to support domestic economic activity (Österreichisches Nationalrat,

November 12, 1975, 157; October 21, 1976, 3154): the budget deficit exceeded 4 percent in both 1975 and 1976.

As in the three other countries, then, Austrian economic policies after the oil crisis were expansionary, based on the assumption that there would only be a short-term crisis and that "steadiness of final demand" was a prudent policy in these circumstances (Rothschild 1994, 120). Unlike fiscal policies in Denmark and Sweden in the mid-1970s, however, which were to a large extent based on tax cuts designed to stimulate private consumption, Austrian economic stimulus plans in the 1970s were largely based on public investments. As the former finance minister Hannes Androsch puts it, the government pursued "a policy-mix of demand management supported by appropriate supply-side measures, where both were designed to be consistent with an overriding hard currency policy" (interview with Hannes Androsch, Vienna, November 22, 2007).

Monetary policy was also relaxed in the mid-1970s, but this was a less prominent feature of Austrian macroeconomic management, and in the course of the 1970s monetary policy was used less and less to influence the domestic economy. A failed attempt to keep interest rates lower than the German Bundesbank's in 1979 was the last time that Austrian monetary authorities treated the interest rate as an instrument of domestic economic management (Unger 2001, 346). While fiscal policy was used to keep unemployment low in the adverse international circumstances of the mid-1970s, exchange rate policy—and therefore in the long run also monetary policy—was assigned to maintaining a fixed exchange rate between the Austrian *schilling* and the West German *mark*.

This "hard currency policy" (*Hartwährungspolitik*) was implemented gradually after the breakdown of the Bretton Woods system in the early 1970s: a trade-weighted currency index was introduced in August 1971 (Androsch 1985, 78–9), then more and more currencies were dropped until only the German *mark* remained (Mooslechner, Schmitz, and Schuberth 2007, 25–6), and from 1981 to the creation of Europe's Economic and Monetary Union in the late 1990s, the Austrian *schilling* was practically fixed to the German currency (Handler and Hochreiter 1998, 24). The hard currency policy was initially controversial, but it had the support of the central bank, the trade unions, and the finance minister, and it was therefore maintained even if some influential political actors—including the chancellor, Bruno Kreisky—had their doubts. From 1979 onward, the policy was rarely questioned politically (Hochreiter and Winckler 1995, 92–3).

The man behind the hard currency policy was Heinz Kienzl, a former chief economist at the Austrian union confederation ÖGB (*Österreichischer Gewerkschaftsbund*), who, by the 1970s, had become the first executive director of the Austrian central bank. He still had links to the unions, especially to the powerful leader of ÖGB, Anton Benya (ÖGB president from 1963 to 1987), who was also the speaker of the parliament, and who in turn had a close relationship with the finance minister, Hannes Androsch (Mr Androsch referred to Benya as his "fatherly friend"— *väterlicher Freund*—in a speech in 2006). Hannes Androsch, Anton Benya, and Heinz Kienzl were key supporters of the hard currency policy. In 1978, the former Finance Minister Stefan Koren, a Christian Democrat, joined this group of important backers when he became central bank governor.

A hard currency policy—pegging the national currency to the currency of a low inflation country (in this case, Germany)—is primarily a policy for price stability, and it may therefore seem surprising that the Austrian trade unions were committed to such a policy. As I will show later, for instance, the Swedish trade union confederation LO supported the big Swedish devaluation in 1982, since the LO leadership believed that it would help to preserve full employment. However, both Hannes Androsch and Heinzl Kienzl said in interviews with the author that they did not believe that devaluations were useful. "We did not want this instrument," Mr Kienzl says (interview with Heinz Kienzl, Vienna, June 7, 2006), and according to Mr Androsch, "The idea that the exchange rate can be used as an active instrument to achieve low unemployment is an illusion," for although a devaluation can increase competitiveness and therefore also exports and employment in the short run, "this benefit won't last long" (interview with Hannes Androsch, Vienna, November 22, 2007).

The underlying concern of the unions and the Social Democrats was by all accounts that the hard currency policy made it easier for the trade unions to control wage formation. "The main reason for the trade unions was that we wanted to keep inflation down," according to Günther Chaloupek, an economic adviser at the chamber of labor (a social partnership institution closely connected to the trade union confederation). "We wanted to avoid the kind of inflationary spiral that developed in Italy and the United Kingdom" (interview with Günther Chaloupek, Vienna, June 8, 2006). Hannes Androsch also believes that the hard currency policy "forced the export-oriented Austrian economy to modernise," since there was "pressure to innovate" (interview with Hannes Androsch, Vienna, November 22, 2007).

The fact that the Austrian government relinquished the possibility of devaluing the *schilling* should not, however, be interpreted as an underlying change in the objectives of economic policy. Full employment would remain the main objective of economic policy until the mid-1980s, and when the hard currency policy was established, Austrian politicians appear to have been confident that they had other instruments at their disposal that would be sufficient to maintain low unemployment. This conviction meant that the hard currency policy was not seen as a fundamental change in economic policy at the time (unlike in Denmark in the early 1980s and Sweden in the early 1990s, where the adoption of hard currency pegs represented a transition from employment-oriented to low inflation-oriented policies). As Georg Winckler (1988, 226) has noted, the fact that "the government declared time and again that its goal was to preserve full employment made it easy for the trade unions to accept a hard currency policy that would increase real wages, without having to fear job losses."

One alternative instrument was the incomes policy of the social partners: it was assumed that the trade unions would be able to adjust their wage demands to the fixed exchange rate regime, containing inflation and maintaining the competitiveness of Austrian export-oriented firms (Rothschild 1994, 121). Countercyclical fiscal policy was also an important part of the policy mix that the Austrian government and its advisers had in mind when they formulated the hard currency policy. Heinz Kienzl himself believed that expansionary fiscal policy could be used to maintain low unemployment in the recession (Kienzl 1978, 178), and he says today that "fiscal policy in these years was more or less an instrument to keep full employment, to keep demand for commodities and services" (interview with Heinz Kienzl, Vienna, June 7, 2006). Demand management through interventionist fiscal policies—particularly policies designed to influence investment behavior—had a long history in Austria, being the basis of an economic strategy that went back to the first years of the Second Republic (Guger 1998, 47). This incidentally makes Austria different from Sweden, where social democratic governments in the 1950s and 1960s relied more on active labor market policy programs (see Marterbauer 2001 for a comparison of Austria's and Sweden's economic policy models).

The combination of employment-oriented fiscal policies, a hard currency policy *vis-à-vis* the West German *mark*, and price stability- and competitiveness-oriented incomes policies controlled by the social partners, has often been referred to as *Austro-Keynesianism*—after the short essay "Austro-Keynesianismus," which was written by the economist Hans Seidel in 1982 (at the time, Mr Seidel was state secretary in the finance ministry). It is important to not underestimate the third component of Austro-Keynesianism, the centrally negotiated incomes policy, which provided for real wage flexibility and inflation control (Marterbauer 2001, 227; Unger 2001, 343). Hannes Androsch says that "tacit agreement with the ÖGB, and Anton Benya, in particular," was an important condition of the government's policies in the 1970s. "The ÖGB agreed to keep wage demands moderate, and thus ensure the success of the programme. The basis of this agreement was mutual trust" (interview with Hannes Androsch, Vienna, November 22, 2007). The close cooperation between the government and the unions would prove especially important when some of the negative effects of the highly expansionary fiscal policies of the mid-1970s became apparent.

With the budget for 1977, presented in the autumn of 1976, Austria's social democratic government adopted a more cautious fiscal policy. The immediate crisis was over, and the government said that it would pay more attention to fiscal balance, while maintaining sufficiently high demand to support full employment (Österreichischer Nationalrat, October 21, 1976, 3151). A year later, in 1977, a rapidly increasing balance of payments deficit had become a major concern for the Austrian government, which presented a first policy package to deal with the balance of payments crisis on October 5, 1977. This first package was followed up by a national budget that continued to emphasize the need for fiscal consolidation (Österreichischer Nationalrat, October 18, 1977, 6301–2). In its efforts to reduce the deficit, the government was helped by its close ties with the unions and by the centralization of Austrian wage bargaining. The fact that the trade unions agreed to moderate wage demands after two years of high wage increases in the mid-1970s was a clear example of the high flexibility and coordination capacity of the Austrian social partnership system at this time, as I will show in more detail later in this chapter.

Hans Seidel, who was an economic adviser to the finance minister in the 1970s and early 1980s, has written that the high current account deficit was seen as a sign that the generally expansionary economic strategy could not be sustained indefinitely. There was a "rethinking" of budgetary policy in the late 1970s, Seidel noted, and after the second oil crisis—in a recession that began in 1980 and deepened in 1981—fiscal policy was less expansionary than it had been in the mid-1970s. Yet Mr Seidel also wrote that full employment would remain the top priority (Seidel 1982a, 18–21), and well into the 1980s, the government declared that full employment, or *Vollbeschäftigung*, came first (Österreichischer Nationalrat, October 18, 1978, 10223; see also October 23, 1979, 685 and October 22, 1980, 4560), even if fiscal policy was not based on generally expansionary policies, as in the mid-1970s, but on a more complex policy mix. Mr Androsch says today that compared to the first half of the 1970s, "the period from 1977 to 1981 was the more successful part, in the context of the more difficult external environment and the need for fiscal consolidation" (interview with Hannes Androsch, Vienna, November 22, 2007).

The policy program that was used to bring down the large current account deficit in the second half of the 1970s was developed jointly by the central bank, the trade union confederation ÖGB, and the finance ministry. In Austrian economic policymaking, the government had primary responsibility for fiscal policy, the central bank had primary responsibility for monetary policy, and the social partners had primary responsibility for wage formation, but powerful political mechanisms allowed for the coordination of policymaking in all these domains, and cooperation and consensus across institutions were expected (Mooslechner, Schmitz, and Schuberth 2007, 22–4).

In the late 1970s and early 1980s, many other measures, apart from general economic policies, contributed to the maintenance of low unemployment in Austria. For example, Austria had long operated a guest-worker system managed by the social partners, and used these workers as a buffer in economic downturns—from a peak of 227,000 foreign workers before the first oil crisis, the number of foreign workers declined to 139,000 in 1984 (Schweighofer 1995, 31). Moreover, the state-owned industries—which still accounted for a large proportion of Austrian business in this period (see Chapter 3)—pursued countercyclical policies of their own, and were instructed not to lay off workers in recessions. Like a number of other European states—including the Netherlands—Austria also began to use early retirement programs to remove older workers from the labor force, again reducing unemployment rates in the short term (Unger and Heitzmann 2003, 376; on the political economy of early retirement in Europe and the United States, see Ebbinghaus 2006).

Nevertheless, many leading policymakers believed that macroeconomic policy played an important role well into the 1980s. For example, in a paper written in the early 1980s, Hans Seidel wrote that fiscal policy was a key instrument, for in Austria, deficit spending was practiced "with more faith in the beneficial effects of such a policy than elsewhere" (Seidel 1982*a*, 18).

In January 1981, finance minister Hannes Androsch, who had been in office since 1970, stepped down. On the level of political rhetoric, the government kept emphasizing the objective of full employment in even stronger terms than it had in the past. "The budget is restrictive enough to retain the budgetary room for maneuver of the early 1970s," the new finance minister, Herbert Salcher, declared in 1981 (Österreichischer Nationalrat, October 22, 8663). "But it is also expansive enough to contribute to securing full employment." The next year, the finance minister said that the "Austrian Way" was defined by the pursuit of active employment policies almost at any cost: "All economic policy instruments are used to prevent unemployment, even if we have to pay the price of additional pressure on the Federal Budget" (October 20, 1982, 12791).

Although the political rhetoric was defiant, Hans Seidel says that the last years of social democratic single-party government in the early 1980s was a kind of "interregnum" when "no clear-cut economic policy was made" (interview with Hans Seidel, Vienna, November 23, 2007). The background to the government's economic policy stance in this period, Mr Seidel says, was that "Kreisky insisted on big budget deficits" whereas the minister of finance—who was "a practical man with no macroeconomic ambitions"—did not object.

In 1983, the Social Democrats lost their absolute majority and Bruno Kreisky resigned. In 1983–6, Austria was ruled by a coalition between the social democratic SPÖ and the liberal FPÖ. In this period, Austria began its transition from the employment-oriented macroeconomic policies of the 1970s and early 1980s to a policy of budget consolidation, which would become the predominant target from 1987 onward. The government's annual economic policy statements changed: whereas the 1970s and 1980s had been about absolute targets such as *Vollbeschäftigung*, the goal in 1984 was "a high level of employment" (*eines hohen Beschäftigungsniveaus*; October 19, 1984, 5225; see also October 23, 1985, 9270). The employment target lost some of its prominent status. "Verbally, it was never given up," according to Ferdinand Lacina, finance minister in 1986–95, "but you had to change the wording to 'as high as possible' some time in the early 1980s" (interview with Ferdinand Lacina, Vienna, June 6, 2006).

"The Keynesian strategy continued," says Werner Teufelsbauer, a former head of the economic policy department at the federal chamber of commerce.

But it was not as explicit, it was not programmatic, it just happened then. When there was a problem, everybody got together in the parity commission [the *Paritätische Kommission für Preis- und Lohnfragen*, a central feature of the Austrian social partnership system]—the chancellor and the presidents [of the unions and employer organizations] and the leading advisers—and said "Let's do something." But it increasingly turned out that the real effect somehow disappeared. So we lost the faith then. But only in the end of the 1980s. (interview with Werner Teufelsbauer, Vienna, June 5, 2006)

Austrian Choices

Austria ended the 1970s with an unemployment rate that was no higher than it had been in 1970. This was a remarkable achievement in a decade when other countries suffered both high inflation and high unemployment. It was the result of a concerted political effort, involving a mix of policies, where a prominent role was given to fiscal policy. The Austrian government's strategy was possible for several different reasons. One was the strength of the social democratic single-party majority government. Another reason was that the centralized social partnership system made it possible for the government to achieve low inflation without having to pursue disinflationary fiscal and monetary policies. However, neither of these factors can account fully for the Austrian experience. As Peter Nannestad (1991, 65) noted in a comparative study of crisis management in the 1970s, the "system of mutual dependencies" that the complicated Austrian policy mix was based on could not have been maintained for long without "the glue of a basic consensus keeping distributional conflicts at bay." Institutions were not enough. For example, by all accounts the social partnership system remained intact well into the 1990s, and in some ways even today, yet the strategy of employment-promoting fiscal policies were given up already in the 1980s.

There is a deeper historical and political explanation, I think, for Austria's approach in the 1970s and the early 1980s. In the early 1970s, Austria was still a relatively poor Western European country, and its political system, the Second Republic, was still young. Postwar reconstruction was still ongoing, and importantly, there was a high degree of faith in Austria's integrated political model, which was based on the social partnership system and on substantial government involvement in the economy. As Chapter 3 will show, economic policies only changed in the mid-1980s, when the comprehensive political model that seemed to be successful in the 1970s had become increasingly contested.

Sweden

Sweden is similar to Austria in the sense that full employment was the primary objective of economic policy in the 1970s and 1980s. By all accounts, Swedish governments in this period hardly even considered economic policies that might have resulted in high unemployment. According to Kjell-Olof Feldt, social democratic minister of trade in 1970–6 and minister of finance in 1982–90, full employment was the "absolutely dominant objective of economic policy," and other objectives "came much further down the list" (telephone interview with Kjell-Olof Feldt, March 31, 2003). When a center-right coalition consisting of the Centre Party, the Liberal Party, and the Conservative Party won power in 1976, it proved to be just as committed to employment-oriented economic policies as the social democratic government that preceded it. Sten Westerberg, who was state secretary in the budget ministry and the ministry of economic affairs in 1976–82, says that "unemployment was seen as something incredibly evil—so evil that you couldn't even write about it in the fiscal plans [the government's main economic policy document]" (interview with Sten Westerberg, Stockholm, June 3, 2002).

What is interesting about the comparison between Austria and Sweden is that Swedish governments in the 1970s and early 1980s lacked two distinct advantages that the Austrian social democratic governments enjoyed in this period.

First, governments in Sweden were weaker. The 1973 election resulted in a hung parliament, so from 1973 to 1976, 175 Social Democrats and Communists faced 175 representatives of the Centre Party, the Liberal Party, and the Conservatives, which meant that it was no longer enough for the social democratic government to get the support of the Communists; it also had to seek the support of one or more center-right parties. Then, from 1976 to 1982, Sweden was ruled by four relatively short-lived center-right governments. In Austria, by contrast, Bruno Kreisky's government could rely on a majority in parliament from 1971 to 1983. Hannes Androsch, finance minister in 1970–81, says that this mattered greatly to the government's room for maneuver: "We enjoyed an absolute majority. When the chancellor or I, or both of us together, said 'we are going to do this,' it was as if the parliament had already decided on it" (interview with Hannes Androsch, Vienna, November 22, 2007).

Second, by the 1970s, Sweden's centralized wage bargaining system no longer allowed for the effective coordination of wage bargaining. Unlike

Austrian governments, therefore, which could rely on the social partners to control real wage costs in the late 1970s, Swedish governments had to resort to currency devaluations and other political interventions to ensure that their employment-oriented economic policies did not lead to unsustainable increases in real wage costs. The fact that Swedish governments nevertheless maintained employment-oriented policies into the late 1980s suggests that institutional capacity may matter less to the choices of governments than historically defined expectations on what governments can and should do.

Economic Policies in the 1970s

Just like governments in Austria, Denmark, and the Netherlands, the Swedish government initially responded to the recession of the mid-1970s by means of expansionary fiscal policies. In the spring of 1974, the social democratic government and the center-right opposition agreed on a number of policies that were designed to counteract the deflationary effects of the oil crisis. The government wrote in the introduction to the 1975 budget bill that although many other OECD countries had given priority to low inflation and external balance, Sweden would accept temporary inflation and trade deficits in order to maintain full employment—which was, the government said, an absolute requirement (Swedish parliamentary papers, Prop. 1975:1, 2, 16, 23).

The means of attaining full employment in the mid-1970s were twofold. First of all, the government used expansionary policies with general effects on demand, such as tax cuts. These policies were favored by the center-right opposition. Second, there were selective, targeted policies—more favored by the Social Democrats—such as support for investment and production. Taken together, these policies were referred to as "bridging policies" (*överbryggningspolitik*), since the idea was to "bridge" the economic downturn and maintain high economic activity until the expected international recovery began.

The government and the center-right parties agreed that full employment was the primary objective of economic policy. Although the government recognized that both inflation and the current account deficit were high, "[f]ighting inflation and the current account deficit through the forced decrease in demand that unemployment and economic stagnation would lead to" was simply not an option (Prop. 1975/6:100, 47). These policy priorities were also reflected in a series of major economic policy agreements between the government, the Liberal Party, the trade unions, and in one case the Centre Party that were concluded in the years immediately following the oil crisis (Bergström 1984).

In 1976, the three center-right parties won the election, and for the first time in forty years, the Swedish prime minister—the Centre Party leader Thorbjörn Fälldin—was not a social democrat. Between 1976 and 1982, Sweden had three different center-right coalition governments and one Liberal minority government. From the 1976 election until the autumn of 1978, the three center-right parties formed a majority government, which broke down over the issue of nuclear energy; then a Liberal minority government was in power until 1979. After the election in 1979, the three parties again formed a majority government, which lasted until the spring of 1981, when the Conservatives left because of disagreements over tax policy; then the Centre Party and the Liberal Party formed a minority government, which remained in power until the election in 1982, which the Social Democrats won.

In its first budget, the new center-right government declared its continued support for the expansionary fiscal policies that had been adopted after the first oil crisis (Prop. 1976/7:100, 7, 18). It did not take long, however, before the government resorted to currency devaluations in order to prevent a further decline in the export industry, whose situation was soon seen as a major economic problem because of high wage cost increases in the mid-1970s. On April 4, 1977, Sweden asked for special consultations with the other members of the "Snake" system, which Sweden had joined in 1973, although it was not a member of the European Community. Sweden originally requested an 8 percent devaluation, but the other Nordic countries persuaded Sweden to accept 6 percent. According to the revised budget bill in April, the reason for the devaluation was that Sweden's effective exchange rate had *de facto* appreciated in 1976, when Sweden's *krona* was pegged, through the Snake, to the German *mark*. At this stage, the government explicitly stated that the devaluation did not take care of the high wage costs paid by export-oriented firms (which was the underlying concern); this problem would have to be solved "internally" (i.e., through moderate wage agreements) (Prop. 1976/7:150, 12).

In the late spring and summer of 1977, there were intense discussions within the government about the need for yet another, larger devaluation, which in effect would force Sweden to leave the Snake (Eklöf 1990, 46–7)—a step that the Danish government never took in this period. On August 29, 1977, Sweden devalued by another 10 percent against the *mark*. A devaluation of this size was not acceptable to the other Snake countries. The central bank's board of governors therefore decided, after consultations with the government, to withdraw from European exchange rate cooperation. From August 1977 to May 1991, the Swedish *krona* was pegged to an exchange rate index, which was trade weighted and contained the currencies of all countries that accounted for more than 1 percent of Sweden's foreign trade.

The reasons for the large devaluation in 1977 were, according to the government, that Sweden did not expect to profit from international economic recovery any time soon, and an internal adjustment of the Swedish economy was "entirely unrealistic" since it would have led to high unemployment (Prop. 1977/8:45, 6). While exchange rate policies became looser, fiscal policies initially got more austere (Prop. 1976/7:150, 9). But there was no definite break with the previous fiscal policy stance: as the government pointed out in 1977, it did not rely on exchange rate policy alone to keep unemployment low, and a year later, the government again started to pursue more expansionary fiscal policies (Prop. 1978/9:50, 13).

Apart from devaluations and expansionary fiscal policies, center-right governments in the late 1970s and early 1980s relied heavily on subsidies and loans to firms and to entire economic sectors in order to prevent further economic decline and unemployment. At this time, large parts of the Swedish economy were scaled back: production at the shipyards halved in the mid-1970s, and steel production declined by 30 percent (Magnusson 2002, 476–7). The fall in industrial production was exceptionally steep: production growth went from being considerably higher than the European average in 1975 to being almost 8 percent lower in 1976 and 1977 (Jonung 1999, 126). Many ambitious industrial programs were launched, and many new government agencies were established to implement them.

This all shows how far the center-right governments in the late 1970s were prepared to go to maintain full employment—further, perhaps, than the Social Democrats. An interpretation of Swedish policies in the 1970s and 1980s requires an explanation of this puzzling fact. One possible explanation is that the center-right parties pursued these policies for tactical reasons. Nils Åsling, the minister for industry, says that employment had top priority, for since the new government was "the first center-right government in many, many years, we did not want to seem worse—in terms of the labor market—than the Social Democrats" (interview with Nils Åsling, Stockholm, August 21, 2002). Ingemar Mundebo, the budget minister, confirms that the government was sensitive to any objections to its employment policies: "In less sophisticated political debates, people said that the center-right parties *wanted* high unemployment. Elsewhere, people said that the center-right parties lacked the necessary competence and skill to deal with the problem." This explains the employment-oriented economic policies of the center-right, Mr Mundebo says (interview with Ingemar Mundebo, Stockholm, April 4, 2002).

But there is also evidence that the center-right parties excluded the option of permitting an increase in unemployment for ideological reasons, and because of expectations on government, ingrained in Sweden's political culture. Thorbjörn Fälldin, the prime minister, describes his views at the time in the following way:

It was quite normal for Sweden to have practically full employment. If you've gotten used to that, it's hard to change. People asked, "Why should we give up a society that works this well? Shouldn't we do something to make the future society work like this also?" (interview with Thorbjörn Fälldin, Ramvik, May 2, 2002)

The ambitious employment policies of the center-right parties cannot be interpreted as simple electoral tactics—the Centre Party and the Liberal Party, and perhaps the Conservatives also, were genuinely committed to full employment.

The economic policies of the new center-right coalition after the 1979 election were quite different from those pursued in 1976–9. Fiscal policy got tighter, and more importantly, it was no longer seen as an instrument of macroeconomic stabilization. Instead of adopting "bridging policies," the center-right governments in the early 1980s argued—much like the Danish and Dutch governments did in the same period—that trade and budget deficits must be brought down, and that keeping economic activity high could only be achieved through increased international competitiveness. From 1980 to 1982, all economic policy documents contained sections on the need for decreased public spending. A first major budget-cutting bill (Prop. 1980/1:20) was sent to parliament in October 1980. The main aim of fiscal policy was now to reduce the budget deficit and reduce government expenditures.

But this fiscal policy change did not mean that governments gave up on full employment. On September 14, 1981, the government devalued the *krona* by another 10 percent. The main rationale for this devaluation was, according to government bills, high labor costs, and it would have been "unrealistic," the government said, to wait for unions and employers to strike moderate wage deals, for in the short term, this would have led to large increases in unemployment (Prop. 1981/2:30, 5). Rolf Wirtén, who was budget minister and minister of economic affairs at the time, believes that the policy package presented in 1981 was an important step, politically: "It initiated more offensive policies, while retaining the insight that we had to get rid of the budget deficit," he says (interview with Rolf Wirtén, Linköping, May 13, 2002). Sten Westerberg, Mr Wirtén's state secretary for economic affairs, says that the devaluation was intended to complement the austere fiscal policies adopted in 1980–1.

There was a wish to follow up the cost-cutting policies—which were seen as defensive—with a real 'offensive' measure. ... If the public sector couldn't be the engine of the economy anymore, you needed something else to be the engine. (interview with Sten Westerberg, Stockholm, June 3, 2002)

In other words, for the Swedish government, fiscal austerity only, a policy pursued by Danish and Dutch governments from 1982 onward, was not an option. That was why the government devalued the currency. When the Social Democrats regained power in 1982, their policy was based on similar considerations.

A "Third Way" for the 1980s

On October 8, 1982, its first day in office, Olof Palme's new social democratic government devalued the Swedish *krona* by another 16 percent. The devaluation was originally supposed to be 20 percent (in a last-minute memo, one of the architects of the social democratic economic program, Michael Sohlman, even suggested that it should be 25 percent; see Lindvall 2004, 74). This was an unusually large devaluation at this time, and it testifies to how important the goal of full unemployment was in Sweden as late as the early to mid-1980s.

The economic policies of the social democratic government from 1982 onward were in many ways different from the policies that social democratic governments had pursued in the 1970s. Yet, although some of their policies were new, the Social Democrats were determined not to make the kinds of concessions that social democrats in other European countries (such as Denmark and the Netherlands) had made in the 1970s and early 1980s. The government was well aware that Sweden's approach to economic policy was increasingly unique. "We felt that bourgeois forces—business—were on the march for the first time in many years," says Ingvar Carlsson, a leading social democrat who went on to become prime minister after the murder of Olof Palme in 1986. "But we did not want to give up, as they did in some other countries" (interview with Ingvar Carlsson, Stockholm, January 29, 2003).

This defiance comes out strongly in an internal memo from 1982, which was written by Michael Sohlman, one of the architects of the new social democratic government's economic strategy. "Conservative forces in the world," Mr Sohlman remarked, "use the international economic crisis as a pretext for a broad campaign against welfare societies of the social democratic (USA: liberal) kind. Since Mitterrand has run into considerable difficulties after the first year's policies, the eyes of the world will turn to Sweden." A failure in Sweden would have serious repercussions. On the other hand, Mr Sohlman wrote, "If we succeed, that would be a major blow to conservative parties in Europe" (Sohlman 1982*a*, 13; translation by the author). By changing course slightly, the Social Democrats hoped to remain a viable political alternative while preserving their core values.

The new government argued that fighting inflation through austere policies, allowing unemployment to rise, was an unacceptable solution to Sweden's economic problems: the welfare costs would be large, and yet it was not certain that balance would return to the economy (Prop. 1982/3:50, 18). Expansionary policies such as the "bridging" policies that the Social Democrats pursued in the mid-1970s were not considered either (Prop. 1982/3:50, 16–17). The government instead opted for a "third way": a big, final devaluation, followed by austere fiscal policies that would enable a transfer of resources from sheltered economic sectors (including the public sector) to the competitive, export-oriented sector (Prop. 1982/3:100, 7). Domestic demand must be kept low enough for the transfer of resources to the non-sheltered sector to take place; hence, the government's intention was to pursue austere fiscal policies for a period of several years (Prop. 1982/3:100, 13–17).

The details of the policy changes that the new social democratic government made in 1982—including the big devaluation—were prepared in the spring of 1982 by two young economic advisers: Michael Sohlman and Erik Åsbrink. They operated independently, without a clear mandate. In the summer of 1982, Mr Sohlman and Mr Åsbrink presented their ideas to a small group of policymakers, including the future finance minister, Kjell-Olof Feldt, and they seem to have had no difficulties selling their ideas to the party leadership. "In the party," Erik Åsbrink says, "nobody had a clear idea of what the economic strategy after the election should be, so you could get things done if you said 'let's do it this way' " (interview with Erik Åsbrink, Stockholm, October 15, 2001).

On one point, however, the strategy that Mr Sohlman and Mr Åsbrink had prepared was not implemented. Apart from the devaluation and a general policy of fiscal restraint, they proposed that Sweden should adopt a hard currency policy, pegging the Swedish *krona* to the West German *mark*. The idea was to stabilize inflation expectations, much like the Austrians had used a hard currency policy to control inflation in the 1970s (in fact, Mr Sohlman and Mr Åsbrink consulted social democratic economists in Vienna while they were preparing their reports in 1982).

In one of the reports that Michael Sohlman wrote in 1982, the choices that the incoming social democratic government faced were presented in great detail. Sohlman (1982*b*, 10–12) noted that there were four ways to restore the competitiveness of Swedish export-oriented firms, which was seen as a necessary condition of economic recovery. The best solution would have been for unions and employers to reduce real wages (which incidentally is what Austrian unions did in the late 1970s). In his opinion, this level of real wage flexibility might have been how "the Swedish wage bargaining model worked in its golden age in the 1950s and 60s," but in his judgment, this model was long gone by the early 1980s. Another method was to let unemployment increase, but this would take too long and the costs would be unacceptably high. A third option was to simultaneously reduce the payroll tax and increase the sales tax, but this method would take time, and the effects would come slowly. He therefore advocated the remaining, fourth option, which was a big devaluation.

"We had to improve our competitiveness," Mr Sohlman said in an interview with the author. "The question was if it would happen quickly, or over a long period of time, during which the weakest members of society would suffer" (interview with Michael Sohlman, Stockholm, October 31, 2001). Although the economic strategy of the 1980s was different from earlier social democratic policies, the main aim was to achieve the traditional goal of social democratic economic policy: full employment. The premise was that full employment was "the purpose and soul of social democracy," as he put it.

With respect to growth, employment, and the balance of payments, the government's economic strategy appeared to be successful in the first half of the 1980s. But within the ministry of finance and the government more generally, there was some concern about the side effects of the employment-oriented macroeconomic policies early on. The ministry of finance therefore prepared a series of special economic policy bills, in an attempt to address the problem of inflation (for much of the 1980s, inflation was relatively high in Sweden, compared to other West European countries, as I show in Chapter 3). In the spring of 1983, for example, the government announced that it would pursue a "forceful anti-inflationary policy" and bring down inflation to 4 percent in 1984 (Prop. 1982/3:150), and in the spring of 1984 the government announced a series of measures to keep inflation below 3 percent in 1985 (Prop. 1983/4:200). The outcomes were 8 percent in 1984 and 7.4 percent in 1985. The trade unions had promised wage restraint when they were consulted about the big devaluation in 1982, and whereas wage agreements were in fact moderate in the early 1980s, from 1984 onward they caused more trouble for the government (Carlsson 2003, 196). By the late 1980s and early 1990s, these sorts of problems had accumulated, leading the Swedish social democratic government to change its economic policies in important ways. Those policy changes will be described and accounted for in Chapter 3.

Swedish Choices

For longer than any other country considered in this book—indeed, for longer than any other country in Europe, except perhaps Norway—Sweden used macroeconomic policies to keep unemployment low. In the 1970s, Swedish governments relied on expansionary fiscal policies (regardless of whether they were social democratic, as in 1973–6, or center-right, as in the period from 1976 onward). In the late 1970s and early 1980s, on the other hand, Swedish governments relied on large devaluations of the *krona* (again, regardless of party composition). The last two devaluations, in 1981 and 1982, were large enough to carry Sweden through the 1980s without an increase in unemployment. In 1990, Sweden's unemployment rate was approximately as high as it had been in 1970.

There are many possible explanations for the political priorities of Swedish governments in the 1970s and 1980s. One is that Sweden has been ruled by a social democratic party for long periods of time. However, the center-right governments that ruled Sweden in 1976–82 were just as eager to maintain full employment as the Social Democrats were. Another explanation is that Sweden's centralized wage bargaining system, which was only decentralized in 1983, allowed governments to concentrate their efforts on employment while unions and employer organizations contained inflation. However, nominal wage increases in the mid-1970s were high and the only reason Sweden did not experience a rapid deterioration in competitiveness was the devaluations. As I will show later, Swedish labor market institutions in the 1970s did not compare favorably with the centralized and efficient wage bargaining institutions in Austria. As Nannestad (1991, 116) has observed, the Swedish policy mix in the 1970s showed little evidence of being the result of an efficient social and economic model.

Yet full employment remained the main aim of economic policy. My view is that there were underlying political reasons for the economic policy choices of Swedish government in the 1970s and 1980s. There was still strong faith in the political model that had emerged after the war: the idea of a "strong state" that was expected to produce continuous social reform (Lindvall and Rothstein 2006). In Chapter 3, I will show that when this political model declined in the late 1980s, economic policies also changed.

The Difference that Politics Makes

One might reasonably have expected Denmark to have more in common with Sweden than with the Netherlands, and the Netherlands to have more in common with Austria than with Denmark. Scholars of the welfare state—and of comparative political economy more generally—typically regard the Scandinavian countries as similar to one another, just as the continental states north of the Alps, such as Austria and the Netherlands, are seen as institutionally and politically alike. Moreover, the political left has traditionally been stronger in the two Scandinavian countries, where the social democratic parties had clearly been dominant between the end of the Second World War and the autumn of 1973. In this period, Sweden had three prime ministers, all social democrats, and of Denmark's nine prime ministers, six were social democrats (between 1945 and 1973, the Danish Social Democrats were out of power for less than nine years). The Austrian Social Democrats, by contrast, had been the junior partner in a series of grand coalitions, and they were out of office in 1966–70. In the Netherlands, the Christian Democrats were even more dominant, taking part in all coalition governments (although the Netherlands had social democratic prime ministers in 1945–6, 1948–58, and again from May 1973).

It is noteworthy, then, that in the area of economic policy, Denmark and the Netherlands had much in common in the 1970s and 1980s.

1. Both Danish and Dutch governments adopted expansionary fiscal policies in 1974–5, but they changed policies again in 1975–6,

giving higher priority to budget balance and balance on the current account.

2. After these initial attempts to support economic activity, economic policymaking in Denmark and the Netherlands was characterized by political conflicts within parties, within governments, and between governments and interest organizations. Whereas finance ministries and central bankers wanted to give priority to external balance, incomes policies, and a reduction of public spending, other influential politicians, groups and institutions wished to do more to increase employment in the short run, support the unemployed, and avoid conflicts with the trade unions.

3. As I show below, corporatism and wage bargaining were deadlocked since the trade unions and the employer organizations failed to overcome their political differences. Governments in both countries were constrained by the extensive indexation of wages and social benefits (Hemerijck 1992, 291, 298), which was in itself a symptom of the inability of different interest groups to resolve distributional conflicts in a pragmatic manner.

4. As a result of these conflicts within governments, and between unions and employers, the late 1970s and early 1980s were characterized by mixed and rather inconsistent economic policy strategies.

5. In both countries, new center-right governments were formed in 1982. By then the economic situation had deteriorated so much that the new governments were able to pursue austere fiscal policies without the risk of a severe political backlash (see Chapter 3).

In Austria and Sweden, governments did things differently. Instead of withdrawing fiscal stimulus in the mid-1970s, they pursued expansionary fiscal policies well into the 1980s, and when Swedish governments gave priority to budget consolidation in the early 1980s, they used currency devaluations as an alternative instrument of employment promotion. The emphasis on full employment in Austria and Sweden was relatively uncontroversial at this time.

The similarities between Denmark and the Netherlands are especially striking when one considers the fact that these two countries faced different economic challenges in the 1970s. Whereas most Danish policymakers and economic advisers believed that the current account deficit was the main constraint on economic policy, without which expansionary fiscal policies would have been both possible and desirable, the Netherlands had a current account surplus until the early 1980s, as a result of the country's natural gas exports. Dutch politicians were more concerned with rising wage costs and the trend of yearly increases in government spending, which was not a major concern in Denmark. In some sense, of course, the economic challenges that Danish and Dutch governments faced can be seen as symptoms of the same underlying problem complex, but the fact that their economic circumstances were different still suggests that one must go beyond purely economic circumstances to explain why Danish and Dutch governments made similar policy choices in the 1970s and 1980s.

In this section, I present evidence in support of the argument that domestic political arrangements mattered to the economic policy strategies of governments in the 1970s and 1980s, concentrating on Denmark and the Netherlands, since the postwar political settlements in these two countries were already disintegrating by the early 1970s. Already before the first oil crisis, changes in the Danish and Dutch party systems—and in the relationship between the state civil society—had fatally undermined the stable political arrangements that the postwar settlement depended on. As a result, the objective of full employment was no longer an overriding imperative. Austria's and Sweden's tightly coupled political models, on the other hand, were still intact when Europe's employment crisis began. When the Austrian and Swedish political models started to unravel in the mid- to late 1980s, economic policies changed in these two countries as well (see Chapter 3).

Party Politics

Figure 2.1 uses one of the most common measure of the number of significant parties in the party system—the *effective number of parties*, originally proposed by Laakso and Taagepera (1979)—to describe the development of the Austrian, Danish, Dutch, and Swedish party systems from 1960 to 2006. As the figure shows, there were big changes in the Dutch party system in the late 1960s and early 1970s, when the effective number of parties increased from around 5 to around 7 (the reduction of the effective number of parties in the late 1970s was a result of the merger of the three main Christian democratic parties). Figure 2.1 also identifies a structural break in Denmark in 1973, when the number of parties increased from 4.5 to 7, but it suggests that the transformation of the Danish party system had already begun in the mid-1960s. In the two other cases, Austria and Sweden, changes were smaller and occurred

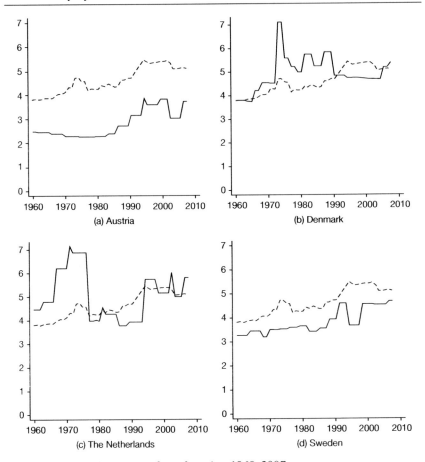

Figure 2.1 The effective number of parties, 1960–2007

Data source: Armingeon et al. (2009). The effective number of (elective) parties is defined by $N = 1/\sum_{i=1}^{m} v_i^2$, where N is the effective number of parties, m is the number of parties, and v_i is party i's vote share. The dotted line represents the mean effective number of parties in the thirteen European countries that have been democracies since the Second World War, excluding countries with a population of less than 1 million. One property of N is that if all parties have the same size, the effective number of parties is the same as the actual number ($N = m$). In all other cases, the effective number of parties is lower than the actual number ($N < m$). The effective number of parties can be calculated on the basis of the number of votes that parties receive or the number of seats that they win. Following Lijphart (1990, 483), who claims that data based on vote shares allow for a better description of the "long-term nature of the party system," I use the first measure, but it makes little difference since all four countries have proportional electoral systems (the correlation between the two alternative measures is in the 0.97–1.00 range for this sample of countries; in majoritarian countries such as the United Kingdom and the United States, it is as low as 0.60–0.70).

Table 2.1 New political parties, 1960–79

	1960s	1970s
Austria	*No new parties*	*No new parties*
Denmark	Socialist People's Party (1960–)	Progress Party (1973–2001)
	Independent Party (1960–6)	Centre Democrats (1973–2001)
	Liberal Centre (1966–8)	Christian People's Party (1973–94, 1998–2005)
	Left Socialists (1968–71, 1975–87)	Communist Party (1973–9)
		Justice Party (1973–5, 1977–81)
Netherlands	Farmers' Party (1963–81)	Democratic Socialists '70 (1971–81)
	Democrats 66 (1967–)	Political Party Radicals (1971–89)
		Christian Democratic Appeal (1977–)
Sweden	*No new parties*	*No new parties*

Note: All parties that entered parliament between 1960 and 1979 are listed, excluding parties that never held more than two seats. The Dutch party *Christen Democratisch Appèl* is a merger of the country's three main Christian democratic parties: the *Anti-Revolutionaire Partij*, the *Christelijk Historische Unie*, and the *Katholieke Volkspartij*.

later: there was a small but significant increase in the effective number of parties in Austria in the mid-1980s and in Sweden in the late 1980s and early 1990s. The cross-country differences in the timing of party system change that Figure 2.1 describes were probably the result of a combination of social circumstances and institutional factors: electoral thresholds are lower in Denmark (2 percent) and the Netherlands (an effective threshold of less than 1 percent) than they are in Austria and Sweden (both have 4 percent thresholds).

Table 2.1, which lists all new parties that entered parliament in the 1960s and 1970s, confirms that the stability of the postwar party system ended much earlier in Denmark and the Netherlands than in Austria and Sweden. In order to move beyond simple, numerical criteria, I will examine each of these countries in greater detail. In this chapter, I will concentrate on Denmark and the Netherlands. A discussion of Austria and Sweden will follow in Chapter 3. In the two latter countries, as Table 2.1 shows, no new parties entered parliament in the 1960s, the 1970s (or the first half of the 1980s, for that matter), which makes them very different from Denmark and the Netherlands.

In Denmark, the transformation of the party system began with the reform of the Communist Party in the late 1950s and early 1960s (which resulted in the formation of the Socialist People's Party), and the formation of some new, relatively small parties later in that decade. However, the most significant event in the history of the postwar party system by far was the 1973 election, which is often referred to as the "landslide" election (*jordskredsvalget*) since five new parties entered parliament, unsettling the previous balance of power between the Conservatives, the Social Democrats, the Liberals, and the Social Liberals. The new parties that entered parliament included the anti-tax Progress Party (*Fremskridtspartiet*)—which transformed into the anti-immigrant Danish People's Party (*Dansk Folkeparti*) in the early 1990s—the Center Democrats (*Centrumdemokraterne*), and the Christian Democrats (*Kristeligt folkeparti*).

In the Netherlands, the late 1960s and early 1970s was a period when the old Dutch political culture declined and a new era of more competitive politics began (Lijphart 1975, Chapter 10). Several new parties emerged that were only weakly connected to old social categories, including the progressive-liberal D66, the progressive Political Party Radicals (which were included in the center-left government of the mid-1970s), and the socialist DS70. When the confessional parties merged in 1977 to form a new Christian democratic party (CDA, *Christen Democratisch Appèl*), this was at least partly a response to these changes within the party system, and as Lijphart pointed out, the creation of the CDA was itself a break with the old consociational logic, since the Catholics and the Protestants used to belong to different "pillars" in Dutch society, and since it contributed (along with left-wing mobilization in the early 1970s) to more competitive politics.

The traditional parties were particularly weak in the early 1970s, just before the oil crisis. From 1946 to 1967, the dominant parties—the three Christian democratic parties, the Liberal Party, and the Social Democrats—held between 86.2 and 91.6 percent of the seats in the Dutch parliament; after the 1967 election, they controlled 78.9 percent of the seats, and in the 1971 and 1972 elections they won only 71.7 and 73.1 percent (Andeweg and Irwin 2009, 54). In other words, whereas the party system was completely dominated by the Social Democrats, the Christian Democrats, and the Liberals until the late 1960s, other types of political parties have since become politically relevant (Andeweg and Irwin 2009, 56–7), especially green and new left parties, progressive-liberal parties, and—more recently—various populist far-right parties.

Both in Denmark and the Netherlands (and later also in Austria and Sweden, as I show in Chapter 3), the most significant economic policy changes that occurred in the period that I am concerned with here—that is, when full employment was replaced by low inflation and balanced budgets as the main economic policy objective—were implemented soon after structural changes in the party system. Party politics probably did not have a direct effect on economic policies, but they arguably had indirect effects: the decline of established structures of party destabilized the institutions and norms that governed postwar policymaking, and made politics more uncertain.

It is important to note that party systems changed *before* the policy shifts that I seek to explain. In other words, to the extent that there is a relationship between economic policy decisions and underlying political developments, as I think there is, economics did not drive politics. In the Netherlands, new parties entered parliament in the late 1960s and early 1970s, before unemployment became a major issue. In Denmark, the party system changed more suddenly, in the "landslide election" of 1973, but as Jørgen Elklit (2002, 49) has demonstrated, there were early signs of movement in the party system as early as 1966: the dramatic events in 1973 appear to have been the result of underlying political changes that accumulated over a period of several years.

Corporatism

By the early 1970s, as I showed in the first chapter, Austria, Denmark, the Netherlands, and Sweden all had highly developed corporatist policy-making institutions. That is, not only did these countries have a history of more or less coordinated wage bargaining; trade unions and employer organizations were also involved in the development and implementation of public policies, especially in the social and labor market policy domains. As I will show in Chapter 3, corporatism was stable in Austria and Sweden in the 1970s and 1980s. This, however, was not the case in Denmark and the Netherlands, where corporatist institutions were deadlocked as a result of divisive conflicts between unions and employers.

In Denmark, the weakening of corporatism in the 1970s was a result of the political debate over economic democracy, which I mentioned in the section on Denmark above. The fact that the unions and the employer organizations—and the political parties—disagreed on this fundamental issue of economic power and distribution led to policymaking stalemates in many different areas. For example, interest organizations and political parties failed to reach agreement on any reforms of the pension system before the late 1980s, since the unions and the political left favored a state-run pension system (similar to the one introduced in Sweden in the 1950s), whereas the employers and the political right opposed any such reform since they were concerned that it might lead to economic democracy in disguise (Anthonsen and Lindvall 2009, 179; on the historical development of the Danish pension system, see Green-Pedersen 2003 and Green-Pedersen and Lindbom 2006).

As previous studies of Danish economic policy have shown, the disagreements over economic democracy did not only result in a temporary decline of corporatism; it also had direct consequences for economic policymaking in the 1970s, since the trade unions would only accept low wage increases if they got economic democracy in return (Nannestad 1991; Nannestad and Green-Pedersen 2000). Denmark's neighbor Sweden had its own debate on economic democracy—in the mid-1970s, the trade union confederation LO proposed the creation of so-called "wage-earner funds" that would increase the power of unions in large Swedish firms—but in Sweden, the conflict over wage-earner funds did not lead to a decline in corporatism until the late 1980s and early 1990s (Anthonsen, Lindvall, and Schmidt Hansen 2009, Section 4).

The Netherlands is similar to Denmark in the sense that there was a crisis of corporatism in the 1970s and early 1980s as a result of ideological and distributional conflicts. As Steven Wolinetz (1989, 79) has observed, postwar politics in the Netherlands had been characterized by "a strong and persistent partnership among trade unions, business associations and government," but in the 1960s this close cooperation "gave way to disagreements on wages and wage regulation," and in the 1970s, the social partners "were unable to agree on either wages or the overall direction of social and economic policy." The main corporatist institutions—the Foundation of Labor and the Social and Economic Council—could no longer play the coordinative role that they had played in the past. Indeed, "rather than operating as a forum for discussion and the discovery of an underlying consensus, the Social and Economic Council functioned more like a British-style Parliament in which opposing sides stated positions known in advance" (Wolinetz 1989, 84, 87; see also Hemerijck 1992, Chapter 8, Hemerijck 2002, and Jones 2008, 109–10). Today most scholars agree that Dutch and Danish corporatism resurged in the 1980s and 1990s, but before that happened, many scholars believed that corporatism in the Netherlands had become "increasingly residual" as Gladdish (1991, 146) put it (see also Kurzer 1993, 68–9).

Since the postwar settlement did not only depend on stable party systems but also on a historic compromise between labor and capital, institutionalized through corporatism, the decline of Danish and Dutch corporatism in the 1970s was a break with the past, and there are strong reasons to believe that this event mattered to economic policymaking, just as the party system changes that I described earlier.

The Purpose of Political Authority

There was another important difference between the Danish, Dutch, Austrian, and Swedish political systems in the 1970s and 1980s, which becomes clear when one considers the political rhetoric that Austrian and Swedish governments used when they explained their economic policy choices in the 1970s and early 1980s. This rhetoric, which was based on the idea of a specific Austrian Way (*der österreichische Weg*) or Swedish Model (*den svenska modellen*), would hardly have been possible in Denmark or the Netherlands. Whereas Austrian and Swedish postwar politics were based on a sense of shared national purpose—in Austria, the idea of social partnership as a basic national principle; in Sweden the idea of the strong society, or strong state—Danish and Dutch politics were always better understood as fluid systems of continuous negotiations among and between political parties and interest groups (Pedersen 2006). In the Netherlands, the internal organization of the cabinet itself used to reflect the balance of power in Dutch society: there were traditional links between the Ministry of Social Affairs and the unions on the one hand and between the Ministry of Economic Affairs and the employers on the other, with the Ministry of Finance representing a certain *raison d'état*. This arrangement went back to the establishment of a special economic cabinet committee in the early 1950s (Hemerijck 1992, 286): central government decision-making was, in itself, an aspect of the permanent negotiation among interest groups.

In Chapter 3, I will show that when Austrian and Swedish governments changed the main objective of economic policy from full employment to low inflation and balanced budgets in the mid-1980s and early 1990s, this policy choice was closely related to more or less simultaneous decisions to apply for membership in the European Community. The reason was not merely that joining the European Union forced the Austrian and Swedish governments to adapt their economic policies to what had by then become the European mainstream; more importantly, both the decision to apply for membership and the decision to give lower priority to full employment were consequences of internal changes in the Austrian and Swedish political models.

Alternative Explanations

The empirical evidence that I have presented so far suggests that political circumstances mattered to the economic policies that governments pursued in the decade after the first oil crisis. Before concluding the analysis of political responses to the threat of unemployment, I will consider two other factors that might conceivably explain why governments in Austria, Denmark, the Netherlands, and Sweden made different choices in the 1970s and early 1980s: on the one hand, economic circumstances; on the other hand, political institutions and labor market institutions.

Economic Circumstances

When governments in Denmark and the Netherlands explained their economic policy choices, they referred to pressing economic problems: in the Danish case, the endemic current account deficit; in the Dutch case, the growth in public spending (an issue that was related to labor market trends since automatic indexation mechanisms immediately translated wage increases into increases in social benefits). It is therefore important to consider whether governments in Denmark and the Netherlands faced specific economic constraints in these areas.

In Denmark, concerns with the trade balance featured prominently in policy documents in the 1970s and 1980s, and the deficit on the current account is a common explanation for the hesitant policies that Danish governments pursued in the 1970s. Knud Heinesen, social democratic finance minister in 1975–9 and 1981–2, believes that this was the main difference between Denmark and countries that pursued more expansionary policies: "I don't think we had a sufficiently good balance of payments situation to pursue more expansionary policies than we did" (interview with Knud Heinesen, Copenhagen, March 18, 2005; see also the OECD *Economic Surveys* of Denmark in 1973, 29–31, and in 1977, 49). Many scholars, notably Lars Mjøset (1987, 426–8), have also argued that Denmark's large deficits on the current account made expansionary fiscal and monetary policies impossible since an increase in domestic demand would immediately lead to larger imports, and thus to a further deterioration of the balance of payments. Denmark started to experience balance of payments problems already in the 1960s (Trier 1997, 37–8) and ran current account deficits until the early 1990s (Andersen 1999, 16).

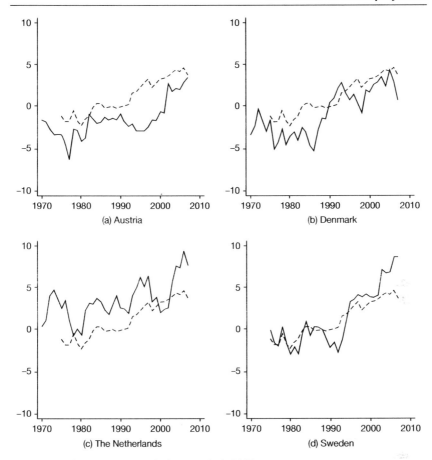

Figure 2.2 Current account balance, 1970–2008

Data source: OECD (2009*a*), except for the data for Denmark before 1988, which are from Mikkelsen (1993, 422). The dotted line represents the mean current account balance in the thirteen European countries that have been democracies since the Second World War, excluding countries with a population of less than 1 million. The data are missing for many observations before 1975, so the reference series only begins in that year.

Figure 2.2 describes the development of the current account balance in Austria, Denmark, the Netherlands, and Sweden from the early 1970s onward. The figure confirms that Denmark had large current account deficits in the 1970s and 1980s. But so did Austria, and although these deficits were seen as a major economic problem at the time (see, e.g., OECD's *Economic Survey* of Austria in 1977, 20–1), they did not stop the Austrian government from pursuing employment-oriented and often expansionary fiscal policies well into the 1980s (when active demand management was given up in Austria in the mid-1980s, the current account was actually in balance). Moreover, Denmark's Scandinavian neighbor Sweden dealt with its relatively minor current account deficits in the late 1970s and early 1980s by devaluing its currency, and as I argued above, the Danish government's reluctance to follow a similar course was largely a result of political factors. In conclusion, the fact that the export-oriented sector of the Danish economy was relatively small mattered to economic policy making, but an account of the differences between Austria, Denmark, the Netherlands, and Sweden must take other factors into account.

Figure 2.2 also shows that the Dutch current account was in surplus throughout the 1970s, which incidentally meant that Dutch governments were under constant pressure from the OECD, whose *Economic Surveys* argued that the Netherlands should adopt more expansionary policies; yet Dutch governments were reluctant to do so. This brings us to the Netherlands, where governments in the 1970s and 1980s were concerned with high wage increases and high annual growth in public spending. Again, however, an analysis of objective indicators (in this case of wage costs and public debt) suggests that economic circumstances were interpreted differently in different countries. The OECD (2009*a*) publishes measures of unit labor costs (wages and salaries, including employer contributions to social security, per unit of output, relative to other countries) that go back to the 1970s, and these data show that whereas Austrian relative unit labor costs increased by 16 percent between 1970 and 1980, Dutch relative unit labor costs were more or less constant throughout the 1970s and only increased by 1 percent between 1970 and 1980 (there was a marked increase in the early 1970s, before the oil crisis, and a marked decrease in 1979–80). Yet Austrian governments pursued employment-oriented macroeconomic policies longer than Dutch governments.

Turning to government budgets, Figure 2.3 describes the development of government debt—defined as the gross financial liabilities of general government—from the early 1970s onward. This figure shows that the Netherlands started out with a higher level of accumulated debt than Austria and Sweden (using alternative debt measures that have been compiled by Franzese, 1999), one can also show that Denmark had lower debt than the Netherlands in the 1970s), so it is possible to argue that Dutch governments were more constrained than governments in Austria, Denmark, and Sweden by the need to consolidate public finances. However, the figure also shows that unlike the three other countries, the Netherlands had falling levels of debt until 1977–8 (although spending

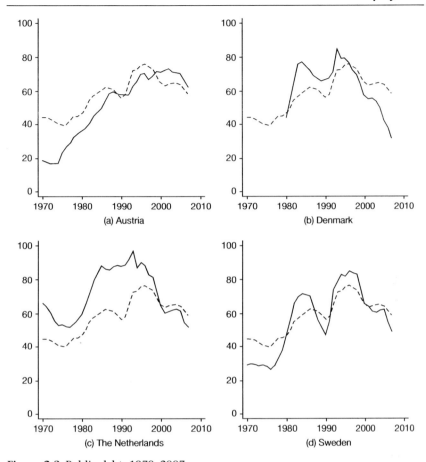

Figure 2.3 Public debt, 1970–2007

Data source: OECD (2009a). In this figure, public debt is defined as general government gross financial liabilities. The dotted line represents the mean level of debt in the thirteen European countries that have been democracies since the Second World War, excluding countries with a population of less than 1 million.

increased in many areas, so did the revenues from natural gas). This should have eased the constraints on economic policy, and probably explains why international observers such as the OECD encouraged the Dutch governments of the 1970s to pursue more expansionary policies. The decision to give priority to fiscal restraint already in the mid- to late 1970s was at least partly a political choice: pursuing more expansionary policies would still have been possible (the situation in the early 1980s was more difficult), but Dutch governments believed that it was more useful and important to bring about structural changes in wage formation and in the development of public spending.

Political Institutions and Labor Market Institutions

The most common explanation for the divergence of economic policies in Western Europe after the first oil crisis is that political institutions and labor market institutions, particularly the authority of central banks and the character of the wage bargaining process, determined the ability of governments to use economic policies to pursue objectives such as low unemployment and low inflation (at least their ability to pursue these objectives simultaneously).

As I showed in Chapter 1, quantitative indicators of central bank independence do not provide a consistent ranking of the Austrian, Danish, Dutch, and Swedish central banks in the 1970s and 1980s. A closer examination suggests that the Danish and Dutch central banks may well have had more influence in the 1970s and 1980s, but this influence largely derived from political circumstances, endogenous to the political story I am telling.

The Danish central bank—with its long-standing governor Erik Hoffmeyer, who headed *Nationalbanken* for almost thirty years, from 1965 to 1994—was an important institution, but when the government tried to get European support for a large devaluation in 1982, against the central bank's will, there was little that the central bank could do to stop it. In the Netherlands, central bank independence was also limited, since the finance minister was authorized to instruct the central bank (Jones 1998, 151–2), and as the former central banker André Szász notes, "the law gave them the authority to issue directives, and even if they didn't issue a directive—and that has never happened in practice—they were responsible" (telephone interview with André Szász, April 18, 2006). When Paulette Kurzer (1993, 138, 141–5) argues that the Dutch central bank was highly independent in the 1970s and 1980s, she bases this claim on the fact that Dutch ministers of finance normally support the central bank's policies, which is a feature of Dutch politics and history, not of Dutch institutions *per se*.

The Austrian central bank is politically dependent in the sense that the social partners are represented on the board and a majority of the board members are appointed by the government (Müller 2003, 245), but as I showed in Chapter 1, some scholars still rank the Austrian central bank as more independent than the Danish and the Dutch central banks.

Concerning Sweden, finally, it is true that the central bank was politically dependent until central bank independence was introduced in the late 1990s, but only in the sense that the parliament had the opportunity to appoint a new governing board, which could then appoint a new governor, and this mechanism has never been used to dismiss a central bank governor that the government disapproved of (furthermore, the Swedish central bank was *de facto* independent from 1982 onward, long before it achieved *de jure* independence in the late 1990s; see Lindvall 2004, Chapter 3).

Another alternative explanation that must be considered is that the relatively low level of coordination and centralization in Danish and Dutch wage bargaining explains the differences between Danish, Dutch, Austrian, and Swedish economic policymaking in the 1970s and 1980s. The Netherlands is often mentioned as an example of how the absence of centralized wage bargaining made macroeconomic management more difficult after the first oil crisis. No successful wage accord was concluded without government intervention between 1970 and 1982 (Hemerijck 1992, 290), and Bart Snels (1999, 137, 143) has argued that the lack of effective wage bargaining coordination explains why the Dutch social democratic government in the 1970s could not do more about employment. The Danish case has similar characteristics, as Peter Nannestad (1991) and Torben Iversen (1998) have documented.

The Austrian case was different (Iversen 1999, 151–5). The union confederation ÖGB and the employer organization WKÖ were able to maintain central control over wage bargaining, which made the coordination of economic policies easier to accomplish. For example, in the second half of the 1970s, after a few years of excessive wage increases in the mid-1970s—which led to current account deficits—the Austrian government could rely on the social partners to restore economic balance. Werner Teufelsbauer, a former head of the economic policy department at the chamber of commerce, mentioned this event in an interview with the author, and noted that "the trade unions accepted to be very moderate in the next years, and that worked quite well" (interview with Werner Teufelsbauer, Vienna, June 5, 2006).

However, the wage bargaining argument is less helpful in the Swedish case. Although it is often argued that the formal decentralization of wage bargaining in 1983 undermined Sweden's macroeconomic regime (Iversen 1999; Wallerstein and Golden 1997), there was a *de facto* decentralization of wage formation in Sweden already in the 1970s, in the sense that agreements between LO and SAF no longer determined wage increases in the entire labor market (Calmfors and Forslund 1990, 79). The main reason was the increasing heterogeneity in the Swedish labor force: the white-collar unions grew in prominence, as did public sector unions, since the public sector (especially social services) expanded so much in the 1970s (Elvander 1988, 36–8; Nycander 2002, 156–62). Moreover, changes in the organization of industrial production increased the heterogeneity in the manufacturing sector as such (Swenson and Pontusson 2000).

There is little evidence that formal decentralization as such had any effects on Sweden's capacity for wage moderation (Hibbs and Locking 1996, 133–7). Unsustainable wage increases were a problem already in the 1970s. Relative unit labor cost increases between 1975 and 1978 were higher than any increases in the 1980s, and the devaluations in 1981 and 1982 were the main reasons why labor costs did not increase more rapidly in the early 1980s. In fact, developments in the 1980s— after the decentralization of wage bargaining—were quite similar to those in the 1970s: an increase in relative unit labor costs in the second half of the decade compared to the first (Lindvall 2004, Chapter 2).

In spite of these developments, Swedish governments continued to pursue employment-oriented macroeconomic policies well into the 1980s. In that sense, the importance of wage bargaining institutions for the distinctive trajectory of Swedish economic policies in the 1970s and 1980s may have been overstated. The disintegration of the wage bargaining system was one of several structural changes that set the stage for economic policymaking throughout the 1970s, 1980s and 1990s; it does not explain the timing of the transition from full employment-oriented policies to disinflationary policies.

It is interesting to note that although Swedish wage bargaining outcomes were inconsistent with macroeconomic stability already in the 1970s, policymakers kept their faith in the virtues of the centralized wage bargaining system well into the 1980s, especially within the social democratic party. In one memo written before the party's social democratic election victory in 1982, for example, the economic adviser Erik Åsbrink wrote that he expected unions to restrain wage increases, and that the centralization of wage bargaining was one of the conditions for this strategy (Åsbrink 1982). Kjell-Olof Feldt, the finance minister between 1982 and 1990, says that it was simply taken for granted, in 1982, that inflation would be kept in check by means of "political solidarity" between the unions and the social democratic party, although he now believes that the wage-setting model disintegrated already in the mid-1970s: "the centralized wage bargains that we had in the early 1970s and which fell apart more and more after that were just a memory in the 80s" (interview with Kjell-Olof Feldt, Stockholm, October 30, 2001).

Similarly, Ingvar Carlsson, who became deputy prime minister in 1982 and prime minister in 1986, has written that "it is obvious that the social democratic leadership tried for too long to maintain something that was already lost. Our inability to face this new reality probably had a negative effect on our ability to adjust and develop policies to the requirements of a new age" (Carlsson 2003, 207). "The wage-setting model didn't break down in the 80s; it had already broken down in the early 70s," Mr Carlsson said in an interview with the author (interview with Ingvar Carlsson, Stockholm, January 29, 2003).

Conclusions

When the European economies went into a deep recession in the mid-1970s, after the first oil crisis, countries responded differently. Although many European states—particularly the smaller ones—initially followed the OECD's advice and took expansionary fiscal policy measures in order to maintain economic activity, some countries, including Denmark and the Netherlands, changed policies relatively quickly. But other countries, such as Austria and Sweden, tried for a long time to avoid any policy decisions that might result in higher unemployment.

In this chapter, I have tried to explain why governments made different choices. Political circumstances—specifically, the stability of the political arrangements that had been established after the Second World War—mattered greatly to the actions of governments. In Austria and Sweden, where political arrangements were stable and political agents simply assumed that the "Austrian Way" must be followed and the "Swedish Model" preserved, governments did not only have the institutional capacity to coordinate active policy responses to the crisis of the 1970s; more importantly, governments took for granted that everything must be done to maintain full employment, since it was the linchpin of these political models (about which I will have more to say in Chapter 3).

In Denmark and the Netherlands, things were different. The institutional and normative structures that had supported postwar political arrangements were crumbling, and the rules of the game were changing. Previously stable party systems had changed beyond recognition, as new types of parties had entered parliament, and corporatist models of political decision-making were undermined by intensified ideological conflicts. In these circumstances, full employment—which was an overriding imperative in Austria and Sweden—became but one policy objective among many. For a few years, governments pursued mixed and rather inconsistent policies, until new center-right governments in the 1980s made more decisive breaks with the past, imposing austere policies in Denmark and the Netherlands.

3

New Regimes

By the 1980s, few West European countries, apart from Austria and Sweden, tried to use macroeconomic policy to sustain full employment. By now, most other countries in the region had given priority to low inflation and balanced budgets. The French U-turn in economic policy in 1983—when François Mitterrand's new administration abandoned its ambitious economic policy strategy less than two years after taking office—made a big impression in political circles across Europe (on the "Mitterrand Experiment," see Hall 1986, Chapter 8). Furthermore, "sound" economic policies, with low inflation and balanced budgets as their main objectives, had become the new orthodoxy in international organizations such as the International Monetary Fund (IMF) and the OECD.

The economic policies of the 1970s, when many governments attempted to achieve economic recovery by means of expansionary fiscal programs, were widely regarded as failed. In the aftermath of the second oil crisis, which occurred in 1979, the OECD Secretariat did not recommend a policy of domestic expansion, as it had done after the first oil crisis in 1973 (see Chapter 2). Among academic economists, monetarist and neoclassical ideas—which emphasized the drawbacks or even the futility of expansionary, interventionist fiscal policies—had become increasingly influential. The conservative election victories in Britain and the United States in 1979 and 1980 increased the political prominence of such beliefs.

This chapter documents the consolidation of new macroeconomic regimes in Denmark and the Netherlands in the early 1980s, and the end of employment-oriented macroeconomic policies in Austria and Sweden in the late 1980s and early 1990s. In the 1990s and 2000s—until the crisis of 2008–9—macroeconomic policy in these countries was largely the domain of central banks. To the extent that governments tried to reduce unemployment, they used other instruments, such as wage restraint (to improve the competitiveness of national firms on international markets) or supply-side labor market reforms (which is the topic of Chapter 4). There have been a few exceptions—for example, in the first half of the 1990s, the Austrian and Danish governments used expansionary fiscal policies in attempts to reduce unemployment—but overall, in the last two decades, the economic policy statements of governments have had relatively little to say about macroeconomic policy in the traditional sense of the word. They have been more concerned with issues of taxation, government spending, the distribution of income, and regulatory reforms.

Whereas Chapter 2 concentrated on analyzing and explaining the development of economic policies in Denmark and the Netherlands in the 1970s and early 1980s, this chapter is mainly concerned with explaining the economic policy changes that occurred in Austria and Sweden in the mid- to late 1980s and early 1990s. I will argue that these policy changes were associated with wider changes in the Austrian and Swedish political models in the late 1980s and early 1990s—a period when Austria and Sweden became, in a certain sense, ordinary European states.

Denmark

In 1982, Denmark's prime minister Anker Jørgensen, whose Social Democrats had governed alone or in coalition with the Liberal Party since 1975, resigned without calling new elections. Following Mr Jørgensen's resignation, the Conservative leader Poul Schlüter formed a new center-right coalition with the Liberal Party and two center parties, the Center Democrats and the Christian Democrats. The new government also relied on the support of the Social Liberal Party, *Det Radikale Venstre*, whose unwillingness to back up the social democratic government had led to the government's downfall.

Economic Policies in the 1980s

The new government was generally expected to be short-lived, but the Conservatives and the Liberal Party went on to rule Denmark, in coalition with various other parties, until 1993. During that period, the deficit on the current account and the high level of unemployment continued to be the country's main economic problems: in the early to mid-1980s, unemployment declined and the current account deficit increased; in the late 1980s and early 1990s, on the other hand, the current account deficit was finally replaced by a surplus, but unemployment increased to even higher levels than in the early 1980s.

On three points, the new center-right government changed Danish economic policy decisively, establishing the main elements of an economic policy regime that has lasted to this day (Asmussen 2007, 91). First, the government abolished the indexation of wages and social benefits. Second, the government declared that public sector consumption growth would be halted. Third, the government announced that it would pursue a fixed exchange rate policy, making no further devaluations. Following a meeting at the central bank on September 10, 1982, before the new government took office, the leaders of the two main coalition parties— the conservative Poul Schlüter and the liberal Henning Christophersen— declared that "the government has no intention of devaluing the *krone*" (Budgetdepartementet 1982, Appendix 8).

The central bank governor Erik Hoffmeyer believed that a devaluation at this time would have been "entirely pointless" since the Danish economy had "gone through an adjustment of real costs—real wages had declined—and there was no reason to inject more inflation into the system" (interview with Erik Hoffmeyer, Copenhagen, March 17, 2005). Yet, this was not an uncontroversial view, for in its annual report, published in October 1982, the economic advisers in the Danish economic council recommended a large devaluation, continuing the policy of labor cost reductions that had begun in 1979 (Det økonomiske Råd 1982, 55–60). The fixed exchange rate regime that was introduced in 1982 endured, however. The exact arrangement was not explicitly defined, but the German *mark* was implicitly understood to be the reference point (Andersen, Hougaard, and Risager 1999, 14), until the creation of the euro.

As I showed in Chapter 2, the previous social democratic governments had already changed Denmark's economic policies in the course of the 1970s and early 1980s, and full employment had ceased to be the primary target of fiscal policy before the Social Democrats lost power. The center-right government's economic program went further still (Nannestad and Green-Pedersen 2000, 10–11), signaling that it was now up to the unions and employer organizations to set wages that were consistent with lower unemployment (Andersen, Hougaard, and Risager 1999, 7). In 1983, the finance ministry's annual report on fiscal policy said that the government's economic policy targets were balance on the current account within three to four years, an elimination of the budget deficit, and a reduction of inflation (Budgetdepartementet 1983, 12). Lower unemployment was not included in this list of economic policy targets—it was expected to follow, once the other economic problems had been dealt with.

The politicians who were responsible for these policies believed that other economic problems were more pressing. Poul Schlüter, who was prime minister from 1982 to 1993, says that low unemployment was a long-term goal:

> It was one of our objectives, but it was difficult, because some of the things we did led to an increase in unemployment in the short term, even if the effect was the opposite in the long term.... I don't think you can say that we ranked unemployment low on our list of objectives. We were very preoccupied with this all along, but it was difficult to find the right balance. (interview with Poul Schlüter, Frederiksberg, August 26, 2005)

Similarly, Palle Simonsen, a centrist Conservative politician who became finance minister in 1984, says that the government had to pay attention to many goals, and low unemployment was one of them, but other problems were more urgent:

> The goal was to get a budget surplus and a surplus on the current account. It was quite clear that we could not live with the deficit on the current account— and not the deficit on the budget either. So that was the goal, and we were well aware that employment might take longer. And you could say that the condition for succeeding with these things was low inflation. But it is not fair to say that low inflation was given higher priority than employment. (interview with Palle Simonsen, Frederiksberg, March 16, 2005)

These statements exemplify an approach that many governments have taken to economic policy from the 1980s onward. The policies of the mid-1970s, when low unemployment was the main objective, also in the short term, were now seen as counterproductive. According to the new way of thinking, governments should pay attention to the budget balance, the balance of payments, and inflation. Given balanced budgets, external balance, and low inflation, the economy would sooner or later return to a low unemployment equilibrium, or so it was hoped. This change in thinking was gradually institutionalized through organizational and procedural changes across Europe, whereby economic policymaking was transferred to finance ministries and central banks, who made policy decisions on the basis of economic objectives only, rather than the mix of social, political, and economic considerations that had guided policy in the past.

In the first part of the center-right's term in office—from 1982 to 1986—interest rates declined rapidly, the Danish economy was booming, and unemployment fell from approximately 8 to around 5 percent. The current account deficit remained high, however, and by the mid-1980s it became clear that the government would have to adopt more restrictive fiscal policies if it were going to meet its main target, external balance. In spite of widespread protests against the government, several austerity packages were passed in 1985–6. They included restrictive incomes policies, cuts in municipal government spending, and the abolition of certain tax deductions for interest payments. The consequence of these measures was a reduction of the current account deficit—subsequently, except for the year of 1998, the Danish current account has been in surplus—but the downside was another phase of rising unemployment in 1987–93 (Asmussen 2007, 104).

Economic Policies in the 1990s

The second part of the center-right government's term in office—from 1987 to 1993—was less eventful. According to Palle Simonsen, who remained finance minister until 1989, "we had already accomplished most of the things we could accomplish, and it was not easy to find new things that could attract the support of a majority" (interview with Palle Simonsen, Frederiksberg, March 16, 2005). There were also mounting conflicts within the government, between more centrist politicians, such as Mr Simonsen, and more market-liberal politicians, such as the minister for taxation, Anders Fogh Rasmussen (who would later become prime minister in the 2000s).

In 1993, the center-right government had to resign over a political scandal related to immigration policy, and a new center-left government was formed, based on a coalition between the Social Democrats, the Social Liberal Party, the Center Democrats, and the Christian Democrats. In some ways, the new center-left government's economic strategy was similar to its predecessor's (Palle Simonsen even says that its economic policies were "identical," the only difference being that the surplus on the current account allowed for more expansionary policies; interview with Palle Simonsen, Frederiksberg, March 16, 2005).

The social democrat Mogens Lykketoft, who was finance minister in 1993–2000, says that there were "elements of consensus," since some of the policy changes that the center-right government had made in the early 1980s were maintained when the center-left took over in 1993— particularly the fixed exchange rate policy, the anti-inflation policy, and the abolition of indexation. But Mr Lykketoft also points out that the new social democratic–social liberal coalition adopted a more expansionary fiscal policy.

We combined it with an easing of fiscal policy–moving public investments forward, under-financing the income tax cut, and introducing a particular form of expansionary credit policy, converting old high-interest mortgages. This last measure probably had the most powerful stimulus effect on private demand in 1993, 1994, and 1995. (interview with Mogens Lykketoft, Copenhagen, March 14, 2005)

The fiscal expansion in 1993, which the government embarked on in spite of a projected 5.9 percent budget deficit, is an interesting event, for it is one of relatively few examples of a deliberate strategy of expansionary fiscal policies in any of the four countries covered in this book between the mid-1980s and the Great Recession of 2008–9. Within the finance ministry, whose civil servants were opposed to the new finance minister's "one-off Keynesianism," there was a great deal of skepticism about this policy (Nannestad and Green-Pedersen 2000, 14, 17; Asmussen 2007, 165, 167), but according to economists such as Andersen, Hougaard, and Risager (1999, 7), it played an important economic role, since it triggered an economic boom of the 1990s and contributed to a fall in unemployment. However, it was only a temporary measure—it was known as a "kick-start"—and fiscal policy later in the 1990s became more restrictive, the most notable measure being the so-called "Pentecost agreement" (*Pinsepakken*) in 1998 (Asmussen 2007, 169; Nannestad and Green-Pedersen 2000, 17).

The Danish Macroeconomic Regime

The macroeconomic regime that was established in the early 1980s—the fixed exchange rate and the commitment to low inflation and external balance—was consolidated in the course of the 1980s and 1990s. Over time, as a result of Denmark's strong economic performance in the 1990s and 2000s, this regime acquired broad domestic support. This was noticeable in the economic crisis of 2008–9, during which the Danish government was concerned with protecting the country's economic policy framework. A report from the danish ministry of finance in 2008 said that any policy that risked undermining the fixed exchange rate policy was unwise since the fixed exchange rate was the foundation of all "economic policy results that we have achieved in the last twenty years" (Finansministeriet 2008, 29).

The Netherlands

In Chapter 2, I showed that Dutch governments scaled back their expansionary fiscal programs already in the mid- to late 1970s. I also showed that the conflict between politicians who wished to use fiscal policy to support economic activity and employment and politicians who wished to consolidate the budget and limit the growth of wages and benefits was finally resolved around 1980, when the second view became broadly accepted. The new center-right government that was established in 1982 continued to follow this course. Just as in the 1970s, political developments in the Netherlands were remarkably similar to developments in Denmark: in both countries, the new center-right governments that were formed in late 1982 adopted important changes in macroeconomic policy and introduced new ways of thinking about economic affairs.

Economic Policies in the 1980s

In the autumn of 1982, the leader of the Christian democratic party, CDA, Ruud Lubbers, formed a coalition with the Liberal Party. This coalition went on to win the election of 1986 and remained in power until 1989. The first priority for the new center-right coalition—according to an early speech by Onno Ruding, the new finance minister—was to control the "almost explosive growth of the financing deficit," and reduce public spending (Ministerie van Financiën 1982, 3). Just as in Denmark, taking measures that might increase unemployment in the short term was seen as a condition for a reduction of unemployment in the long term. Mr Ruding said in parliament that the government was "convinced that economic growth can be restored and employment increased only if the steady deterioration in the government's finances is checked," and he predicted that putting the government's finances in order would be the main objective of economic policy for the foreseeable future (Ministerie van Financiën 1982, 3, 7). The government did go on to take radical budgetary measures in 1982–3—ending the indexation of wages and benefits and cutting public sector pay (Wolinetz 1989, 91–2).

According to experts on the Dutch case, such as Bart Snels (1999, 121), the Lubbers government definitively gave up demand-managing fiscal policy. The new finance minister, Onno Ruding, confirms that, in his view, there was little room for expansionary fiscal policies in the early 1980s:

I am not against that under all circumstances. That is a normal measure that frequently works in the short term (I am not so sure that it always works in the long term). But we didn't have the money. There was a rapidly rising deficit. We couldn't follow stimulatory policies, because they would by definition have further destabilized the already unstable budgetary situation in the short run, and I think also in the long run. (interview with Onno Ruding, Brussels, March 21, 2006)

Apart from fiscal consolidation, the new government based its economic strategy on wage restraint, which was greatly facilitated by an agreement between the main Dutch union confederation, FNV (*Federatie Nederlandse Vakbeweging*) and the employer association. This agreement, commonly known as the Wassenaar Accord (Stichting van de Arbeid 1982), is often credited with laying the foundation for the Dutch economic "miracle" in the 1980s and 1990s (Visser and Hemerijck 1997; Nickell and van Ours 2000).

Before the Lubbers government was even formed, the leading center-right politicians communicated to the unions and the employer organizations that in the absence of a voluntary agreement, it would impose a mandatory wage freeze, Mr Lubbers said in an interview with the author:

We threatened the social partners—the trade unions, led by Wim Kok, who later became prime minister, and the employers, represented by van Veen—and we said that if you don't agree, in the Dutch tradition, on a policy that is acceptable to us, we will go in by law. The idea that the government would control wages was horrible for both of them. (interview with Ruud Lubbers, Rotterdam, March 21, 2006)

Wim Kok confirms that the government's threat played an important role. The unions had unsuccessfully protested against a previous, mandatory wage freeze under the Van Agt government a few years earlier. "I asked my colleagues, 'What should we do?'" Wim Kok said in an interview with the author. "We will lose influence in Dutch society if we keep organizing protests without winning them" (telephone interview with Wim Kok, March 30, 2006). But Mr Kok also points out that the Wassenaar agreement was the result of a change of thinking within Dutch trade unions: "The concern about the high level of unemployment, especially youth unemployment, was so widespread within the trade union movement that people were more inclined to accept a deal with the employers than they had been in the 1970s."

One premise of the Wassenaar agreement was the assumption that the problem of unemployment could only be solved in the long term. "Even if economic growth recovers," the main labor market organizations said in their joint statement in 1982, "it will not be possible in the medium term to assist the entire existing labor force and the growth in the labor force in finding paid employment in the near future" (Stichting van de Arbeid 1982). The agreement therefore contained some provisions for the redistribution of available work. It seems likely that the shared understanding of unemployment as a long-term, structural problem facilitated the adoption of important labor market reforms in the late 1980s, and in the 1990s (see Chapter 4).

During the center-right governments in the 1980s, the current Dutch macroeconomic regime was established, with budget consolidation and wage restraint as its two main components. The main legacy of the Lubbers government, as Anton Hemerijck has noted (1992, 335), was broad agreement on the general direction of macroeconomic policy from the early 1980s onward, when economic policy revolved "around relatively straightforward quantitative budget cutting proposals." Wage restraint has also been an important theme in Dutch economic policy ever since the early 1980s (just as it was in the first postwar decades). When unemployment rose temporarily in the early 1990s, the government's immediate response was to emphasize the need for wage restraint (Rijksvoorlichtingsdienst 1991, 83–4; Ministerie van Financiën 1993, 4). The same thing happened a decade later, during the recession in the early 2000s (Rijksvoorlichtingsdienst 2002, 5).

Compared to the 1970s, there were few conflicts within the government over the direction of macroeconomic policy in the 1980s. The only exception was a small devaluation in 1983, when the Dutch *guilder* depreciated by 2 percent against the German *mark*. The devaluation had the support of prime minister Lubbers and the minister of social affairs, Jan de Koning, but it was opposed by the central bank and the finance minister (Szász 1999, 199–201). Ruud Lubbers says today that he thought that "being a bit more flexible on the currency would allow us to maintain our overall policies," and he still believes "even in retrospect, that it was the right thing to do" (interview with Ruud Lubbers, Rotterdam, March 21, 2006). After this event, however, the Dutch stuck to their fixed policy *vis-à-vis* the German *mark* until the creation of the euro.

Economic Policies in the 1990s

Just as the Danish center-right governments became more market-liberal in the late 1980s and early 1990s, the second Lubbers government, formed in 1986, had a more liberal agenda, with objectives such as "slimming down" the civil service and promoting "less government" (Ministerie van Financiën 1986, 10–11). Within a few years after the 1986 election, however, there was a change in government: the social democratic PvdA joined Ruud Lubbers's Christian Democrats in government in 1989, and the liberals joined the opposition. The previous finance minister, Onno Ruding, was replaced by the former trade union leader Wim Kok, who became the leader of PvdA in the mid-1980s. The change in government did not lead to a change in macroeconomic policy priorities, however. "Now and then, we took some selective fiscal measures to support purchasing power," Wim Kok said in an interview with the author, "but in general, the room for fiscal and monetary policy to create additional demand was very limited" (telephone interview with Wim Kok, March 30, 2006).

In 1994, there was another change in government, as the Social Democrats entered into a coalition with the Liberal Party VVD and the progressive-liberal D66 (*Democraten 66*). The Christian Democrats found themselves out of office for the first time since the Second World War. In economic and labor market policy, the motto of the new "purple" coalition, which was in power from 1994 to 2002, was "jobs, jobs, jobs" (Ministerie van Financiën 1997, 5). However, macroeconomic policy only had an indirect role, in job creation, providing for "sustainable economic growth" by means of a "consistent financial and economic policy that will inspire confidence" (Ministerie van Financiën 1994, 1). The main instrument, in addition to wage restraint, was a combination of social and labor market policy reforms, which I will examine in Chapter 4.

In fiscal policy, the purple governments introduced a new set of medium-term budgeting principles, popularly known as the *Zalmnorm* after the minister of finance in 1994–2002 and 2003–7, Gerrit Zalm (Zalm 2009, 117). Mr Zalm says that his aim was to provide for a more long-term perspective on the development of public finances: "What I did was to base the budgetary room of maneuver on a cautious scenario for a four-year period, set the ceilings in real terms, and stick to the ceilings whatever happened with the economy" (interview with Gerrit Zalm, Amsterdam, February 8, 2010). The idea was to gradually reduce public spending, while also making budgetary policy more neutral to short-term economic fluctuations. Low unemployment was an "important goal" for the government, Mr Zalm notes, "but we didn't quantify goals for employment. The budget policy was based on medium-term considerations. We didn't have an activist, cyclical policy."

The Dutch Macroeconomic Regime

The Dutch case is in many ways similar to the Danish. In both countries, center-right coalition governments gained power in 1982 and imposed tougher fiscal policies, and in both countries new kinds of coalitions between social democratic and liberal parties in the 1990s and early 2000s pursued labor market reforms and presided over big falls in unemployment, as I will explain further in Chapter 4. The main difference was that the Danish center-left government that was formed in 1993 also used expansionary fiscal policies temporarily to stimulate domestic demand in the mid-1990s, in an attempt to bring down the high level of unemployment. In the Netherlands, there had been a more or less continuous decline in unemployment from the early 1980s to the early 1990s, which probably explains why the Dutch government in the early 1990s preferred to stick to the wage restraint strategy that was credited with this significant accomplishment.

Austria

In the mid-1980s, the Austrian government decided to give priority to the stabilization and reduction of the large government debt that had accumulated in the wake of the two oil crises (the gross financial liabilities of the Austrian general government had increased from less than 20 percent of GDP in the early 1970s to almost 60 percent by the late 1980s). As I will show, however, the new fiscal policy was introduced gradually and cautiously, which makes Austria rather different from Sweden, where the economic policy shift in the early 1990s and the ensuing budget consolidation in the mid-1990s occurred more suddenly, and had more dramatic effects.

Economic Policies in the Late 1980s

In the early 1980s, Austrian unemployment started creeping slowly upward, and as Peter Katzenstein (1984, 43–4) has noted, the government now relied less on expansionary fiscal policies than it had in the past. For example, in the recession of 1983, the government opted for a more restrictive fiscal policy than it had in the recessions of 1975, 1978, and 1981 (Marterbauer 2001, 233–5). But expansionary policies were not given up entirely. Franz Vranitzky, who was finance minister from 1984 to 1986, says that he was "a little more hesitant than my predecessors" about countercyclical fiscal policies, but he believed that "it was still possible, with public investments, to stimulate parts of the economy" (interview with Franz Vranitzky, Vienna, June 7, 2006).

The main change in economic policy change occurred in the mid-1980s. Some scholars, such as Emmerich Tálos (1987, 131–53), date the shift to as early as 1984. However, the openly declared, programmatic policy change came in 1987, following the formation of a new grand coalition between the Social Democrats and the Christian Democrats in 1987, with two social democrats, Franz Vranitzky and Ferdinand Lacina, as prime minister and finance minister (Unger 2001, 347; Penz 2007, 65).

When he presented the new government's first budget to the Austrian parliament in February 1987, Ferdinand Lacina said that it no longer made sense to fight unemployment by "increasing government expenditure, compensating for the lacking private demand," since Austria's problems were long term and structural (Österreichischer Nationalrat, February 25, 1987, 424). The budget must be consolidated, the government believed, in order to preserve the "functions of the modern state for the future" (Österreichischer Nationalrat, February 25, 1987, 430).

Although the new government was concerned with budget consolidation, however, it said that it would allow the consolidation process to take place over a number of years, since a quicker deficit reduction was seen as "unrealistic" (Österreichischer Nationalrat, February 25, 1987, 423). The idea, Ferdinand Lacina says today, was to prepare for "a soft landing." The goal was to lower the deficit gradually, "let's say by 0.5 percent a year, on average, to ensure that the negative effect on employment and economic growth would be rather weak" (interview with Ferdinand Lacina, Vienna, June 6, 2006). In Mr Lacina's view, the government had a mixed strategy, "maintaining a high level of employment—it was not full employment of course, even at that time," but also "making some progress with the consolidation of the budget."

When the government launched its new program, it said that one of the aims of consolidating public finances was to provide for a subsequent return to active fiscal policies. To some extent, this was rhetoric—Franz Vranitzky claims that he "thought it was over" (interview with Franz

Vranitzky, Vienna, June 7, 2006), and Ferdinand Lacina points out that "it was easier for the Social Democrats to say that now we have to concentrate on the consolidation of the budget, in order to have more room of maneuver at a later time when it was really necessary" (interview with Ferdinand Lacina, Vienna, June 6, 2006)—but as I will show below, the government did pursue more expansionary fiscal policies in the early 1990s.

To sum up, the new grand coalition government believed that it had become necessary to reduce the debt, but it allowed for a gradual process of budget consolidation. This meant that although full employment was no longer treated as the dominant goal, keeping employment as high as possible—"die Erhaltung eines möglichts hohen Beschäftigungsniveaus"— was still important, as the finance minister said in the autumn of 1987 (Österreichischer Nationalrat, 21 October, 3586). Judging from the finance minister's speeches on economic policy in the late 1980s and early 1990s, the government took pride in the fact that unemployment was lower in Austria than in most other European countries.

In 1988–90, the government's economic strategy did appear to be very successful in the sense that government debt was stabilized without any adverse employment effects. One policy that may have contributed to this outcome was a tax reform in 1988–9, which was designed to stimulate private demand (Österreichischer Nationalrat, October 19, 1988, 8536). Günther Chaloupek, an economic adviser at the chamber of labor, says that the grand coalition's policies at first amounted to a "change in emphasis" rather than a break with the past, since the income tax cut "supported a boom from 1988 to 1992" (interview with Günther Chaloupek, Vienna, June 8, 2006; see also Unger 1990, 71).

Economic Policies in the 1990s

In the early 1990s, after the unification of Germany, unemployment in Austria increased—as did unemployment in Denmark, the Netherlands, and Sweden—and when the budget for 1993 was developed, a fall in real GDP was expected. In October 1992, the finance minister said that the time had come to use some of the fiscal room for maneuver to "bridge" the recession and support the economy by means of public investments (Österreichischer Nationalrat, October 22, 1992, 9466–7), and in 1993–4, the government allowed the "automatic stabilizers" to work, halting the budget consolidation process temporarily in order to support domestic demand (Österreichischer Nationalrat, October 20,

1993, 15370). Ferdinand Lacina said in an interview with the author that "to decrease the budget deficit at that time would have meant shrinking the GDP by force" (interview with Ferdinand Lacina, Vienna, June 6, 2006).

There were additional reasons for the policy choices that were made in the early 1990s, however. Günther Chaloupek says that although deficits were high in this period, "it was not because of anti-cyclical policy: it was a result of a political struggle. And the government didn't want to do anything to scare people off the EU" (interview with Günther Chaloupek, Vienna, June 8, 2006; cf. Walterskirchen 1997, 6). In the late 1990s, when Austria had become a member of the European Union, the budget consolidation process continued in a (successful) attempt to meet the convergence criteria for joining the Economic and Monetary Union (Rosner, Van der Bellen, and Winckler 1999, 146–8).

The Austrian Macroeconomic Regime

As I discussed in Chapter 2, Austrian economic policy relied for a long time on countercyclical fiscal policies, which were used—in combination with various supply-side policies—to keep unemployment low. The expansionary fiscal policies were phased out from the mid-1980s onward. Even after that, however, especially in the first half of the 1990s, Austrian governments have been more prone to fiscal activism than many other European countries. Ewald Walterskirchen, an economist at WIFO, the Austrian Institute for Economic Research, said in an interview in the mid-2000s, conducted when a right-wing government was in government, that "unemployment seems to be such an important issue that even conservative governments do something in the recession," noting that it was "surprising in this political environment that anti-cyclical policies are still important" (interview with Ewald Walterskirchen, Vienna, June 6, 2006).

The end of "Austro-Keynesianism"—the policy mix that I described in Chapter 2—is normally explained with reference to the increasing openness of the Austrian economy (Marterbauer 2001, 238), or the increasing level of public debt, which made it necessary to change the course (see, e.g., Winckler 1988, 228). These factors mattered, but as the openness data that I reported in Chapter 1 show, economic interdependence actually increased faster in the 1970s (when Austria was still pursuing countercyclical policies), than it did in the early 1980s (immediately before the main economic policy changes), and the debt statistics that I presented in

Chapter 2 demonstrate that there was a continuous, almost linear increase in Austria's public debt from 1974 to 1987. There was no compelling economic reason why the budget consolidation process had to begin in 1987, as opposed to, say, 1982 or 1992.

But there were political reasons. By the mid-1980s, as I show below, Austria's government was in the process of making a number of important changes in the country's basic political arrangements, and party-political conditions had become less predictable, since the Green Party had entered parliament and the old liberal party, FPÖ, had redefined itself as a far-right party, quickly becoming an important challenger to the traditionally dominant *Großparteien*, the Christian Democrats and the Social Democrats. These facts help to explain why Austrian governments were prepared to consider a reorientation of economic policy.

Sweden

In the early 1990s, the Swedish government and central bank went to great lengths to implement a hard currency strategy in order to bring down inflation, which was now significantly higher than inflation in most other countries in Western Europe. This change in policy, in combination with a number of economic shocks, had big consequences: having had one of the lowest unemployment rates in Europe in 1988–91 (only Swiss unemployment was lower), Sweden had one of the highest unemployment rates among Western Europe's old democracies in the mid-1990s. My explanation for the adoption of disinflationary policies in Sweden in the early 1990s is that it was associated with underlying political changes, just as the economic policy changes in Austria in the mid- to late 1980s. However, the two countries followed different paths. Where policy changes in Austria were cautious and gradual, policy changes in Sweden were sudden and dramatic.

Economic Policies in the 1990s

In the second half of the 1980s, the Swedish social democratic government kept following the strategy that it had introduced in 1982. The government's economic policy declarations typically said that its "third way" policies had successfully dealt with some of Sweden's problems, but not all: rising inflation and wage costs were major concerns. "Now, the most important task is to hold back price and wage increases," the government stated in 1987. But it still hoped to accomplish these goals without adverse effects on economic activity and employment.

In many other countries, this has been achieved by means of increasing unemployment. The Swedish government does not want to use that method, and instead wants to find other ways of improving economic performance, increasing savings, and breaking inflation expectations. (Prop. 1986/7:150, 1, 7)

Toward the end of the 1980s, these problems became more and more acute. In January 1988, for example, the government said that its "third way" in economic policy had reached a "critical moment" (Prop. 1987/8: 100, 17). One factor that probably contributed to the overheating economy in the late 1980s was the deregulation of the domestic credit market in 1985 when the lending limits for Swedish banks and financial institutions were abolished (Svensson 1996). The former prime minister Ingvar Carlsson has argued that the deregulation turned out to be ruinous for economic policy in the late 1980s (Carlsson 2003, Chapter 4, 255–60, Chapter 11), and most economists agree that the deregulation had powerful effects on private demand—either directly or indirectly through its effects on asset prices—which would have required very tight fiscal policies (some would say unreasonably tight policies) in order to keep prices and wages under control.

Another problem that complicated the government's efforts to bring down inflation was an unprecedented level of conflict between the social democratic leadership and the blue-collar trade union confederation LO, and between factions within the social democratic party itself. LO and the social democratic left were concerned that austere fiscal policies would punish the poor for the excesses of the rich (Malm 1994, 131–41).

By 1989, the finance ministry foresaw a coming economic downturn and the finance minister and his advisers came to believe that unemployment was inevitable, since the wage costs of Swedish firms were rising so quickly. This made fiscal restraint all the more important, finance minister Kjell-Olof Feldt wrote in his memoirs:

It was politically uncomfortable to bring about unemployment through a drop in domestic demand, as a result of economic policy, but that was, from an economic point of view, far better than achieving the same result by means of a drop in foreign trade. (Feldt 1991, 432)

In early 1989, therefore, the government proposed a program of austere fiscal policies, including an increase in consumption taxes, but failed to get this bill through parliament. One year later, in February 1990, the government attempted to deal with rising inflation through the direct regulation of prices, wages, and trade union activities (Prop. 1989/90: 95), and when the parliament struck down this bill as well, the government resigned. Since no other coalition could be formed, however, the Social Democrats returned to government a few weeks later. In the process, Kjell-Olof Feldt—who had been finance minister since 1982—left the government.

The new finance minister, Allan Larsson, believed that the best way to deal with Sweden's economic problems was to enforce wage restraint through government intervention at an early stage in the wage bargaining process. A special commission that was formed in the spring of 1990 in fact brokered an agreement between the unions and the employer organizations in December 1990, achieving a temporary recentralization of Swedish wage formation institutions (Elvander 2002, 199–200). This emphasis on wage restraint explains why the government resisted all ideas about trying to avert an economic crisis by means of macroeconomic policy in the early 1990s. By 1990, some economists had started to suggest that the Swedish currency was overvalued, and that something should be done to prevent a future economic downturn. As one former civil servant in the finance ministry puts it, however, "the politicians concluded that we couldn't make that kind of adjustment now, since workers would immediately try to compensate by raising wages" (interview with Lars Heikensten, Stockholm, August 16, 2002).

In the summer of 1990, the blue-collar trade union LO's economic research unit suggested in its annual economic report that Sweden should change its exchange rate regime, adapting to the high level of inflation. In the view of the LO economists some of the countries that the Swedish *krona* was pegged to—notably Germany—did not give enough priority to full employment, so Sweden should either float the *krona* or peg it to a different currency index that comprised currencies with wage and price trends similar to Sweden's. This was the only way of safeguarding full employment, according to the union economists (LO 1990, 28–9).

The finance minister disagreed. "I considered it a provocation against our efforts to reduce inflation," Mr Larsson says (interview with Allan Larsson, Stockholm, October 30, 2001). He believed that it was necessary to respond forcefully to LO, which is closely associated with the Social Democrats. This is an important explanation for the strong language that was used in economic policy bills from the autumn of 1990 and early 1991, where the government's commitment to the fixed exchange rate, and to low inflation, was affirmed in no uncertain terms. On

October 26, 1990, following speculation against the Swedish currency, the government introduced a number of measures against inflation, declared that the government would seek membership in the European Community (as the EU was then called), and declared that disinflation would be given priority over "all other ambitions and demands" (Prop. 1990/1:50, 130).

Allan Larsson and other leading social democrats have argued that the phrase "priority over all other ambitions and demands" has often been misinterpreted. As Mr Larsson points out, the government bills say that inflation must be reduced in order to *preserve* employment. "By 'other ambitions and demands,'" he says, "we meant increased public spending, and inflation-driving wage increases. Inflation was the big threat against employment, not our efforts to reduce inflation" (interview with Allan Larsson, Stockholm, October 30, 2001). In a similar vein, Ingvar Carlsson, prime minister in 1986–91 and 1994–6, disagrees with "those who say it was a paradigm shift and it was such a big thing. We had inflation that threatened to put firms out of business quickly." He concludes, "If you wanted full employment, the first thing you had to do was to reduce inflation" (interview with Ingvar Carlsson, Stockholm, January 29, 2003).

It seems clear, however, that the government no longer regarded full employment as the main operative target of economic policy. Unlike politicians like Ingvar Carlsson and Allan Larsson, the director of the finance ministry's economic affairs department in the early 1990s, Lars Heikensten, says that the declarations that were made in 1990 and 1991 in some sense represented a regime change: "*de facto*, the politicians had decided that they were prepared to accept a certain increase in unemployment, in order to secure a stable development in the future" (interview with Lars Heikensten, Stockholm, August 16, 2002). There is no reason to believe that the Social Democrats suddenly cared less about unemployment. However, leading politicians had come to believe that a long-term solution to Sweden's economic problems in general, including the employment problem, required an immediate reduction in inflation (Larsson 1991, 23), just like governments in Denmark and the Netherlands in the 1970s and Austrian governments in the 1980s decided to give priority to other economic policy objectives in the short to medium term.

Inflation declined quickly in 1991–2, probably as a result of the government's efforts to control wage formation. In the spring of 1991, a few months before a general election that the Social Democrats lost, the government reaffirmed its commitment to low inflation by pegging the Swedish *krona* to the European Currency Unit, the *ecu*, on May 17, 1991. Ever since the autumn of 1977, the Swedish *krona* had been pegged to a currency basket that was composed of the currencies of Sweden's major trading partners (although there were two big devaluations in the early 1980s). Gunnar Lund, the state secretary in the finance ministry and a strong advocate of the *ecu* peg, says that this decision was a consequence of the government's economic policy stance: "We believed that we had finally changed economic policy thoroughly, recognized the fight against inflation as fundamental, initiated structural reforms, and we were on our way into Europe," and "definitely pegging to the *ecu*" was a way of demonstrating that Sweden had changed (interview with Gunnar Lund, Stockholm, Stockholm, May 6, 2003). The *ecu* peg was unilateral, and Sweden did not become a member of the European Monetary System. Nevertheless, Sweden was soon drawn into the crisis on European currency markets in 1992.

After the election of 1991, a center-right coalition government was formed, with the conservative Carl Bildt as prime minister. The government included the conservative Moderate Party, the Liberal Party, the Christian Democrats, and the Centre Party, and its macroeconomic strategy was similar to the strategy the Social Democrats had pursued in 1990 and 1991. The most important events during the center-right government's three years in office took place in 1992, when the hard currency policy came to an end since the central bank was forced to adopt a floating exchange rate for the *krona*. This did not mean that the government gave up its attempts to contain inflation, however; it simply chose other means of achieving that aim.

In the summer and autumn of 1992, European currency markets became increasingly volatile, and many European currencies came under pressure. The Swedish central bank went to great lengths to defend the *krona*, and both the government and the social democratic opposition supported this policy. When Britain and Italy floated their currencies in mid-September, the bank even raised overnight lending rates to 500 percent, which—although it was unprecedented—does not seem to have been the upper limit: the bank's former governor, Bengt Dennis, writes in his memoirs that the bank at one point considered raising short-term interest rates to 4,000 percent (Dennis 1998, 53).

While the central bank used its main instrument, the short-term lending rate, to defend the value of the *Krona*, the government and the social democratic opposition negotiated two fiscal policy packages that were meant to increase confidence in the government's commitment to the fixed exchange rate. Preliminary negotiations between the government and the Social Democrats were initiated in August, leading to higher-level negotiations in mid-September. On September 20, 1992, prime minister Carl Bildt and the social democratic leader Ingvar Carlsson held a joint press conference where they presented a program for economic stabilization. The government and the Social Democrats reached another agreement a few days later, on September 30. The first agreement concerned measures that were intended to reduce the fiscal deficit. The second agreement contained an internal devaluation—that is, a tax policy adjustment that lowered payroll taxes and raised indirect taxes in order to improve competitiveness.

There were plans for a third package in mid-November, but the *krona* was floated before the government and the opposition had concluded their negotiations: on November 19, the governor of the central bank released a statement, which declared that as of 2.28 PM that afternoon, the *krona* was no longer pegged to the *ecu*. In the end, then, the efforts of the central bank, the government, and the opposition had proved to be in vain, and the fixed exchange rate strategy had failed. Unemployment was now high, however: according to OECD figures, it reached 6.7 percent in 1992 and 10.9 percent in 1993 (the national figures are slightly lower). It would get higher still, even if the major depreciation of the *krona* in 1992–3 improved the competitiveness of Swedish firms.

When politicians made low and stable inflation the primary target of economic policy in the early 1990s, they foresaw rising unemployment, but they did not imagine that unemployment would increase as much as it did. It would later become clear that the most important cause of the increase in unemployment was not wage-cost increases—which both the social democratic and the center-right government had seen as Sweden's main economic problem in the early 1990s—but a domestic economic collapse, which was the result of a large drop in domestic demand that occurred when a bubble in the real-estate market burst and real interest rates increased in the wake of the reunification of Germany (Jonung 1999, 201–11).

These mechanisms were not well understood before 1992–3. Allan Larsson, finance minister in 1990–1, says that "what we didn't see clearly, and what Bildt's new government didn't see clearly, was what was happening with the German economy—overheating and monetary restraint, which affected the rest of Europe, and the consequences that this had" (interview with Allan Larsson, Stockholm, October 30, 2001). Economic experts in the finance ministry had believed that the downturn in the early 1990s would be similar to previous downturns. Lars Heikensten, who headed the finance ministry's economic affairs department, says that the idea behind the policies that both the Social Democrats and the center-right parties pursued in the early 1990s was "to let the process work itself through just like in earlier downturns. But this time we would not devalue, but accept temporarily higher unemployment; say, an increase from 2 to 4 percent, and then the system would adjust" (interview with Lars Heikensten, Stockholm, August 16, 2002). In other words, the political parties assumed that if the major actors in the labor market could be persuaded that the government would not devalue again, they would seek moderate wage increases, inflation would be reduced, and although unemployment would probably rise somewhat, the situation would improve as soon as everyone understood that the government and the central bank were serious about disinflation.

The Swedish Macroeconomic Regime

In the first period after the floating of the *krona* in 1992, the government assumed that Sweden would return to a fixed exchange rate quite soon. Carl Bildt, who was prime minister at the time, says that a fixed exchange rate within the European system of exchange rate cooperation was an objective from the start, but it could only be done when the Swedish exchange rate and the economic situation in Europe both stabilized (E–mail message from Carl Bildt, January 19, 2003). This turned out to take longer than expected, however, and Sweden's exchange rate has remained floating since November 19, 1992. After a referendum in 2003— when those opposed to joining the Economic and Monetary Union outnumbered those in favor by three to two—it seems likely that Sweden will keep its floating exchange rate for some time.

In early 1993, a few months after the floating of the *krona*, a new monetary policy regime was introduced. The central bank—which acted independently, but had the support of Anne Wibble, the finance minister—set an inflation target of $2 +/- 1$ percent for monetary policy, the most important macroeconomic policy instrument after the turn to a floating exchange rate. The inflation target that was adopted in early 1993 has guided monetary policy since. The central bank today measures inflation expectations and sets interest rates on the basis of prognoses that are based on these measurements. This method of setting interest rates— known as "inflation targeting"—is used by a growing number of central

115

banks, including those in the United Kingdom, Norway, and New Zealand (Truman 2003).

The main economic policy objective of the social democratic government that was formed after the election of 1994 was fiscal consolidation, which was what the Social Democrats had campaigned on in 1994. Just like the center-right government before them, the Social Democrats believed that lower long-term interest rates were best achieved through a rapid consolidation of the government's fiscal position. Helped by lower interest rates, economic activity would pick up again (and the budget deficit would become less of a problem since interest payments would decrease). For most of the 1990s, neither the center-right nor the Social Democrats saw fiscal policy as an instrument of macroeconomic stabilization—unlike governments in Austria and Denmark, which adopted more expansionary fiscal policies in the mid-1990s. The center-right government presented long-term objectives for the reduction of government debt in 1993–4, committing itself to "abolishing the structural deficit in public finances" (Prop. 1992/3: 100). The Social Democrats presented more specific budget-cutting proposals in the 1994 election campaign and introduced their first major cost-cutting program two months after the election, in November 1994 (Prop. 1994/5: 61).

What is especially noteworthy about the Swedish policy changes in the late 1980s and early 1990s is how drastic they were. Unlike the Austrian grand coalition government in the late 1980s and 1990s, which changed fiscal policies gradually, over a period of several years, Swedish governments made sudden shifts and dramatic gestures—from the deregulation of domestic credit markets in November 1985 to the strong statements about the importance of low inflation in 1990, the *ecu* peg in 1991, the 500 percent short-term lending rate in 1992, and the drastic fiscal consolidation in the mid-1990s. Over a short period of time, Swedish governments gave up their rhetoric about a specifically Swedish "third way" and made low inflation and balanced budgets the main objectives of economic policy.

Ordinary European States

This concludes my account of Austrian, Danish, Dutch, and Swedish economic policies from the mid-1980s to the early 2000s. By the early 1990s, all four countries had made low inflation and balanced budgets the primary targets of fiscal and monetary policy. But there were important differences between countries.

1. The main difference, as Chapters 2 and 3 have shown, is that whereas Denmark and the Netherlands gave up on full employment and made the transition to economic policy regimes based on low inflation and balanced budgets in the late 1970s and early 1980s, Austria made this transition in the second half of the 1980s, and Sweden did so in the 1990s.

2. When they made these policy changes, Austria, Denmark, the Netherlands, and Sweden at least initially relied on hard currency strategies, pegging their national currencies to the German *mark*. Later, Austria and the Netherlands—whose currencies followed the *mark* closely already in the mid-1970s—became members of the Eurozone from the start in 1999. Denmark and Sweden, however, did not participate in Stage Three of the EMU, and Sweden has had a floating exchange rate since 1992.

3. In fiscal policy, a policy of budget consolidation and fiscal restraint has been the norm in all four countries ever since the 1980s. Here too, there are some differences, however: governments in Austria and Denmark launched cautiously expansionary fiscal policies during the economic downturn in the early 1990s. The Netherlands and Sweden did not.

In this section, I will present evidence for my claim that governments in Austria and Sweden changed the main objective of economic policy from full employment to low inflation and balanced budgets when they did, some ten to fifteen years later than Denmark and the Netherlands, as a result of the development of domestic political arrangements in the 1980s, just as political instability and uncertainty in Denmark and the Netherlands in the 1970s help to explain economic policy choices in these two countries in the 1970s and early 1980s (see Chapter 2).

One aspect of Austria's and Sweden's political transformation in the 1980s and early 1990s was party system change. Whereas no new parties had entered the Austrian and Swedish parliaments in the 1960s, 1970s, and early 1980s—a period when the Danish and Dutch party systems changed fundamentally, with important consequences for policymaking (see Chapter 2)—the formerly stable Austrian and Swedish party systems also began to change in the late 1980s.

Table 3.1 lists all new parties in the Austrian, Danish, Dutch, and Swedish parliaments in the 1980s, 1990s, and 2000s. The Danish and Dutch party systems kept changing. In 1989, several smaller left parties in these two countries merged to form new left-wing/green parties: the

Table 3.1 New political parties since 1980

	1980s	1990s and 2000s
Austria	Green Party (1986–)	Liberal Forum (1994–9) Alliance for the Future of Austria (2005–)
Denmark	Common Course (1987–8)	Red-Green Alliance (1994–) Danish People's Party (1998–) Liberal Alliance (2007–)
Netherlands	Reformatory Political Federation (1981–2002) GreenLeft (1989–)	Socialist Party (1994–) General Elderly Alliance (1994–8) Christian Union (2002–) List Pim Fortuyn (2002–6) Party for Freedom (2006–)
Sweden	Green Party (1988–91, 1994–)	Christian Democrats (1991–) New Democracy (1991–4)

Note: All parties that entered parliament between 1980 and the present are listed, excluding parties that never held more than two seats. The Austrian party Alliance for the Future of Austria (*Bündnis Zukunft Österreich*) is a splinter group from the Freedom Party.

Red-Green Alliance in Denmark (which won representation in parliament in 1994) and the GreenLeft in the Netherlands. Another significant development was the formation of new far-right parties with anti-immigrant platforms in both countries in the late 1990s and in the 2000s. In Denmark, the Danish People's Party was formed in 1995 by a splinter group from the old anti-tax Progress Party and won representation in parliament for the first time in 1998 (by the late 2000s, it had become the third largest party in *Folketinget*). In the Netherlands, the populist party List Pim Fortuyn won twenty-six seats in the *Tweede Kamer* in 2002, and the Party for Freedom—formed by Geert Wilders, formerly a member of the conservative-liberal party VVD—won nine seats in 2006.

In Austria, the Christian Democrats (ÖVP) and the Social Democrats (SPÖ) dominated party politics until the mid-1980s, with the liberal Freedom Party (FPÖ) playing a relatively minor role. The most significant event in the development of the postwar party system in Austria was the "earthquake election" in 1986, when two significant events occurred: the Green Party entered parliament, and the Freedom Party redefined itself as a far-right populist party, becoming a political force to be reckoned with under its new leader, Jörg Haider (Gerlich and Müller 1989, 147). In the 1990s and 2000s, there were further developments: a new liberal party was represented in the Austrian parliament in the second half of the 1990s, and in the 2000s—while it was a part of the governing coalition—Jörg Haider's Freedom Party split, which resulted in the formation of a new right-wing party called Alliance for the Future of Austria (with Haider as party leader). The far-right parties have become an increasingly important force in Austrian politics: in the 2008 elections, their combined vote share was approximately 28 percent.

In Sweden, the old five-party system changed greatly in the late 1980s and early 1990s (Demker 2006, 477). The Green Party (*Miljöpartiet*) became represented in parliament for the first time in 1988–91. The Christian Democrats (*Kristdemokratiska samhällspartiet*, later renamed *Kristdemokraterna*) and the right-wing populist New Democracy (*Ny demokrati*) entered parliament in 1991. This meant that Sweden turned from a five- to a seven-party system: although New Democracy were voted out in 1994, the Greens returned, and there have thus been seven parties in the Swedish parliament from 1991 onward. The appearance of new parties had important political effects. For example, the 1988 election—the last election before the social democratic government decided to give priority to a reduction of inflation in 1990–1—was completely dominated by environmental politics, since the Green Party had become a threat to the old parties (Esaiasson 1990, 442; Gilljam and Holmberg 1990, 32–3). Moreover, coalition formation was less predictable in the 1990s and early 2000s than it had been in the 1960s, 1970s, and 1980s.

In both Austria and Sweden, then, the number of parties increased, new issue dimensions emerged, and the dynamics of party competition changed in the second half of the 1980s, *before* governments in these two countries announced that they would change economic policies. But those were not the only political changes in Austria and Sweden at this time. The economic policy shifts that I have described in this chapter were also associated with deeper changes in Austrian and Swedish political arrangements, two of the most distinctive and integrated of all the political models that were created in Europe after the Second World War.

The two countries were different in many ways—the state was more dominant in Swedish political culture whereas the Austrian political model was based on more corporatist structures (Katzenstein 1984, 1985a; Kunkel and Pontusson 1998; Lindvall and Rothstein 2006)—but in both Austria and Sweden, powerful political mechanisms supported the coordination of policymaking across policy domains. In my view, the wish to preserve these political arrangements is an important part of the explanation for the fact that Austrian and Swedish governments decided to fight for full employment for so long. This explains why the changes that occurred in the Austrian and Swedish political models in the mid-1980s and early 1990s were followed by the adoption of more mainstream economic policies. The transformation of the Austrian political model from the mid-1980s onward was a negotiated retreat, managed by the main political parties and interest organizations. The transformation of the Swedish political model in the late 1980s and 1990s was more sudden, and more radical. This explains why the *pace* of economic policy change in the 1980s and 1990s was so different in these two countries.

The Austrian Political Model

The main political arrangements of Austria's Second Republic were established in the 1940s and 1950s (Austria's First Republic existed from the end of the First World War to the fascist takeover in 1934). Before the end of the war, the leaders of the prewar political parties met to discuss the organization of politics in postwar Austria, and on the basis of these negotiations, a national government was set up during the occupation by France, the Soviet Union, the United Kingdom, and the United States in 1945–55. Constitutionally, the Second Republic was a continuation of the First: after the liberation of Austria, on May 1, 1945, the 1920 constitution, revised in 1929, was simply reinstated. With the State Treaty, signed in 1955, Austria regained full independence (Jelavich 1987, 245–7, 270).

The remarkable stability of the Austrian political system after the Second World War was a result of two institutional features, which were meant to allow political elites to manage the latent conflict between left and right, avoiding the polarized conflicts that had led to civil war and the breakdown of democracy in the 1930s.

First, there was effectively a two-party system, which was organized around the *Proporz* model, through which the Christian Democrats and the Social Democrats shared power and allocated government appointments among their supporters. There was also a high degree of ideological consensus between the main parties in the first decades after the war: both parties supported the idea of an active state, in the economic as well as the social domain (Tálos 2005b, 58), and even in periods of single-party majority government, such as the long period of social democratic rule from 1970 to 1983, most legislation was passed with big parliamentary majorities, after negotiations with the trade unions and employer organizations (Obinger 2009a, 9).

Second, there was—and is—a strong corporatist system, which was in many ways the defining feature of postwar Austrian politics

(Katzenstein 1984, 59–78). The main actors within the Austrian social partnership system (*Sozialpartnerschaft*)—apart from the political parties and the government—are the trade union confederation *Österreichischer Gewerkschaftsbund* (ÖGB) and three semipublic organizations with compulsory membership that represent different interest groups in Austrian society: the Federal Chamber of Labor (the *Arbeiterkammer*), which represents workers; the Federal Economic Chamber (the *Wirtschaftskammer*), which represents employers and firms; and the Federal Chamber of Agriculture (*Präsidentenkonferenz der Landwirtschaftskammern*), which represents farmers. These organizations have a history of participation in political decision-making, and are still influential.

In the 1950s and 1960s, a network of institutions and organizations was set up to manage the relationship between interest organizations, and between interest organizations and the state. The most important institution was the parity commission on wages and prices (*Paritätische Kommission für Lohn- und Preisfragen*), which was established in 1957 to deal with the problem of inflation. It has been called a "second government for economic affairs" (Jelavich 1987, 275), and along with its powerful subcommittees, set up in the 1950s and 1960s, it was a particularly significant institution in the 1960s, 1970s, and 1980s.

The political culture in Austria's Second Republic was defined by a strong faith in the possibilities of politics, much like Swedish political culture (see below). On the basis of interviews conducted in the late 1960s, William Bluhm (1973, 179–80) concluded that Austria was a country where pragmatic politicians took pride in the fact that Austria was a "stable and prosperous political and economic community," created by "rational politics" (Bluhm 1973, 205). The leaders of the Christian Democrats and the Social Democrats, in Bluhm's view, had developed this approach to politics as a result of "the unhappy experience of the anschluss, the happy postwar escape from partition into East Austria and West Austria, and the success of the pragmatic politicians of the postwar coalition in refuting the myth of economic nonviability by creating an affluent society (Wohlstandsstaat)" (Bluhm 1973, 179).

When it comes to economic policy, the Austrian political model was based on powerful mechanisms for the integration of policymaking networks within the state and between the state and civil society (Jelavich 1987, 280). Werner Teufelsbauer, a former director of the economic policy department in the chamber of commerce, describes Austria's unofficial, tripartite system of economic policymaking in the following manner:

The whole political system in Austria was built on the principle that the Socialists and the Christian Democrats should cooperate in any institution. This means that in the national bank, on the labor side, and on the business side—and of course in the government and the parliament—there was the same system. It cut through all the institutional pillars.... There was, due to this system of parity, of consensus, always a very active interaction and discussion between the formal pillars of the republic. (interview with Werner Teufelsbauer, Vienna, June 5, 2006)

Mr Teufelsbauer also notes that over time, the interaction between the government, the social partners, and the central bank became organized around economic forecasts, developed by Austria's main economic research institute, WIFO (*Wirtschaftsforschungsinstitut Österreichs*). The forecasts allowed for "coordination of the basic economic strategies," Mr Teufelsbauer says, leading to "a kind of joint model of how the economy works."

In an interview with the author, Heinz Kienzl, a former head of the economic policy department in the trade union confederation ÖGB, described the role of the central bank in this policymaking network (by the mid-1970s, Mr Kienzl had left his previous job at ÖGB to become first executive director in the national bank):

We had many instruments. We had contacts with the ministry of finance, we had contacts with the chancellor, we had contacts with the chamber of commerce, we had contacts with the chamber of agriculture and the chamber of labor and the trade unions, and—very, very important—we had very good contacts with the banks.... We had quite a bit of dirigisme in our policy all the time. (interview with Heinz Kienzl, Vienna, June 7, 2006)

This was not the role that central banks in Denmark, the Netherlands, or even Sweden played in the period that I have discussed in Chapters 2 and 3.

One of the most important characteristics of the Austrian political economy from the 1950s to the mid-1980s was the high proportion of state-owned companies. The state-owned sector in Austria was exceptionally large by Western European standards, since many firms ended up in state ownership after the Soviet withdrawal from Austria in 1955. By the early 1970s, public companies represented 20 percent of Austria's gross national product and 29 percent of its labor force (Jelavich 1987, 278). The size of the nationalized industries is not just indicative of the presence of the state in the Austrian economy; it also matters directly to the topic of this book since the state-owned companies were used as instruments of the government's employment policy (Katzenstein 1984,

40), and, more generally, for achieving "social and political harmony" (Jelavich 1987, 278).

In the "Kreisky Era" in the 1970s and early 1980s—when the social democratic government responded so forcefully to the threat of unemployment—all the elements of the Austrian political model that I have described so far were intact. In this period, the Austrian government developed a particularly "integrative" social and economic model, as Otto Penz has put it (2007, 90). Moreover, the party system was still completely dominated by the Social Democrats and the Christian Democrats, the corporatist system was fully developed, the coordination of economic policy between the main institutions and within the social partnership system worked smoothly, and the state-owned sector of the economy was large and uncontested.

By the mid-1980s, however, the Austrian political model had begun to change in important ways. As I have already shown, this was when the party system started to change. Another clear example of underlying political change was the reform of the state-owned sector of the economy. There was a series of political scandals related to the management of the state-owned sector in the mid-1980s, the biggest one being the scandal in the large company *VÖEST Alpine* in 1985. As a consequence of these scandals, the social–liberal coalition depoliticized the holding management of the nationalized industries in 1986, and in 1987 the new grand coalition government approved one last subsidy to the ailing state-owned industries on the condition that future financial difficulties would lead to privatization (Seeleib-Kaiser, van Dyk, and Roggenkamp 2008, 32). In the long run, the scandals led to further changes in Austria's political arrangements and political culture (Sully 1990, 17–18). The privatization of Austria's state-owned companies is therefore often described as a major break with the Austrian postwar model (Rosner, Van der Bellen, and Winckler 1999, 144).

The grand coalition government that was formed in 1987 also changed other policies that had been distinctive of the Austrian approach to economic and social policy, pursuing more liberal policies in general and reducing the role of the state in both the economy and in society (Gerlich and Müller 1989, 154). Under the chancellorship of Frans Vranitzky, in 1987–97, Austria "almost became a 'normal' capitalist economy," as Rosner, Van der Bellen, and Winckler (1999, 146) have observed. There was also a change in political discourse, as the traditional assumptions that political actors had made about the role of the state were weakened (Penz 2007, 89).

One possible explanation for these widespread political changes in Austria is that the Social Democrats lost their majority in 1983, which forced them to cooperate with other parties—first with the Freedom Party in 1983–6 and then with the Christian Democrats from 1987 onward. However, the social democratic party itself was changing after Bruno Kreisky's resignation in 1983. Seeleib-Kaiser, van Dyk, and Roggenkamp (2008, 159) point out that SPÖ's general programmatic shift can be dated to the 1986 election manifesto—that is, before the grand coalition was formed.

According to Franz Vranitzky himself, "1986 changed Austria." In his view, that was not merely the year when Jörg Haider became party leader of the FPÖ and the Social Democrats began to cooperate with the Christian Democrats again: "It was also the end of Kreisky—Kreisky's ideas. His successor Fred Sinowatz, who had been a long-standing cabinet minister in Kreisky's government, still represented the spirit of Kreisky" (Interview with Franz Vranitzky, Vienna, June 7, 2006). Although the formation of a grand coalition with the Christian Democrats contributed to the change in direction in Austrian politics, Mr Vranitzky says that this was not the whole story. "I always said, although I did not say it out loud, that even if we had not had a grand coalition, if we had had a single-party government, we would have been obliged and forced to change."

There are strong reasons to believe that the widespread political changes in Austria in the mid-1980s explain why the change in macroeconomic policy that was announced in 1987 occurred at this particular point in time. The gradual character of this policy change, compared with Sweden, can probably be explained by the fact that the Social Democrats and the Christian Democrats governed Austria together, and by the fact that the social partnership system remained largely intact.

The social partnership system was not unaffected by the political changes in Austria in the 1980s and 1990s. According to Emmerich Tálos (2005b), economic problems and increasing party competition in the course of the 1980s made it more difficult to strike a balance between the large interest groups, which led to a decline in the influence of institutions such as the parity commission. The social partnership system also came under attack as a result of political scandals in the 1990s, which led to important reforms within the chambers. In the 2000s, finally, the formation of a right-wing coalition government seemed to herald major changes in the social partnership system, since the government sought to adopt and implement major reforms without consulting the main interest organizations.

Yet the chamber system survived, and in comparison with other countries, the Austrian social partnership system has been relatively stable over time. The idea of social partnership remains one of the dominant political principles of the Second Republic. In the English translation of the Austrian government's legislative program for the period 2008–13, for example, the term "social partners" was used twenty-two times (Federal Chancellery of Austria 2008). As I will show in Chapter 4, the social partnership system has not only been an important source of continuity in economic policy, but also in social and labor market policy.

The Swedish Political Model

Just like it had become obvious in the mid-1980s that the Austrian political model was changing, it became clear in the late 1980s and early 1990s that Sweden's political arrangements were transforming.

There is nothing new about this argument. Already in 1990, a major study of democracy and power in Sweden, which had been commissioned by the government in 1985, published its main report. The main message of the Swedish power study, or *Maktutredningen*, was that many of Sweden's distinctive institutions and policies had been weakened. The committee of social scientists that led the power study argued that Sweden was undergoing a transition, to a new kind of democracy, more individualistic, and more similar to the political systems of other countries (SOU 1990:44, 21). The final report concluded that the period "that was characterized by strong public expansion, centralized bargaining based on a historical compromise between labor and capital, social engineering and centrally planned standard solutions is over" (SOU 1990:44, 407).

This was a strong claim, and it led to an intense public debate. But when the leaders of the main political parties were invited to give their views on the power study in Swedish newspapers in the summer of 1990, no one disputed it. There was a difference in emphasis. The social democratic prime minister, Ingvar Carlsson, wrote that although the Swedish model had to be reformed, "the entire idea of a unique Swedish way of governing does not have to be abandoned," whereas the leaders of the main opposition parties, the Conservatives and the Liberal Party, believed that the power study had shown why social democracy had failed (Lindvall 2004, 129). However, the idea that Sweden had in some sense reached the end of an era was treated, at this point, as a historical fact.

In the postwar decades, Swedish politics was based on a rationalistic belief in ongoing social reform (Lindvall and Rothstein 2006, 49). The idea was for national politicians to set the main policy agendas, after consultations and negotiations with the main interest organizations. Then government commissions of inquiry were formed, and engaged experts who compiled knowledge about policy problems and possible solutions. The political proposals that were generated by such government commissions were subsequently translated into government bills and sent to parliament for approval. Then an administrative agency with long-term responsibility for a certain policy domain—such as education, social policy, housing, or labor market policy—was asked to implement the resulting policy, which often involved issuing directives to municipal governments.

One important feature of this political model was that it was treated as a coherent whole, not merely a set of individual policies. Foreign observers were impressed with the rationalistic, technocratic nature of policymaking in the Netherlands in the 1950s and 1960s (Abert 1969), but this primarily applied to the area of economic policy. Sweden was different, in the sense that a range of different policy programs were supposed to pull in the same direction, reinforcing one another. The high level of expectations concerning the central government's coordination capacity was backed up by institutions: as (Benner and Vad 2000, 407) have noted, the Swedish political system in the postwar period was characterized by "close links integrating policy fields and many forums for establishing consensus among the most important actors." For example, as Jenny Andersson (2003) has shown, social policy in the 1950s and 1960s was based on the assumption that a concerted political effort would allow the Swedish welfare state to simultaneously realize the goals of economic growth and social security.

Over time, this rationalistic and structured policymaking process appeared to generate important results, and a strong faith in the possibilities of politics and social reform developed. As Cecilia Garme (2001, 137) put it, "to produce welfare reforms of a certain kind became what a Swedish ruler was expected to do, his—or their—raison d'être." Although there were important differences between the main political parties, faith in Sweden's distinctive approach to politics and social affairs was not just a social democratic phenomenon. In the 1976 election, for example, the Liberal Party campaigned under the slogan "social reform without socialism" (Lindvall 2004, 65), and as the Liberal political adviser Sten Westerberg puts it, even the center-right parties regarded the Swedish welfare state as the "Hegelian end of history" (interview with Sten Westerberg, Stockholm, June 3, 2002).

The political model that I have described above was more or less intact in the 1970s, when Swedish governments fought so hard to preserve full employment. In fact, the 1970s was a period when Sweden's economic and social policies began to deviate most from the policies of other rich, Western democracies (Lindbeck 1997, 1275).

In the late 1980s and early 1990s, however, the policymaking model that I described above was transforming. One of the main institutional changes in this period was the decline of corporatist policymaking institutions. In early 1991, the Swedish employers' confederation, SAF (*Svenska Arbetsgivareföreningen*) decided to withdraw its representatives from almost all administrative boards and agencies (for detailed analyses of the causes and consequences of this event, see, e.g., Hermansson et al. 1999; Rothstein and Bergström 1999; Johansson 2000; Lindvall and Sebring 2005). Unlike in Denmark and the Netherlands—where corporatism was in crisis in the 1970s and early 1980s (see Chapter 2) but subsequently resurged (see Chapter 4)—Swedish corporatism appears to be in definite decline. This was an important part of the context of the policy changes in the early 1990s. For example, Ingvar Carlsson, prime minister in 1986–91 and 1994–6, has written that the failed attempt to develop a policy response to Sweden's economic problems in cooperation with the main interest organizations in 1990 made him lose faith in the capacity of the social partners for concerted problem-solving: the "famous Swedish labor market model was stone dead," Mr Carlsson (2003, 293) said in his memoirs.

The end of corporatism was not all. By the late 1980s and early 1990s, Swedish governments had also begun to change many of the distinctive policies that the Swedish postwar model was associated with, much like Austrian governments had begun to change distinctive Austrian policies, notably when it comes to state-owned companies, before they changed Austria's economic policy stance in the mid- to late 1980s. In Sweden, a relatively small share of the economy was state owned. It is therefore more relevant to investigate other policies, which were more closely connected with the reform agenda of Swedish (social democratic) governments in the first postwar decades.

I take my lead from a report to the social democratic party congress in 1964. This report, which was entitled "Results and Reforms" (*Resultat och reformer*) described the results of the social reforms that had been implemented since democratization, discussing the main reform challenges for the future. Among the most important results that the report identified were "education for everyone" and "classless housing" (Socialdemokraterna 1964, 109). An analysis of how policies in the areas of education and housing changed from the 1960s onward reveals the extent of the political transformation that had occurred by the early 1990s. In both of these policy areas, the policies that were developed in the 1960s exemplified the centralized and rationalistic policymaking style of the Swedish postwar model. In contrast, the large reforms that occurred in both areas in the late 1980s and early 1990s represented a different approach to policymaking and the role of the state.

Schools are essential for social reproduction, and Swedish governments in the postwar period regarded education as an important area of social reform (Rothstein 1986). The main event in the development of primary and secondary education in the first decades after the Second World War was the establishment of a national comprehensive school system in the 1960s, when most forms of tracking were abolished. The significance of these reforms is not only the underlying political ambition, which was to create a more egalitarian system of primary and secondary education, but also the fact that they were based on centralized control over the curriculum, and over primary and secondary education more generally, building on the nationalization, professionalization, and secularization of the Swedish school system in the early twentieth century.

The centralized system of comprehensive education (*enhetsskolan*) remained more or less intact in the 1970s and early 1980s. Education policies were adjusted, but only incrementally; governments experimented with decentralization, but radical reform agendas were resisted. In the mid- to late 1980s, however, Sweden's education policies became more politically contested. The central government's management of primary and secondary education was increasingly seen as problematic, and both the Social Democrats and the Liberal Party, which had significant political influence in this area, started to change their education policies in 1984–5, setting the agenda for a broader political debate over education later on (Schüllerqvist 1996).

In the late 1980s and early 1990s, the social democratic government implemented several far-reaching institutional reforms in the area of primary and secondary education. The minister responsible for this was the ascending social democratic politician Göran Persson, who would go on to become finance minister (1994–6) and prime minister (1996–2006). In a speech in 1990, Göran Persson announced that the national school board (*Skolöverstyrelsen*)—the state bureaucracy in charge of primary and secondary education—would be completely dismantled and replaced by a new administrative board with fewer policy instruments at its disposal. Indeed, Mr Persson said, "many of the tasks that are today handled by *Skolöverstyrelsen* will disappear" (Lindensjö and Lundgren 2000, 101). Most of the political responsibility for the management of primary and secondary education was transferred to municipal governments.

In a book about education reforms in Sweden, Bo Lindensjö and Ulf P. Lundgren have described the policy changes in the early 1990s as "probably the biggest in the history of primary and secondary education, and clearly the quickest." As their account of these reforms show, the procedures and beliefs that structured policymaking in the first postwar decades no longer applied. The new policies, Lindensjö and Lundgren note (2000, 116, 128), were characterized by an absence of trust in the scientific basis of political decisions, a low level of consensus, a lack of faith in the central bureaucracy, and increased demands for local participation. "The traditional social democratic doctrine—that the national government should decide the objectives, content and organization of schooling with a high level of consensus and after consultations with organized interests—was in retreat."

The center-right governments took education reform further still, introducing a voucher system that allowed for the development of independent schools alongside the state-run schools. When the Social Democrats returned to power in 1994, they did not reverse these reforms. By the 2000s, therefore, the Swedish system of primary and secondary education was very different from the system that had been created in the 1960s. It is no longer a centrally directed, comprehensive system, but a decentralized system, under municipal control, where public and private providers compete over the provision of education services in local education markets.

Another policy area where there were dramatic changes in the 1980s and 1990s is housing policy, which had been an important part of Swedish social policy until then. Just as in the area of education, there were ambitious reforms in housing policy in the 1960s, when large programs were launched to provide Swedish citizens with modern apartments and houses. In 1964, for example, the government announced that it would oversee the construction of one million apartments in ten years (Benner 1997, 65), and this goal was actually reached (which is quite remarkable for a country with fewer than 8 million inhabitants, as Sweden had at the time). As Ulf Olsson (1991) has pointed out, the construction and housing

129

sectors were subject to extensive regulation, reflecting high political ambitions and a prominent role for the central government: "More attention has probably been paid by politicians to housing than any other sector of the modern Swedish economy" (Olsson 1991, 159).

By the early 1990s, however, the social democratic government in 1982–9 had already begun to dismantle many of the ambitious programs of the past, and the center-right government in 1991–4 completed the transformation of housing policy by simply shutting down the Ministry of Housing. When the Social Democrats returned to power in 1994, they did not reinstate this ministry. One report on Swedish housing policy has argued that "even if the retreat isn't complete, deregulations and drastically diminished public programs in this area have meant that housing construction and administration has been depoliticized to an extent that makes it reasonable to speak of the end of an era" (Strömberg 2001, 44). These observations are similar to the observations that Lindensjö and Lundgren made concerning education policy: again, the main policy changes occurred around 1990; again, the center-right government in 1991–4 continued on a reform path that the Social Democrats had already begun to follow before they lost power in 1991; and again, the Social Democrats did not restore old institutions and policies when they regained power in 1994.

The evidence that I have presented from two key policy areas—education and housing—suggests that Swedish politics was transforming before the large economic policy changes that occured in the early 1990s. The institutions and norms that had defined Swedish policymaking ever since the first postwar decades were changing. The timing is no coincidence: in the 1970s and early 1980s, when both social democratic and center-right governments regarded the maintenance of low unemployment as an overriding imperative, it was widely believed that the Swedish political model must be protected. As late as the mid-1980s, the Swedish prime minister Olof Palme said in an interview that the Swedish government was trying to defend "the highest level of civilization any society has ever achieved" (Ehnmark 2002). In the early 1990s, when both social democratic and center-right governments put low and stable inflation before the maintenance of full employment, at least in the short term, there was less faith in the superiority of the Swedish political model.

As a consequence of these changes in the political context, both the social democratic government that was in power until 1991 and the center-right government that was in power in 1991–4 were less concerned with short-term economic management and more concerned with long-term economic and political reform than either center-right or social democratic governments had been in the past. In 1982, the new social democratic government had emphasized that "economic policy cannot be guided by long-term goals only; it must also be adapted to the current economic situation" (Prop. 1982/3: 50, 26). In the 1990s, on the other hand, Swedish governments explained that short-term macroeconomic stabilization must not be allowed to interfere with the long-term structural reforms that were at this time considered necessary. As Mats Benner (1997, 69) puts it, there was "a dramatic shift from the philosophy of the 'third way', where the growth generated by the devaluation [in 1982] should be used to maintain the social policy system. Instead, changes in social policy should stabilize the conditions for economic growth."

This change in perspective was most pronounced during the center-right government in 1991–4, whose campaign message had been that fundamental political changes were necessary. The government was well aware that the costs of disinflation were going to be high, since it took place in the middle of a severe recession, but any suggestions about keeping demand up and the economy going by means of macroeconomic policy measures were resisted. There were a number of "structural" changes that had to be made, and short-term demand management could not be allowed to interfere with the government's long-term agenda (Prop. 1991/2: 38, 5, 35; Prop. 1991/2: 100, 1–2, 21, 39; Prop. 1991/2: 150, 1–2; Prop. 1992/3: 150, 2).

However, there had been a similar change in perspective under the Social Democrats in the late 1980s. The finance ministry was increasingly preoccupied with "structural" problems and policies, such as a big tax reform that was adopted in 1989–90 (Lindvall 2004, Chapter 4). Finance minister Kjell-Olof Feldt's close aides testify to the minister's, and the finance ministry's, increasing concern with structural policies, as opposed to macroeconomic policy in the narrow sense. The head of the economic affairs department, Lars Heikensten, says, for example, that "a lot of what the Finance Ministry did in the late 1980s had to do with structural policy, especially after the 1988 election" (interview with Lars Heikensten, Stockholm, August 16, 2002). Although it was not as radical as the subsequent center-right government, the social democratic government had begun to give long-term economic and political reform priority over short-term economic management well before the election in 1991.

In conclusion, the economic policy changes that I have described in this chapter took place in a political environment that was different from the 1970s and early 1980s, when even the center-right parties had been reluctant to change economic policies. There are strong reasons to believe that the underlying political changes that I have described in this section explain why Swedish governments tried to maintain low unemployment by means of macroeconomic policies longer than most other West European countries.

Alternative Explanations

The evidence that I have presented on political changes in Austria and Sweden in the 1980s and 1990s suggests that the resilience of Austria's and Sweden's political models in the 1970s and early 1980s was an important reason why Austrian and Swedish governments were so eager to preserve full employment at that time. The evidence also suggests that the political changes in Austria and Sweden in the 1980s and early 1990s explain why governments in the late 1980s in Austria and the early 1990s in Sweden were prepared to change economic policies, adapting to what had by then become the European orthodoxy of low inflation and balanced budgets. Before concluding my analysis of economic policies in the 1980s and 1990s, I will consider three alternative explanations for these cross-country differences: financial interdependence, Europeanization, and economic ideas.

Economic Circumstances

When the Austrian and Swedish governments changed their economic policies in the mid-1980s and early 1990s—giving priority to balanced budgets and low inflation, rather than full employment—they said that these policy changes had become necessary since other economic problems were so serious that they required immediate attention. The Austrian grand coalition government that was formed in 1987 said that a reduction of public debt would be its main goal, and both social democratic and center-right governments in Sweden said that low and stable inflation was first on their lists of priorities.

There is no doubt that government debt had become relatively high in Austria by the late 1980s (see Figure 2.3). Nor is there any doubt that

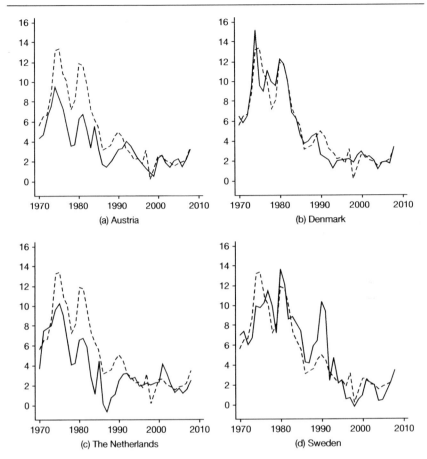

Figure 3.1 Inflation, 1970–2008

Data source: World Bank (2009). Inflation is defined as the annual percentage change in the consumer price index. The dotted line represents the mean inflation rate in the thirteen European countries that have been democracies since the Second World War, excluding countries with a population of less than one million.

inflation was high in Sweden in the late 1980s and early 1990s: Figure 3.1, which describes the development of inflation in Austria, Denmark, the Netherlands, and Sweden in the period from 1970 onward, shows that although Swedish inflation was lower in absolute terms in the 1980s and early 1990s than it had been around 1980, inflation rates had declined in other European countries in the meantime, which meant that the consequences of high inflation were more serious (particularly when Sweden's exchange rate was pegged to the exchange rates of countries with lower levels of inflation).

However, it would be an oversimplification to explain the timing of economic policy changes in Austria and Sweden with reference to these underlying economic pressures only. As I noted earlier, Austrian government debt had been increasing continuously since the mid-1970s, and no immediate economic crisis forced the Austrian government to give priority to debt reduction in the mid-1980s (as opposed to the early 1980s or early 1990s, for instance). But as I showed in the section on the Austrian political model, above, there were political reasons why change occurred at this point. Similarly, although inflation was particularly high in Sweden in the late 1980s and early 1990s—at least in a comparative perspective—Swedish governments had been concerned with the high rate of nominal wage increases, which was the main reason for high inflation, ever since the mid-1970s. The political factors that I have identified in this chapter help to explain why governments believed that it was necessary to take radical measures to bring down inflation in the early 1990s.

In sum, although Austrian and Swedish governments could probably not have carried on indefinitely with the employment-oriented economic policy strategies they had followed prior to the late 1980s and early 1990s, it is likely that the policy changes that occurred in that period might have occurred earlier, or later, if the political circumstances had been different.

This political explanation assumes that Austria and Sweden were not protected in some other way from the economic pressures that Denmark and the Netherlands were exposed to in the 1970s and 1980s. One factor that should be considered in this context is the regulation of international capital flows, since some students of Austria and Sweden have argued that their relatively extensive regulation of capital movements explains why they were able to use macroeconomic policy to protect their domestic economies even after other countries had given up such attempts (Kurzer 1993; Moses 1994, 22–3).

It is true that Austria and Sweden only abandoned capital controls in the late 1980s, which was later than Denmark and the Netherlands. In Sweden, the last major step—the deregulation of portfolio investments— was taken in 1989, and in Austria, the last significant controls were only removed in 1991. Indeed, Figure 3.2, which describes the extent of capital account liberalization in Austria, Denmark, the Netherlands, and Sweden from the early 1960s to the late 2000s, suggests that Austria and Sweden still shelter their financial markets to a larger extent than the average Western European country, whereas the Danish and Dutch financial markets have been, if anything, slightly more open.

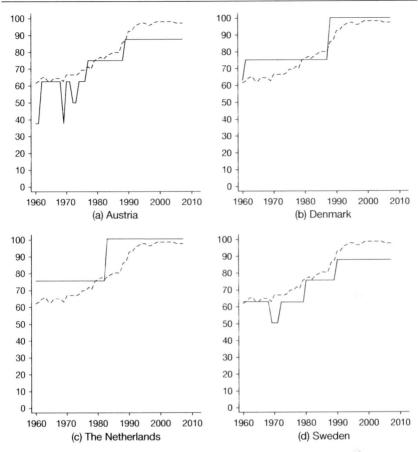

Figure 3.2 Capital account liberalization, 1960–2007

Data source: Quinn (1997). The dotted line represents the mean level of capital account liberalization, on a scale from 0 to 100, in the thirteen European countries that have been democracies since the Second World War, excluding countries with a population of less than 1 million. I am grateful to Dennis P. Quinn for sharing his data on capital account liberalization.

However, there are two reasons why this should not be seen as evidence that the constraints associated with the liberalization of the international capital market explains why Austria and Sweden waited longer than Denmark and the Netherlands before they adopted economic policies oriented toward low inflation and balanced budgets. First of all, the degree of capital account regulation is itself a political choice. If regulations had sheltered Austria and Sweden and governments had believed that this shelter was necessary for pursuing their macroeconomic objectives, they could have refrained from deregulating (just as Danish and Dutch governments could have).

Second, and perhaps more importantly, the regulation of international capital flows did not actually provide much shelter for the Austrian and Swedish economies: beginning in the late 1970s, even states that retained capital controls were constrained by the increasing freedom of capital movements. In Austria, monetary policy was not seen as a part of domestic demand management after 1979, when it became clear that Austria was open to capital movements in a "policy-relevant" sense, as Eduard Hochreiter, an economist at the central bank, puts it (interview with Eduard Hochreiter, Vienna, June 9, 2006; see also Hochreiter and Tavlas 2004). In Denmark, the former governor of the central bank, Erik Hoffmeyer (1993, 40), notes that from 1969, the role of monetary policy was primarily to support the exchange rate.

Regarding the Netherlands, the Dutch central banker André Szász says that in the 1970s, Dutch economic policy authorities were still under the "illusion" that they had room for maneuver, but although the Netherlands regulated short-term capital flows, "within the board I was the one who was in charge of this, and therefore I was the one most directly confronted with the difficulties, and I was increasingly aware that this was theory rather than practice" (telephone interview with André Szász, April 18, 2006). In Sweden, finally, Lars Wohlin, who became governor of the central bank in 1979, says that with a fixed exchange rate, which Sweden had at the time, "the aim of monetary policy was to maintain balance in currency flows" (Lars Wohlin, Stockholm, April 3, 2002). This evidence suggests that all four countries had similar experiences, and were similarly restricted, already in the 1970s.

The European Dimension

The macroeconomic regime changes in Austria and Sweden in the late 1980s and early 1990s coincided with policy changes concerning membership of the European Community. Whereas the Netherlands was a member from the start and Denmark joined in the early 1970s, Austria and Sweden only joined the EU in 1995. The main reason was that in the late 1980s and early 1990s, the end of the Cold War permitted these two neutral states to join without compromising their policies of neutrality. Moreover, European integration intensified in the second half of the 1980s, which made membership seem more important and attractive: the Single European Act established a single European market in 1986, and the

European Monetary System, initiated in 1979, proved to be more resilient than previous attempts at European monetary cooperation, such as the "Snake" system of the 1970s (McNamara 1998, Chapters 6 and 7).

The fact that governments changed both economic policies and policies *vis-à-vis* the European Community between the mid-1980s and the mid-1990s can be explained in at least three ways. One possible interpretation is that the desire to join the European Union forced governments to change their economic policies, in order to adapt to the policies that other European countries pursued, and to the requirements of the Economic and Monetary Union (for two different versions of this argument, see Moses 1997 and Ingebritsen 1998). Another interpretation is that the same set of economic pressures forced Austrian and Swedish governments to change both economic policies and foreign policies.

However, there is a third view, which is that economic policymaking was largely separate from the issue of EC membership, and that to the extent that there was a connection, it was that EC membership—or the prospect of membership—helped governments to commit to economic policy changes that they wanted to adopt for other reasons (Soskice 2000, 61). A close inspection of the decision-making process in Austria and Sweden suggests that this explanation has important merits.

In response to the question whether economic policies would have been different if Austria had *not* decided to join the European Union, the former Austrian chancellor Franz Vranitzky replied, "No, clearly no," pointing out that "even if we had not decided to join, we were faced with the situation that two thirds of our external transactions were with the twelve European Union countries" (interview with Franz Vranitzky, Vienna, June 7, 2006). Furthermore, the economic policy changes in Austria began in the mid-1980s, but the application for membership was only handed in in 1989. This was earlier than in Sweden, but after the change in economic policy that I have discussed in this chapter.

Concerning the Swedish case, Jakob Gustavsson's comprehensive study of EU membership (1998) shows that the wish to join the EC was at least partly caused by disappointment with the performance of the domestic economy: it was thus, in this sense, an outcome, not a cause, of the economic policy changes that I am concerned with here. The prime minister at the time, Ingvar Carlsson, says that the "basic thing" was the end of the Cold War, which meant that Sweden's policy of neutrality was no longer an obstacle to EU membership, but beyond that, Mr Carlsson believed that joining the EU would allow Sweden to make desirable domestic policy changes.

For me, in this situation, membership was also an element in the modernization of our economic policy. I felt that we were conceited in Sweden, thinking that we were so good at everything. (interview with Ingvar Carlsson, Stockholm, January 29, 2003)

Allan Larsson, finance minister in 1990–1, regarded domestic economic policies as primary: the application for EC membership was a "signal that Sweden was not going to go on with high inflation and then devalue," he said in an interview with the author (interview with Allan Larsson, Stockholm, October 30, 2001).

In conclusion, the decision to join the European Community was separate from or endogenous to the political processes that this book examines. When Austria's and Sweden's membership applications were submitted, Austrian and Swedish governments had already decided to change their economic policies, making them more similar to economic policies in other European states.

The Role of Economic Ideas

The final alternative explanation that I will consider in this chapter is the argument that the transition from high-employment-oriented to low-inflation-oriented macroeconomic policies in Austria, Denmark, the Netherlands, and Sweden was the result, at least in part, of the decline of Keynesianism and the appearance of alternative approaches to macroeconomics. An important literature in comparative politics has argued that these intellectual changes shaped the economic policies of governments in the 1970s, 1980s, and 1990s (McNamara 1998; Marcussen 2000; Blyth 2001, 2002). Other scholars claim, by contrast, that politicians merely use economic ideas to rationalize policies that they wish to adopt for other reasons (Notermans 2000, 37–41).

My own view is that expert ideas—that is, shared beliefs about cause-and-effect relationships, developed and disseminated by actors who are widely recognized as having special knowledge about a certain policy's target area—have real but limited effects on policies (Lindvall 2009, 704): when governments consider second-order policy changes, they often turn to experts for advice, but experts have less influence over routine decisions, such as first-order policy changes, or over fundamental, third-order policy changes, such as a change in the goals of economic policy (see the section "Models of Politics" in Chapter 1).

Among the four countries considered in this book, the case for the political influence of economic ideas is perhaps strongest when it comes to the Netherlands. By tradition, economic experts have played an important role in Dutch economic policymaking, and the Netherlands bureau for economic policy analysis (*Centraal Planbureau*, CPB) occupies a central position in the Dutch state. The bureau for economic policy analysis was created after the Second World War, with the famous economist Jan Tinbergen as its director (Tinbergen was the recipient of the Sveriges Riksbank Prize in Economic Sciences in Memory of Alfred Nobel the first time it was awarded, in 1969). Since the coalition agreements of new governments are routinely submitted to the CPB for analysis, the policymaking process in the Netherlands is more technocratic than policymaking in Austria, Denmark, or Sweden.

There is some evidence that the economic policy shifts in the Netherlands in the 1970s were associated with changes in CPB thinking. Unlike in the three other countries, where Keynesianism remained dominant at least until the early 1980s (and in the cases of Austria and Denmark longer still), non-Keynesian ideas appear to have influenced policymaking in the Netherlands already in the mid-1970s. In an influential paper, which was published in Dutch in 1974 and in English in 1976, two economists at the bureau for economic policy analysis argued that the rise in unemployment in the Netherlands should be attributed to the rise in real labor costs, not to weak domestic demand (Den Hartog and Tjan 1976). This paper is often described as important to the development of Dutch economic thinking, and economic policymaking, in the 1980s and 1990s (Zalm 1990, 2; Jones 2008, 147–9). In the 1970s, there were other economists who favored a more Keynesian approach to economic problems (de Klerk, van der Laan, and Thio 1977), but within a few years, the views of the Den Hartog and Tjan paper had become more generally accepted (interview with Kees van Paridon and Dirk Wolfson, Rotterdam, 21 November 2007).

The central planning bureau was also important in the 1990s, when it produced reports suggesting that tax policies and unemployment compensation policies mattered to the levels of employment and unemployment (see Chapter 4). According to Gerrit Zalm, who was the director of CPB in the early 1990s and finance minister in 1994–2002 and 2003–7, the economic models that are used by the bureau for economic policy analysis matter to the political debate since the political parties routinely send their policy proposals to the CPB and ask the bureau to calculate the likely economic effects. In the 1990s, Mr Zalm argues, this meant that parties began to develop ideas about how to make social policies more employment-efficient.

When benefit income ratios became effective in the model, then left wing parties brought up tax credits and right wing parties reduced benefits. One thing is delivering money and one thing is costing money, but in terms of incentives the effect is more or less the same. I think that this may be one of the reasons that this incentives idea is now accepted by all political parties. (interview with Gerrit Zalm, Amsterdam, February 8, 2010)

Going back to the 1970s and 1980s, the new macroeconomic analyses that were being developed at the bureau for economic policy analysis by scholars such as Den Hartog and Tjan may have had some effect on some key policy choices in the 1970s, such as the center-left government's decision to adopt its 1 percent policy in 1975–6. But it was not a major cause. As the section on the Netherlands in Chapter 2 showed, the political debate between those politicians who regarded themselves as Keynesians and those who did not continued throughout the 1970s, and when Ruud Lubbers's new center-right government was formed in 1982, adopting austere fiscal policies and enforcing a policy of wage restraint, new economic ideas were not the main motivation, according to Onno Ruding, finance minister from 1982 to 1989:

We did not pretend to be a new Keynes or something like that. No, it was more about new political priorities. We said that those policies have failed or are about to fail, and we should do things differently.... That was not only a matter of saving money; it also concerned the state's influence. The government in the mid-70s really wanted to change society in a much more egalitarian direction and with a much larger role for the State. (interview with Onno Ruding, Brussels, March 21, 2006)

A comparison between the Netherlands and Denmark also suggests that the effects of economic ideas on the overall direction of economic policies should not be overstated. Throughout the 1970s and 1980s, and for much of the 1990s, Denmark and the Netherlands pursued relatively similar economic policies, at least compared to Austria and Sweden. Yet, Danish and Dutch economic experts had different views (Danish economists were more Keynesian), and the institutions that governed the relationship between experts and the state were different.

There is little evidence that the gradual reorientation of Danish economic policy was the result of a change in economic ideas, for the economic debate in Denmark was dominated by Keynesians throughout the 1970s and well into the 1980s and 1990s (Asmussen 2007, 57, 65). This difference between the Danish and Dutch cases may help to explain why the center-left government in Denmark chose to adopt a cautiously expansionary fiscal policy program in 1993 whereas the Dutch Christian democratic–social democratic coalition government stuck to a policy of wage moderation and fiscal restraint in this period. But it does not explain the fact that Denmark and the Netherlands have otherwise been so similar.

Concerning Austria and Sweden—the two cases that this chapter is mainly concerned with—a comparison of the development of economic ideas and economic policies in these two countries reveals that contrary to the argument that ideas shape policies, the Austrian government decided to give budget consolidation priority over full employment at a time when Keynesian ideas were still dominant among Austrian economists, whereas the Swedish social democratic government in the early 1980s continued to give priority to full employment at a time when anti-Keynesian ideas had become influential among Swedish economists, and in policymaking circles (Lindvall 2009).

In his essay "Austro-Keynesianismus," Hans Seidel, an Austrian economist and former state secretary in the finance ministry, wrote that Austrian economists had one thing in common: they were all Keynesians (Seidel 1982b). Although monetarist and new classical ideas have gained ground in Austria since Seidel's essay was published, an analysis of articles in the policy-oriented economics journals *Wirtschaft und Gesellschaft* and *Wirtschaftspolitische Blätter* (which are published by the chamber of labor and the chamber of commerce) suggests that Keynesianism has remained stronger in Austria than in many other European countries, especially when it comes to more policy-relevant research. This was almost certainly the case when economic policies changed in the mid-1980s—as late as 1994, both *Wirtschaft und Gesellschaft* and *Wirtschaftspolitische Blätter* published issues on macroeconomics in which most contributions represented broadly Keynesian views (Lindvall 2009).

Gunther Tichy, an emeritus professor at the University of Graz, says that it is important to remember that Austrian Keynesianism was always different from other Keynesian traditions, since it was mainly concerned with the reduction of uncertainty, not with short-term stabilization— "the question of how to fight recessions with fiscal policy was never the main point"—but he also says that "macroeconomic policy and macroeconomic aspects are much more looked at in Austria than anywhere else" and that Keynesianism, in the Austrian sense, has remained relatively influential even in the 2000s (interview with Gunther Tichy, Vienna, November 22, 2007).

The leading Swedish economics experts responded differently to the anti-Keynesian trend in the international economic debate. An analysis of articles published in the Swedish journal *Ekonomisk debatt* suggests that the transition from Keynesianism to predominantly new classical ideas can be divided into three phases. In the first phase (the mid-1970s), some elements of non-Keynesian theories were discussed in connection with particular empirical or theoretical problems. In the second phase (the late 1970s), individual economists presented broad challenges to Keynesianism, describing the problems of Keynesianism as so serious that it should be regarded as inferior to other macroeconomic approaches. In the third phase (the early 1980s), economists started describing alternatives to Keynesianism as commonly held views and took the crisis of Keynesianism to be historical fact. In 1982, an entire issue of the journal dealt with "the need for new strategies in stabilization policy" (Calmfors 1982). In Denmark, non-Keynesian ideas were for a long time associated with a few individual economists, but the opposite was true in Sweden, where, by the mid-1980s, Keynesian ideas were associated with individual economists such as Sven Grassman, an expert on balance of payments statistics.

In 1982, when six years of center-right government were drawing to a close and social democratic economic experts were developing a new economic program, Keynesian ideas were widely regarded as outdated among Swedish economists. This did not lead the Social Democrats to change the main objective of economic policy from full employment to low inflation, however, although it did lead them to change the instruments of economic policy.

The importance of economic ideas for the social democratic policy change in 1982 can be observed in the internal memoranda that two social democratic economic advisers, Michael Sohlman and Erik Åsbrink, wrote in the spring and summer of 1982 (see especially Åsbrink 1982). Sohlman's and Åsbrink's memoranda rejected a strategy based on expansionary fiscal policies, a strategy that they believed had failed in Sweden in the 1970s and in the first year of the Mitterrand administration in France. Having no faith in the favored Keynesian instrument, fiscal policy, the social democratic economic advisers emphasized exchange rate policy. Their idea was not only to make a big devaluation but also to peg the Swedish *krona* to the West German *mark* in order to control inflation.

The second part of the program was never implemented, but the reasoning behind it reveals the influence of new classical economic ideas. Sohlman and Åsbrink based their arguments explicitly on the notion of "rules-based economic policies," which was the version of anti-Keynesian thinking that gained currency in Sweden in the early 1980s. "I believed in rules-based economic policies, and the idea of pegging the *krona* to the German *mark*, which didn't happen, was an obvious example of rules-based policies," Mr Åsbrink says today (interview with Erik Åsbrink, Stockholm, October 15, 2001). Kjell-Olof Feldt—who was finance minister from 1982 to 1990—says that the idea of rational expectations "had become part of our worldview" (interview with Kjell-Olof Feldt, Stockholm, October 30, 2001).

The economic strategy of the Swedish Social Democrats after the party's return to power in 1982 is thus a particularly clear example of the real but limited effects of economic ideas (Lindvall 2009). Leading social democratic economic advisers had decided not to prescribe Keynesian remedies, since they were persuaded by the critique of Keynesianism that had become influential in international economic organizations and among Swedish economists in the early 1980s. Still, there was never any question of changing the objectives of economic policy. Being convinced that Keynesian ideas were not useful, these advisers suggested that a new instrument, exchange rate policy, could be used to meet the objective of full employment. New ideas changed the method, not the goals. The limited effects of ideas on objectives are also apparent in the case of the proposal to link the Swedish *krona* to the German *mark*. Although this was a logical part of the program from the point of view of the ideas that informed it, the leading politicians chose not to implement it since they believed that this might lead to higher unemployment in the medium term.

In conclusion, the dominant ideas among economic experts help to explain particular policy choices in Austria, Denmark, the Netherlands, and Sweden, but economic ideas do not explain why the gradual shift away from full employment policies in the course of the 1970s, 1980s, and early 1990s took so much longer in Austria and Sweden than it did in Denmark and the Netherlands.

Conclusions

By the early 1990s, Austria, Denmark, the Netherlands, and Sweden had all changed their fiscal and monetary policies, making low inflation and balanced budgets the primary objectives of macroeconomic policy. However, Austria and Sweden made this policy change later than Denmark and the Netherlands. Well into the 1980s, Austrian and Swedish governments used fiscal or exchange rate policies to maintain full employment. When governments in Austria and Sweden did give up on full employment, giving priority to budget consolidation (in Austria) and low inflation (in Sweden), this was at least partly a result of underlying changes in the Austrian and Swedish political models—just as the economic policy changes in Denmark and the Netherlands in the second half of the 1970s had been associated with underlying political changes in those two countries.

4

The Fact of Unemployment

Once unemployment rates increase, they tend to remain high. This places new demands on political institutions, for the reduction of unemployment typically requires other policy instruments than the ones governments use when they try to prevent unemployment from increasing. This chapter is concerned with the labor market policies that Austria, Denmark, the Netherlands, and Sweden have pursued after the emergence of high unemployment. It attempts to explain why these countries have followed different reform paths, and why political conflicts over labor market reform have played out differently.

Beginning in the early 1990s, European governments have increasingly treated unemployment as a microeconomic problem. Instead of trying to encourage growth, expecting employment to follow, governments have pursued labor market policy reforms designed to increase the likelihood that unemployed individuals will seek, find, and accept new jobs. This was the theme of the OECD's influential *Jobs Study* (1994), and the idea that labor market policies matter to employment and national economic performance has remained popular ever since—both in domestic politics and within the institutions of the European Union (Weishaupt 2008, Chapter 5).

This change in political emphasis in the 1990s and 2000s was a consequence of the persistence of high unemployment in many Western European countries. Long after the shocks that destabilized the postwar economic order had occurred, average unemployment in Europe remained high. But unemployment rates varied greatly across countries. This suggested to experts and policymakers alike that certain features of labor market policy—notably the character of unemployment compensation schemes and active labor market programs—might explain why it was so difficult for many countries to bring unemployment down (Blanchard 2006, 25–6).

The differences between Denmark, the Netherlands, Austria, and Sweden were stark in the 1990s and 2000s, just as they had been in the 1970s and 1980s. In the 1990s, Danish and Dutch governments negotiated comprehensive labor market reforms with the main labor market organizations. Due to the apparent success of these policies—unemployment declined sharply in both countries from the mid-1990s onward—Denmark and the Netherlands have come to be regarded as the two main examples of "flexicurity," the idea that successful employment policies must simultaneously provide for flexible labor markets and social security (Viebrock and Clasen 2009, 313–16). In Austria and Sweden, labor market reforms have been more cautious. That said, there were important differences between Austria and Sweden—as a result, I will argue, of the more pragmatic and gradual character of political and economic reform in Austria from the 1980s onward (see Chapter 3).

The main argument of this chapter is that the relatively high reform intensity in Denmark and the Netherlands in the 1990s was a result of two factors: the early onset of mass unemployment and the renegotiation of postwar political arrangements that had begun in the 1980s. The political circumstances and economic policy choices in the 1970s and early 1980s that I have analyzed in previous chapters thus mattered indirectly to labor market policymaking in the 1990s and 2000s, and new political developments had a direct effect on the choices governments made.

An Overview

This chapter is concerned with cash benefits for the unemployed, active labor market policies, and the interaction between the two. Most advanced countries have two systems of unemployment compensation: unemployment insurance, which is normally earnings-related, and unemployment assistance for the uninsured, which is normally means tested. Active labor market programs aim to reduce unemployment by influencing the "supply, demand, and mobility of labor" (Rueda 2007, 23), using a variety of instruments, such as employment agencies, labor market training schemes, and employment subsidies.

In recent years, many European governments have sought to encourage the integration or reintegration of the unemployed in the labor market (i.e., "activate" the unemployed, in contemporary political jargon) through various reforms in the two policy areas that I have just mentioned. Eichhorst et al. (2008, 4–7) distinguish between "demanding" and "enabling" activation policies. (Weishaupt 2008, 55–6, 255 distinguishes between "negative" and "positive" work incentives; the underlying idea is similar.) One distinctive feature of labor market reforms in Denmark and the Netherlands is that they have combined "demanding" and "enabling" policy measures. Austrian and Swedish governments have done this to a lesser extent.

Labor market reforms that make policies more "demanding" are designed to increase the job-search activity of the unemployed and the likelihood that they will accept job offers. Many labor economists believe that less generous unemployment benefits, and particularly benefits of limited duration, encourage the unemployed to increase their efforts to find a new job (Nickell 1997; Nickell and Layard 1999; Layard, Nickell, and Jackman 2005; Fredriksson and Holmlund 2006), and several European countries—including Denmark and the Netherlands—have therefore reduced the duration of unemployment benefits in the 1990s and 2000s. Other examples of "demanding" policy reforms are increased administrative control over the job-search behavior of the unemployed, harsher penalties for those who fail to look for a new job, and compulsory training or work ("workfare") for the long-term unemployed.

Labor market reforms that make policies more "enabling" are designed to increase the employability and productivity of the unemployed, and to ease the transition from unemployment to gainful employment. Policies that fall into this category include traditional active labor market programs—employment agencies, training, and employment subsidies—but also other instruments, such as "in-work-benefits" that allow the unemployed to keep some of their benefits temporarily if they start a new job, and childcare services that allow workers to combine work with family responsibilities. The expansion of public sector employment can also be categorized as an enabling activation policy, as can the promotion of part-time and flexible working arrangements, which is particularly relevant here since part-time work has become very common in the Netherlands, especially among women (Visser 2002).

Although this chapter is mainly concerned with unemployment benefits and active labor market policies, other social policies are also mentioned if they have mattered greatly to labor market strategies and employment outcomes in Austria, Denmark, the Netherlands, and Sweden. This includes early retirement in Austria and Denmark, disability benefits in the Netherlands, and sickness benefits in Sweden. These programs are relevant since the long-term unemployed have sometimes been transferred from unemployment compensation schemes to other forms of social protection (on disability benefits in the Netherlands, see Hemerijck, Unger, and Visser 2000, 218; on sickness benefits in Sweden, see Green-Pedersen and Lindbom 2005, 69–70, and Stensöta 2009, 14). The fact that welfare state programs are connected in this manner suggests that it matters greatly whether countries undertake simultaneous reforms across policy domains or if reforms are more decoupled.

Before I examine the development of labor market policy within each country in detail, I will present an overview of important policy changes in Austria, Denmark, the Netherlands, and Sweden using available quantitative indicators. Figure 4.1, which is based on Lyle Scruggs's widely used social insurance dataset (2004), describes the development of typical replacement rates (the ratios of net benefits to net incomes for average production workers) in unemployment insurance between 1980 and 2002. With the exception of Austria, where the replacement rate has been only slightly higher than the average replacement rate in Western Europe, the countries featured in this book all belonged to the most generous welfare states in Europe by the early 1980s. Figure 4.1 also shows that governments in Denmark and the Netherlands have reduced replacement rates significantly, starting with large reductions in the mid-1980s and continuing with a series of smaller reductions in the 1990s and early 2000s. In Sweden, replacement rates have also declined, but only after the economic crisis of the early 1990s. Unlike governments in the three other countries, Austrian governments appear to have made relatively few changes over time, although there has been a gradual reduction of replacement rates in unemployment insurance from 1993 onward (Tálos 2005a, 67–8).

The data from the social citizenship indicator program (Korpi and Palme 2008) are largely consistent with Scruggs's data, confirming that there were "major cuts" in unemployment insurance in Denmark, the Netherlands, and Sweden in the 1980s and 1990s (Korpi and Palme 2003, 444). The main difference between Scruggs's dataset and the SCIP dataset is that the Danish benefit reduction in the 1980s only shows up in 1986–7 in Scruggs's data (see Figure 4.1), as opposed to 1982 in SCIP. The explanation is probably that the Danish policy changes were more indirect: Walter Korpi and Joakim Palme (2003) categorize the Dutch (and Swedish) policy changes as "straightforward cuts in benefit levels" whereas the Danish policy change is categorized as a "freezing or reduction of benefit ceilings."

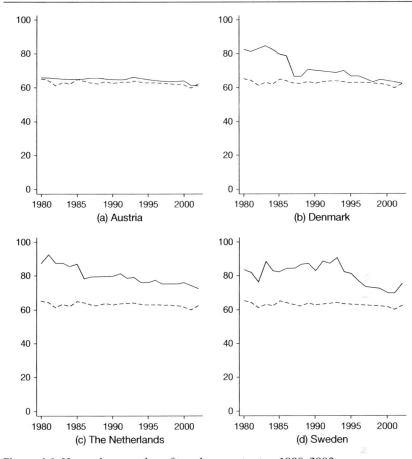

Figure 4.1 Unemployment benefit replacement rates, 1980–2002

Data source: Scruggs (2004). Scruggs's dataset includes two separate measures of the unemployment benefit replacement rate: one concerns unmarried individuals earning the average wage; the other concerns households with an average production worker, a dependent spouse, and two dependent children aged 7 and 12. The figures above report the mean of these two ratios. The dotted line represents the mean replacement rate in the thirteen European countries that have been democracies since the Second World War, excluding countries with a population of less than one million. These replacement rates are calculated for "average production workers." It is important to note that since the earnings ceilings are quite low in Denmark and Sweden, only low wage earners are entitled to the full 70 or 80 percent replacement rate; those who earn higher wages may in some circumstances be entitled to lower benefits than similar categories of Austrian and Dutch employees. See the indicators published in OECD (2007) for details on replacement rates for different earnings categories. (I am grateful to Johan Davidsson for pointing these cross-country differences out to me.)

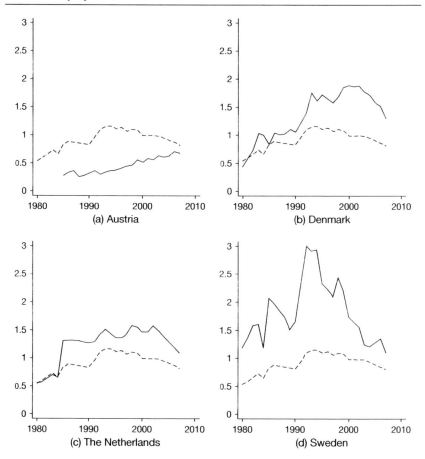

Figure 4.2 Active labor market policy spending as a percentage of GDP, 1980–2007

Data source: OECD (2009*b*). Data for 1980–4 are from Armingeon et al. (2009). The dotted line represents the mean level of ALMP spending as a percentage of GDP in the thirteen European countries that have been democracies since the Second World War, excluding countries with a population of less than 1 million.

Figure 4.2 uses data from the OECD *Social Expenditure Database* to describe the development of government spending on active labor market policies in the four countries from 1980 to 2007. Denmark stands out. Throughout the 1980s, active labor market policy spending in Denmark was close to the average rate in the thirteen European countries that I have used as a reference group throughout this book. Beginning in the early 1990s, however, Danish active labor market policy spending increased greatly. Governments in the Netherlands also increased active labor market policy spending in the mid-1980s and early 1990s, and active labor market policy spending in the Netherlands remained relatively high even if unemployment rates decreased considerably in the late 1990s and early 2000s.

Although Sweden pioneered modern active labor market policies in the 1950s and 1960s, Swedish governments have, interestingly, reduced active market policy spending after the deep economic crisis of the 1990s, and by the 2000s it was back at the same level as in the 1980s, when unemployment was much lower. In recent years, Sweden has actually spent a smaller percentage of its national income on active labor market policy programs than Denmark and the Netherlands in some periods. Austrian governments, finally, have increased their spending on active labor market programs slightly, but Austria's programs remain small compared to the three other countries in this study—and compared to the West European average.

If one takes into consideration that unemployment declined in Denmark and the Netherlands between the 1980s and the 2000s, but increased in Austria and Sweden in the same period, it becomes clear that governments in Austria, Denmark, and the Netherlands have raised the profile of active labor market policies in their policy mixes (this is especially clear in Denmark and the Netherlands), whereas Swedish governments have moved in the other direction. The ratio of spending on active labor market policies and spending on ("passive") unemployment benefits, for example, suggests that whereas the "active" component of labor market policy has become larger in Austria, Denmark, and the Netherlands, Swedish policies have become more passive in the sense that a larger proportion of labor market policy spending has gone to cash benefits for the unemployed.

Although this chapter is mainly concerned with unemployment compensation and active labor market policies, I note in passing that governments in all four countries have liberalized certain aspects of employment protection legislation. As in most other European countries, almost all of these changes concern temporary contracts, not permanent contracts (the only significant exception being the elimination of severance pay in Austria in the early 2000s). Governments in Denmark, the Netherlands, and Sweden increased the scope for temporary work agencies in the 1990s. The Netherlands and Sweden have also increased the scope for fixed-term contracts (OECD 2004, 119–20).

Denmark

The overview that I have just presented identified important labor market policy changes in all four countries, particularly in Denmark, the Netherlands, and Sweden. But it is necessary to examine policy-making in each country in more detail before drawing any conclusions about similarities and differences among countries (or about the political circumstances that led to, or prevented, significant changes in policy).

In the 2000s, the Danish labor market model became the envy of the world and a blueprint for labor market reform across Europe. The question that concerns me here is how and why the most important labor market reforms in Denmark, which occurred in the 1990s, became politically possible. I will show that these reforms depended on new political bargains—both within the party system and between interest organizations—and I will argue that these political conditions resulted from the economic and political processes that I examine in this book.

Denmark has a voluntary unemployment insurance scheme, operated by unemployment funds affiliated with the trade unions. By the early 1980s, benefits had become both generous and long-lasting: in 1967, the replacement rate reached 90 percent of previous earnings, up to a certain maximum rate (Korpi and Palme 2008, country notes, Denmark 1970), and although benefits were in principle of limited duration, the law on job offers to the unemployed (*Lov om arbejdstilbud til ledige*), which had been adopted in 1978, meant that the duration of unemployment benefits was practically unlimited (Green-Pedersen 2002, 71; Paulsen 1992, 71). The uninsured unemployed in Denmark are entitled to means-tested social assistance. In the early 1980s, the levels of social assistance payments were still determined by individual case workers, but a maximum benefit was introduced by the social democratic government in 1981. The maximum benefit was reduced considerably by the center-right government in 1983 (Paulsen 1992, 74).

In contrast to its Scandinavian neighbor, Sweden, Denmark does not have a long history of active labor market policies, and as Figure 4.2 shows, active labor market policy spending was fairly low in both absolute and relative terms in the early 1980s. For much of the 1990s and 2000s, Denmark spent a larger share of its national income on active labor market policies than any other country in the world, but this is a relatively recent phenomenon; the 1990s was arguably the first time that the Danish government operated extensive active labor market programs (Benner and Vad 2000, 451).

Danish Reforms

By the early 1990s, Danish unemployment had increased to somewhere between 9 and 11 percent of the labor force, depending on which defin-ition of unemployment you rely on, and Denmark had lived with high unemployment ever since the late 1970s. The long history of persistent, high unemployment was an important explanation for the labor market reforms of the 1990s, which were explicitly designed to reduce long-term unemployment. The retrenchment of unemployment benefits by center-right governments in the 1980s—which brought the typical replacement rate in Danish unemployment insurance closer to the European aver-age (Figure 4.1)—were mainly about cost-cutting (see, however, Pedersen 2007, 88). The benefit ceiling freezes that the government imposed from 1982 onward led to significant reductions in the overall generosity of unemployment insurance—especially for medium- to high-income earn-ers (Green-Pedersen 2002, 71–2; Korpi and Palme 2008, country notes, Denmark 1985).

In the early 1990s, while Poul Schlüter's center-right coalition was still in power, the Danish government set up a commission of inquiry, chaired by the economist Hans Zeuthen, to investigate the "structural problems" in the Danish labor market. The commission's report, published in 1992 (Zeuthenudvalget 1992), provided the blueprint for the main reforms of the 1990s. There was broad political agreement, at this time, that unemployment had become a structural problem in Danish society, in the sense that economic upswings did not translate into higher levels of employment, and that this was a result of misguided labor market policies (see Torfing 1999, 13–14 and Larsen and Andersen 2009, 244–9). In particular, the reforms of the late 1970s, when unemployment benefit duration had in practice become unlimited, were now widely regarded as flawed.

The head of the secretariat of the Zeuthen committee, Jørgen Rosted—a senior civil servant in the ministry of finance—says that the unem-ployment compensation schemes in Denmark had become too generous and too long lasting, giving the unemployed no incentive to look for new jobs. It was necessary, he believed, to limit duration and reduce the replacement rate after a few years of unemployment. But "to accomplish this in a Nordic country at that time was very difficult," according to

Mr Rosted. The unions were reluctant to give up forms of social protection that many of their members relied on. "You need a lot of guts if you are going to convince the trade unions that they must tell their members that the country will never get back on its feet if they do not give up these things," Mr Rosted says (interview with Jørgen Rosted, Copenhagen, March 18, 2005).

The unions were only willing to accept stricter qualification requirements and shorter benefit duration if they got something else in return, and what they wanted were large investments in Swedish-style active labor market policies. This was the political bargain at the heart of the Danish labor market reforms. In other words, active labor market policies were used to compensate workers for the reduction in benefit generosity, much like Swedish social democratic governments in the 1950s—the pioneers of active labor market policy in Europe—used active labor market programs to compensate workers who lost their jobs because of industrial restructuring (Lindvert 2006, 39).

The employer organizations were initially reluctant to accept this trade-off, but in the end, the unions and employers came to an agreement. It still took some time to pass the first labor market reform, since some of the ministers in the conservative–liberal coalition government that was in power until 1993 disapproved of the strong emphasis on active labor market policy in the committee's proposal. In 1993, however, Poul Schlüter's center-right government was forced to resign, and a new center-left government was formed (see Chapter 3). The new government adopted most of the Zeuthen committee's proposals, combining a series of labor market reforms with the expansionary fiscal programs that they launched in 1993 (Jensen 2008, 65; see also Chapter 3).

The Danish parliament adopted three comprehensive labor market reforms in the mid- to late 1990s: one in 1993, one in 1995, and one in 1998. The first reform meant that from 1994, the maximum duration of unemployment benefits was limited to seven years, the right to re-qualify for unemployment benefits through participation in activation programs was abolished, and long-term receipt of unemployment benefits was made conditional on activation measures such as education and job training. From 1996, the maximum duration of unemployment benefits was reduced further, to five years, while eligibility criteria were tightened, the minimum age for recipients of unemployment benefits was increased from seventeen to nineteen years, and benefits for young people were drastically reduced after six months of unemployment. From 1999, finally, duration was reduced to four years, and new, tighter rules were introduced for the older unemployed. The point in time when the unemployed were required to enroll in active labor market programs was gradually moved forward: subsequent to the 1999 reform, it arrived after one year (Green-Pedersen 2002, 72).

After the center-left parties lost power to a new center-right coalition in 2001, the labor market regime that was established in the mid- to late 1990s remained more or less intact: the 2002 reform "More People at Work" (*Flere i Arbejde*) continued along the reform path of the previous government, taking further measures to encourage early job search (Andersen and Larsen 2004, 202). In 2003, the center-right government also increased the activation requirements in the unemployment assistance system, capping benefit payments in order to increase the incentives to find work (Torfing 2004, 35; Graversen and Thinggard 2005, 7).

In contemporary political rhetoric, the term "flexicurity" often refers to the combination of flexible labor markets—liberal hiring and firing regulations—and generous unemployment benefits. When the Danish case is used as an example of flexicurity (and it often is: see, for example, European Commission 2007), Denmark's liberal employment protection laws are often mentioned. However, whereas the low level of unemployment protection is one core element of Denmark's labor market regime (Kenworthy 2008, 129; Bredgaard et al. 2009), the big reforms of the 1990s did not concern this particular policy area (Calmfors 2007, 3).

The result of the reforms of the 1990s was a labor market policy regime that combined what Eichhorst et al. (2008) have termed "enabling" and "demanding" activation. It was enabling since spending on active labor market policies increased greatly, and it was demanding since the pressure on the unemployed to find new jobs increased. There was a "dual aim," as Jon Kvist (2003, 242) argues: to encourage unemployment benefit recipients to seek new jobs while at the same time improving their qualifications and employability.

Danish Choices

As several authors have noted, the labor market reforms in Denmark were not merely a series of discrete policy changes but a gradual "third-order" policy change (Hall 1993), in the sense that labor market and social policy have become oriented toward new goals and informed by new ideas (Cox 1998, 2001). In the 1970s and 1980s, the main idea was that there were not enough jobs for everyone, so work should be shared and the unemployed should be protected. The introduction of early retirement, *efterløn*, in 1979 was one consequence of this way of approaching the unemployment problem. This way of thinking, Jon Kvist (2001, 5) claims, has largely been abandoned. Instead, most social insurance schemes are now designed to encourage the reintegration of the unemployed in the labor market.

The one part of the Danish social and labor market policy regime in the late 2000s that seemed to be at odds with the employment-oriented, activating stance that had been the norm since the mid-1990s was the system of early retirement, or *efterløn*. The *efterløn* reform that was introduced in the 1970s allowed workers, under certain conditions, to retire early on unemployment benefits, and it was an attempt, typical of its time, to redistribute available work from the old to the young. The center-left government undertook a partial reform of the *efterløn* scheme in 1998, seeking, at a great political cost, to encourage people to work longer by making the conditions for early retirement stricter, reducing benefit levels, and creating incentives for older workers to remain active in the labor market (Larsen and Andersen 2009, 253–5), but Denmark has retained some early retirement programs for employees older than 59 (Auer 2002, 91). As a consequence, the labor market participation rate of 55–64-year-olds is lower in Denmark than in neighboring Sweden, even if the overall employment rate in Denmark has been higher ever since the mid-1990s (Eichhorst and Hemerijck 2009, 206–12).

The Netherlands

Just like Denmark, the Netherlands was celebrated as an employment miracle in the 1990s and 2000s. Ever since 1998—with the exception of two years in the 2000s, when the Danish unemployment rate was marginally lower—the Netherlands has had lower unemployment than either of the three other countries covered in this book (see Figure 4.2). In fact, there were long periods in the 2000s when the Netherlands had a lower unemployment rate than any other country in Europe. The Dutch employment miracle is commonly attributed to a combination of policies, including, prominently, the policy of wage restraint that was initiated with the Wassenaar Agreement in 1982 (see Chapter 3), regulatory reforms that allowed for a high proportion of part-time and fixed-term employment, and the "activation" of Dutch social policies (van Ours 2006, 152–3). I am concerned, here, with the political conditions that made the third set of policy changes possible.

The Netherlands had, no significant tradition of active labor market policies before the 1980s, although there were the beginnings of active labor market policy in the mid-1970s (Seeleib-Kaiser, van Dyk, and Roggenkamp 2008, 25). Generous social protection for the unemployed was implemented gradually in the Netherlands from the early 1950s to the mid-1960s. A system of short-term unemployment insurance (WW, *Werklosheidswet*), which paid 80 percent of previous earnings for a period of six months, was introduced in 1952. A further, tax-funded unemployment benefit, which provided unemployment compensation for an additional period, whose length depended on the employment record of the unemployed individual, was introduced in 1964. The replacement rate in the second scheme was 75 percent. When these two benefits were exhausted, a third form of unemployment compensation, which was not earnings-related, was available, before an individual was consigned to social assistance (Einerhand, Eriksson, and Hansen 1993, 19–20). The disability insurance program that was created in the 1960s, which provided benefits that were in effect even more generous than unemployment benefits, played an important part as an instrument of labor shedding in the Netherlands, and should also be mentioned here (Seeleib-Kaiser, van Dyk, and Roggenkamp 2008, 24–5; Green-Pedersen 2002, 74).

Dutch Reforms

The center-right governments in the 1980s made a series of cuts in the unemployment benefit system. Ruud Lubbers's first two governments—which were in power between 1982 and 1989—halted the automatic indexation of benefits, froze benefit levels, reduced the duration of benefits for young unemployed, reduced the replacement rate in unemployment insurance (to 70 percent of the previous wage), and restricted eligibility. The Christian democratic–social democratic coalition that was in power between 1989 and 1994 continued on this course, freezing social benefits on several occasions (Cox 1993, 180; Green-Pedersen 2002, 75; Rueda 2007, 193).

The motivation for most of the reforms in the 1980s was fiscal: Dutch governments wished to reduce the budget deficit, and the only way to accomplish this was by limiting social spending. In the 1990s, however, employment as such became an important goal, not least because the government's Scientific Council for Government Policy (WRR, *Wetenschappelijke Raad voor het Regeringsbeleid*) argued that the only way to preserve generous social policies was to increase labor market participation (Rueda 2007, 194; Sol et al. 2008, 165).

There were several reforms in the unemployment benefit system under the "purple" (social democratic–liberal) governments in the mid- to late 1990s and early 2000s. In 1995, for example, the Unemployment Insurance Act extended the qualification period for unemployment benefits, and other pieces of legislation that came into force in 1995 and 1996 increased the activation requirements in the unemployment benefit system and the social assistance system (Rueda 2007, 198). Other significant pieces of legislation from the mid-1990s led to an increased emphasis on monitoring and sanctions, forcing the unemployed to look for new jobs (de Mooij 2004, 31–3; van Ours 2006, 145–7). With the Jobseekers Employment Act in 1998, the government introduced a new set of administrative procedures for the treatment of individual unemployed by municipal governments, which were instructed to conduct assessment interviews and make individual action plans on the basis of these interviews (Hemerijck and Marx, forthcoming). These new policies were elements in a wide-ranging strategy to encourage the reintegration of the unemployed in the labor market.

The unemployment benefit reforms continued under the center-right governments in the mid-2000s. In the most recent reform—implemented in October 2006—the two Dutch unemployment benefit regimes were merged into a single, income-related benefit, which is paid for a maximum of three years and two months (for workers with long contribution histories; others are covered for a shorter period), a reduction from five years, which used to be the maximum duration. One interesting element of this reform is that whereas the maximum duration was reduced, and entitlement conditions were tightened, the replacement rate was increased from 70 to 75 percent in the first two months of unemployment (Sol et al. 2008, 176–82; Andeweg and Irwin 2009, 222). According to Marko Bos, the director of economic affairs at the social and economic council, this was one of several reforms in the 1990s and 2000s where there was "more or less agreement between the social partners" (interview with Marko Bos, The Hague, November 20, 2007).

The 1990s also saw important reforms in active labor market policy, just as in Denmark—although the expansion of active labor market programs did not go as far in the Netherlands. Moreover, whereas the Danish government spends more on training, aiming for general improvements in human capital, active labor market policies in the Netherlands are distinguished by high spending on public employment and employment subsidies for vulnerable groups (Rueda 2007, 164–6).

As Figure 4.2 showed, the Netherlands had already increased spending on active labor market policies in the mid-1980s, but a new institutional framework for active labor market policy was only created during the Christian democratic–social democratic coalition in 1989–94. Many workers had become "unemployable," the government believed, and new policies were introduced to address this problem, in collaboration with the social partners (Rijksvoorlichtingsdienst 1990, 94). Following the introduction of the new Public Employment Service in 1991, the Christian democratic–social democratic government adopted other important pieces of active labor market policy legislation, such as the 1992 Guaranteed Youth Employment Act (Seeleib-Kaiser, van Dyk, and Roggenkamp 2008, 60).

The purple governments in the mid- to late 1990s continued to expand active labor market policy. For example, the social democratic minister for social affairs and employment in 1994–8, Ad Melkert, introduced new types of subsidized employment for the long-term unemployed—so-called "Melkert jobs"—and reduced social security contributions for low-income earners and long-term unemployed (Rijksvoorlichtingsdienst 1997, 45–6; Hemerijck and Marx, forthcoming).

Just like the Danish center-left governments in the 1990s, then, the Dutch governments in 1994–2002 combined "demanding" and "enabling" activation reforms, by making it more difficult (or costly) to remain on benefits, while at the same time assisting the long-term unemployed through various forms of employment subsidies and training measures. Gerrit Zalm, a liberal politician who served as finance minister in the "purple" governments in 1994–2002, says that this combination of policies was a "trade-off" between the Social Democrats and his own Liberal Party. Personally, he did not find active labor market programs very useful—"I am from the Liberal Party; I was more in favor of tax incentives for work." He also says, however, that being able to offer subsidized employment allowed the public authorities to put more pressure on the unemployed: "The way you execute the benefit schemes can become more harsh. And of course, from the point of view of a liberal, that is not a bad thing" (interview with Gerrit Zalm, Amsterdam, February 8, 2010).

Active labor market programs were cut back after 2002, when the liberals joined the Christian Democrats in a new center-right coalition. The Christian Democrats had been critical of the subsidized employment programs that the Social Democrats had introduced in the 1990s (Hemerijck and Marx, forthcoming), and the new government therefore emphasized "demanding" rather than "enabling" activation (see, e.g., Rijksvoorlichtingsdienst 2002, 10–12).

Dutch Choices

In addition to the policy changes that I have described in this section, which is mainly concerned with unemployment benefits and active labor market policies, Dutch governments in the 1990s and 2000s made several other policy changes in other areas that were designed to increase participation and reduce unemployment. For example, Dutch governments have changed employment regulations, allowing for more varied employment arrangements and promoting part-time and temporary work (Seeleib-Kaiser, van Dyk, and Roggenkamp 2008, 61).

A series of reforms of disability insurance have also been important since the number of disability insurance claimants rose sharply in the 1980s. In 1993, the first significant piece of legislation that was designed to deal with this problem—the Act on Reducing Disability Claims—came into force (Rueda 2007, 195–7). It is noteworthy that the Netherlands has reversed the trend of low participation rates among older workers (whereas Austria, for instance, has not been able to improve employment in this group, as Seeleib-Kaiser, van Dyk, and Roggenkamp 2008, 73 note).

In conclusion, the Netherlands has much in common with Denmark, in the sense that a large number of interconnected reforms in the area of unemployment compensation and active labor market policy in the 1990s and 2000s—and policy changes in other policy areas—were explicitly designed to reduce unemployment and increase employment.

Austria

Compared to Denmark and the Netherlands, there were relatively few labor market reforms in Austria in the 1990s and 2000s, as Figures 4.1 and 4.2 suggest: typical unemployment benefit replacement rates have only declined very slightly, remaining close to the European average, and spending on active labor market policy remains relatively low, although it has been increasing more or less continuously since the 1980s.

The current Austrian unemployment insurance legislation, the *Arbeitslosenversicherung*, was introduced in the late 1970s. Unemployment insurance is mandatory and funded by contributions from employees and employers. Compared with countries like Denmark and Sweden, there has traditionally been less pressure on the unemployed to find a new job quickly, and typically for the continental economies, "suitable jobs" have been defined narrowly, allowing the unemployed to wait for jobs that correspond to their training and experience.

The unemployment benefit has two components: a basic rate and a supplement for workers with families. Although the basic replacement rate has always been relatively modest compared to the three other countries covered in this book, it should be noted that unemployed workers with dependants receive significantly higher benefits. Comparative data (Scruggs 2004) show that the difference between typical replacement rates for single individuals and typical replacement rates for unemployed workers with dependants is significantly larger in Austria than in Denmark, the Netherlands, and Sweden.

The duration of unemployment insurance benefits is relatively short— ranging from twenty weeks for workers with short contribution records (the shortest duration used to be twelve weeks) to one year for workers with long contribution records—but those who no longer qualify for unemployment benefits become entitled to unemployment assistance, or *Notstandshilfe*, which is of unlimited duration and only marginally less generous (although unemployment assistance benefits are means tested in the sense that they are not paid to unemployed individuals whose partners are working).

The legislative framework for active labor market policy in Austria— the Labor Market Promotion Act, or *Arbeitsmarktförderungsgesetz*—dates back to 1969 (Weishaupt for a summary, see 2008, 77). As I showed in Chapters 2 and 3, however, Austria pursued employment-oriented macroeconomic policies for a long time. This meant, among other things, that general economic policies were expected to provide for such a high employment rate, and such a low unemployment rate, that no special measures needed to be taken to integrate the unemployed. Active labor market policy therefore played only a small role in Austria prior to the 1980s (Seeleib-Kaiser, van Dyk, and Roggenkamp 2008, 17).

Austrian Reforms

The grand coalition government in the 1990s began a series of gradual reforms of unemployment benefits, starting in 1993. From 1993 to 2000, the net replacement rate was gradually reduced from 57.9 to 55 percent.

It has also become more difficult to qualify for unemployment benefits. Initially, the benefit was calculated on the basis of income in the last four weeks before becoming unemployed, but during the 1990s this period was extended, first to six months and then to one year (Grillberger 1996, 116; Grillberger 2001, 110–11).

In 1993, when the replacement rate was reduced for the first time, the grand coalition government also implemented further reforms, which were the results of compromises between the main political parties and the interest organizations: job-search requirements became more stringent and the concept of "willingness to work" was redefined, in the sense that the unemployed were required to participate in various active labor market programs, and to show evidence of having taken steps to increase the likelihood of new employment (BGBl 502/1993). In 1996 and 2004, the sanctions for low job-search activity were increased from four to six weeks without benefits, and to eight weeks for repeated offences (BGBl 201/1996, BGBl I 77/2004). These reforms in the early 1990s were linked to the creation of a new administrative organization for the implementation of active labor market programs (see below).

In 2004, new legislation relaxed the definition of a "suitable job." After 100 days of unemployment, an unemployed person may now be asked to take a job that does not correspond to his or her previous job (in the first 100 days, a job is considered unsuitable if it makes it difficult for the unemployed to return to his or her previous profession). However, new provisions were also introduced to guarantee job-seekers that they would not have to accept a job if the pay was more than 20 percent less than they earned in their previous jobs (Tomandl 2009, 243). In other words, although the right-wing government that was in power at this time removed the principle that no one should be forced to take a job outside his or her occupation, this provision was replaced with new rules that were meant to protect incomes (Obinger 2009b, 8).

On the basis of the changes that I have just described, Seeleib-Kaiser, van Dyk, and Roggenkamp (2008, 34) conclude that whereas there were only marginal changes in the Austrian unemployment insurance before 1993, there has been a liberal tendency ever since: eligibility criteria have been tightened and the pressure on the unemployed to provide evidence of looking for new jobs has increased. From a political point of view, however, it is noteworthy that the labor market reform process in Austria has been gradual and consensual, compared with the three other countries studied in this book. This feature of Austrian labor market reforms is perhaps not so surprising when it comes to the period before 2000, when the Social Democrats and the Christian Democrats were both included in the governing coalition, but it is more surprising that it continued under the right-wing government in the early to mid-2000s.

The most likely explanation is Austria's social partnership system. The minister of economics and labor in 2000–8, Martin Bartenstein, his predecessor Lore Hostasch, a social democrat, and the head of the economic policy department in the chamber of labor, Günther Chaloupek, all confirm that the main reforms of the 2000s—such as the new definition of a "suitable job"—were negotiated with the unions and the employer organizations and supported by both (interview with Martin Bartenstein, Vienna, February 10, 2010; interview with Lore Hostasch, Vienna, February 11, 2010; interview with Günther Chaloupek, Vienna, February 11, 2010). In other policy areas, such as old age pensions, the relationship between the government and the trade unions became significantly more adversarial in the 2000s, but in labor market policy, all reforms were negotiated with the social partners.

A first step toward an expansion of active labor market policy in Austria was taken in 1983, when new legislation provided for the development of an "experimental" approach to labor market policy that was meant to encourage the development of new policy instruments, and some new programs were also initiated in the 1980s as a result of this initiative (Weishaupt 2008, 117). However, the most important phase in the expansion of active labor market policy in Austria was the 1990s. In 1994, the labor market administration was reformed. The new Public Employment Service Act provided for the reorganization of the labor market administration, which was outsourced from the federal ministry of employment to a new, tripartite agency—the *Arbeitsmarktservice*, where the social partners play a dominant role.

A wide array of active labor market policy instruments are used in Austria. When unemployment began to increase in the first half of the 1980s, the government introduced new training measures (Bundesministerium für soziale Verwaltung 1983, 223). The training programs were expanded in the late 1980s, when the privatization of public companies resulted in turbulence in the labor market: in 1988, the Unemployment Insurance Act was amended to allow for the possibility of so-called labor foundations (*Arbeitsstiftungen*), designed to assist the reintegration of laid-off workers by means of training and job-search assistance. Today, the *Arbeitsmarktservice* distinguishes between four types of training measures: orientation, qualification, active job seeking, and training (Bundesministerium für Arbeit, Soziales und Konsumentenschutz 2009, 72, 112).

Austria also has important provisions for subsidized employment during periods of economic difficulties. One important instrument is the short-term working allowance (*Kurzarbeitshilfe*), which dates back at least to the early 1980s (Bundesministerium für soziale Verwaltung 1981, 58). This program subsidizes employment during temporary economic difficulties provided that the employer agrees not to lay off workers for a certain period. In the economic crisis in 2008–9, such programs were used extensively, which helped to keep the unemployment rate in Austria low, compared to many other countries. There are also various provisions for subsidized employment for the long-term unemployed, both in nonprofit organizations and in private companies.

Austrian Choices

According to Emmerich Tálos (2005*a*, 39–40), Austrian social policy was characterized by pragmatic compromises between the major parties and interest organizations until the late 1990s, with no programmatic change in the overall character of social policies. With the formation of the right-wing coalition in 2000, however, Tálos argues that things changed considerably, since the new government sought radical changes, based on a new understanding of the ideas and aims of social protection.

In the area of labor market policy, however, there does not appear to have been a radical break with the past, at least not when it comes to actual legal changes and spending priorities.

One factor that must be taken into account is that Austria's unemployment insurance system was never as generous as in the three other countries in this book. In spite of the fact that the Social Democrats were so powerful in the 1970s and early 1980s, for example, the effective replacement rate in unemployment insurance was never higher than approximately 60 percent. Martin Bartenstein, who was minister for economics and labor in the ÖVP–FPÖ coalition in the 2000s, says that his party does not believe that the unemployment benefit system contributes to significantly higher levels of unemployment, so there is little demand for reform (interview with Martin Bartenstein, Vienna, February 10, 2010). On the other hand, the Austrian Christian Democrats appear to have been more willing than the Dutch center-right parties to support the gradual expansion of active labor market programs. As I have already suggested, the social partnership system—and especially the fact that the social partners participate in the implementation of active labor market programs—is likely to be an important part of the explanation for the gradual and pragmatic nature of labor market reform in Austria.

Austria's main problems lie elsewhere. As in many other countries, early retirement programs were an important element in the Austrian labor market strategy in the 1970s and 1980s. Although some programs were abolished in the mid-1990s, when the government declared that the early retirement strategy had come to an end (Seeleib-Kaiser, van Dyk, and Roggenkamp 2008, 34; Auer 2002, 91), Austrian governments have not reformed early retirement programs as forcefully as Dutch governments (Ludwig-Mayerhofer and Wroblewski 2004, 489), and older workers are more likely to have left the labor force than they are in the other three countries covered in this book. According to data from the 2007 European Labor Force Survey, the employment rate among 55–64-year-olds was 69.6 in Sweden, 67.5 in Denmark, 48.3 in the Netherlands (an increase of almost 17 percentage points in ten years), and only 35.5 in Austria (Eichhorst and Hemerijck 2009, 212). The low employment rate in the older age groups is regarded as an important problem within Austria, which should be taken into account when evaluating the overall reform capacity of the Austrian government.

Sweden

In Austria, the government's employment strategy was largely based on macroeconomic policy before the 1980s. Sweden's employment strategy in the 1950s and 1960s, however, was organized around active labor market policies (Marterbauer 2001). Sweden's reliance on macroeconomic policies to maintain full employment in the 1970s and 1980s, which I discussed in Chapters 2 and 3, was in this sense a break with the past: in the 1950s and 1960s, governments kept fiscal policies tight in order to contain inflation (and to force firms to increase productivity).

The combination of tight fiscal policies, a "solidaristic" wage policy that reduced wage differentials within economic sectors, and extensive labor market programs was the brainchild of the Swedish trade union economists Gösta Rehn and Rudolf Meidner, and it is often referred to as the Rehn–Meidner model (Lewin 1967, 367–70; Pontusson 1992, 59–68; Erixon 2003). The aim of labor market programs in this policy model was to relocate and train those who became temporarily stranded on "islands of unemployment" in the economy (this term was used in a memorandum that Gösta Rehn wrote in the early 1950s; see Erlander 1974, 236–40).

Given Sweden's history of active labor market policies, it is noteworthy that active labor market policy became a less prominent part of the labor market policy mix in Sweden in the 1990s and 2000s than it had been in the past. Unlike governments in Austria, Denmark, and the Netherlands, Swedish governments increased spending on "passive" labor market policies (unemployment benefits) more than spending on active labor market programs, and active labor market policy spending per unemployed has declined sharply. In the course of the 1990s and 2000s, Swedish governments appeared to lose faith in its traditional, active labor market policy-based policy regime. At the same time, however, the Social Democrats, who were in power until 2006, were unwilling to reduce benefit duration in order to put more pressure on the unemployed to look for jobs, which is what the Danish social democrats did in the 1990s.

This particular reform path was the result of a combination of factors, including the fact that mass unemployment appeared relatively late in Sweden (which meant that governments did not stop hoping that unemployment would decline when the economy grew), the fact that there was no resurgence of corporatism (which reduced the ability of Swedish interest organizations to coordinate and help to implement new labor market reforms, unlike interest organizations in neighboring Denmark; see Martin 2004), and the fact that political conflicts between left and right became more entrenched in this policy domain.

Just like Denmark, Sweden has a voluntary unemployment insurance system, which is managed by unemployment funds associated with the trade unions. The replacement rate in unemployment insurance has traditionally been high by European standards. The duration is formally shorter than in Denmark (it was extended to sixty weeks—or ninety weeks if the recipient was over age 55—in the early 1970s; see Korpi and Palme 2008, country notes, Sweden, 1970 and 1975), but a guarantee against losing unemployment benefits—*utförsäkringsgarantin*, introduced in the 1980s—meant that unemployment benefit duration was (and is) practically unlimited (Lindvert 2006, 88; Davidsson 2009, 19).

From the late 1950s to the 2000s, spending on active labor market policy was high compared to other European countries. Moreover, as Bo Rothstein (1996, 56–64, 74–7) has shown, active labor market policy was an integral part of Sweden's postwar model, and a core part of the political and economic strategy of the ruling Social Democratic Party. Other aspects of labor market policy—such as unemployment insurance—have traditionally belonged to the most politically divisive issues in Swedish politics (Hermansson 1993, 357, 430), but the main feature of active labor market policy was the delegation of authority to bureaucrats and labor market organizations: active labor market policy programs were managed by a powerful administrative organization, the national labor market board (*Arbetsmarknadsstyrelsen*, AMS) in close cooperation with the unions and employer organizations (Rothstein 1992, Chapter 8).

Swedish Reforms

The overall generosity of Swedish unemployment benefits declined in the 1990s and 2000s. The first significant change occurred in 1993, when the center-right government reduced the replacement rate in the unemployment insurance system from 90 to 80 percent of previous earnings. In 1995, the new social democratic government reduced the replacement rate further, to 75 percent of previous earnings. As Carl Dahlström (2009, 224–5, 232) has noted, it is intriguing that unemployment insurance replacement rates were not reduced during the 1992 currency crisis, when the government and the social democratic opposition agreed to make cuts in other important social insurance programs, such as sickness benefits. It seems likely that this was a result of opposition from the Social Democrats, for the cut in 1993 was made unilaterally by the government, following the breakdown of negotiations with the social democratic opposition.

In 1993, the center-right government also lowered the benefit ceiling, introduced five waiting days, extended the qualification period from four to five months, and made some further, structural changes regarding the financing and administration of unemployment insurance. Many of these changes were revoked, however, when the Social Democrats returned to power in 1994 (Davidsson 2009, 18).

Just like the cuts in unemployment benefits in Denmark and the Netherlands in the 1980s, the cuts in Sweden in the 1990s were primarily meant to save money. The activation of the unemployed does not appear to have been an important motive at this time. In the late 1990s, when the social democratic government deemed that the improvement of public finances allowed for an increase in generosity, the government increased the replacement rate to 80 percent once more, which suggests that the social democrats were not guided by concerns with the employment effects of generous unemployment insurance payments when they kept the lower rate after 1999.

A second round of unemployment benefit reforms in the late 1990s and early 2000s, however, were motivated by "activation." In 1997, the government increased the qualification period to six months and made it more difficult to qualify for new benefits by participating in labor market training, and in 2000—in the most important reform in this period—the social democratic government introduced higher job-search requirements and eliminated the possibility of qualifying for new benefits by participating in training programs. Instead of allowing the long-term unemployed to keep re-qualifying for new benefits, the government introduced an activity guarantee (*Aktivitetsgarantin*, which was replaced by *Jobb- och utvecklingsgarantin* in 2007). The idea was to protect the most vulnerable groups in the labor market, but also to increase the pressure on the long-term unemployed to find new jobs by engaging them in full-time training and counseling (Lindvert 2006, 79).

The reform that was implemented in 2000 was prepared by an intra-departmental committee in the ministry of industry, employment and communications. The committee had two aims: to improve the incentives for the unemployed to engage in job search, and to increase the generosity of unemployment benefits for middle-income earners by raising the maximum level of benefits (which happened again in 2001). These two aims were regarded as complementary in the sense that higher demands and tougher sanctions were seen a means of protecting the existing, generous system. It would only be possible to keep replacement rates high if the unemployed were required to accept job offers, the committee argued in its report.

Crucially, however, the reform in 2000 did not lead to a reduction in the duration of unemployment insurance (Prop. 1999/2000: 98, section 8.2; Green-Pedersen and Lindbom 2005, 76). In that sense, the reforms that were passed by the Swedish parliament around 2000 were less radical than the Danish reforms in the 1990s, which clearly limited the duration of unemployment benefit payments, first to seven years, then to five, and finally to four. When the government introduced the reforms that were enacted in 1997, it had floated the idea of limiting to the duration of unemployment insurance—a proposal that was debated extensively and eventually withdrawn (Junestav 2004, 209–10). The 2000 reform was explicitly designed as an *alternative* to the Danish solution of limited benefit duration (Ds 1999:58, 193–6). The intra-departmental committee that prepared the 2000 reform said that it was "not reasonable" to interrupt unemployment benefit payments, since this would make the long-term unemployed dependent on social assistance.

Sten Olsson, who was state secretary in the prime minister's office in 2002–4 and state secretary in the finance ministry in 2004–6, says that he, and many other senior social democrats, found the idea of limiting unemployment insurance unfair. Although he believes that there may have been some people who claimed unemployment benefits although they could have found a job, the main reason for the relatively high level of unemployment in the 2000s, in Mr Olsson's view, was that after the deep economic crisis of the 2000s, "many people were outside the labor market for so long that their employability was very low." What they needed were not economic incentives but new types of "individualized labor market programs, rather than the general programs we had used in the past" (interview with Sten Olsson, Stockholm, September 22, 2009).

The center-right parties had a different view, and the most radical reforms in unemployment insurance in Sweden in the period considered here occurred after the formation of a new center-right coalition government in 2006. The center-right campaign in 2006 was based on the idea that the Social Democrats had failed to increase employment. In unemployment insurance, the main change that was enacted after 2006 was the reduction of replacement rates from 80 to 70 percent of previous earnings, after approximately nine months of unemployment, in order to encourage job search. The new government said that it was in favor of short periods of generous unemployment insurance, but claimed that the existing system meant that the "economic incentives to end unemployment are weak" (Prop. 2006/7: 15–17). The center-right government also reduced income taxes for those in paid employment, lowering the effective replacement rates in all social insurance systems.

When the deep economic crisis of the 1990s commenced in Sweden in 1991, both the social democratic government that was in power in the early phases of the crisis and the center-right government that took over in 1991 increased spending on labor market policy programs (Lindvert 2006, 59–62). However, the economic crisis put the Swedish labor market model under great strain. The active labor market programs grew in volume, with increasing numbers of participants, from only 60,000 in 1990 to more than 230,000 in 1994. In 1993, the nature of active labor market policies changed, as the center-right government introduced new quantitative targets—that is, the national labour market board was instructed to process a certain number of unemployed (Lindvert 2006, 62).

Afterward, the introduction of quantitative targets is widely regarded as a mistake, since it led to lower quality training, and therefore also to a crisis of legitimacy for Sweden's ambitious and costly labor market programs. Within a few years, there was broad agreement that the labor market policies of the 1990s had failed in important ways, even among those who were responsible for these policies (Lindvert 2006, 66–72). Around 1996, the government intended to reform active labor market policies, and there were some ambitious reform ideas, but the report by the government commission of inquiry that prepared these reforms proved to be politically controversial and the only result was a certain degree of decentralization of labor market policy (Lindvert 2006, 75–7). Labor market policies were reformed again in 2000 and individual action plans for the unemployed were introduced in 1996 (Lindvert 2006, 77–81), but these were relatively minor changes.

The most remarkable fact about active labor market policy in Sweden in the 1990s and early 2000s, however, is arguably that it did not change much, even if the economic and social conditions changed greatly. The main labor market programs had been created in a period of full employment and for a type of labor market that allowed for mass-produced training programs. In the 1990s, although neither of these conditions held, there were few major policy changes in this area (Furåker and Blomsterberg 2002, 282–3; Lindvert 2006, 55, 77).

One indication of the low reform intensity in Sweden is that European employment discourse has had little impact on Swedish labor market policy. In her study of Sweden's implementation of the European employment strategy, Åsa Vifell (2006, Chapter 4) demonstrates that Swedish labor market policymaking is decoupled from the EU level. Negotiations with Sweden's EU partners are managed by small groups of civil servants in the ministries of finance and industry, whereas domestic policymaking is managed by other civil servants and by the national labor market board. At the same time, as Lindvert (2006, 101) pointed out in her study of labor market policies from the mid-1990s onward, there has been an important *de facto* change in Swedish labor market policy, since the ratio of active to passive spending has fallen so much.

Swedish Choices

When it comes to unemployment benefits, the Swedish reform path has been relatively similar to the Danish and the Dutch, but with some delay.

First, Swedish governments made general cuts in replacement rates, motivated by fiscal concerns, in the mid-1990s. This happened already in the 1980s in Denmark and the Netherlands. Second, Swedish governments sought to encourage high job-search activity among the unemployed through employment-oriented reforms in the late 1990s and mid-2000s. Such reforms were adopted already in the late 1980s and early to mid-1990s in Denmark and the Netherlands.

But there were also important differences between the politics of labor market reform in Sweden, Denmark, and the Netherlands. First of all, the Swedish reforms have been less radical—for example, Swedish governments have not limited the duration of unemployment insurance, which remains *de facto* unlimited. Second, there appears to have been a higher level of political conflict. Third, the reforms of the Swedish unemployment insurance system have not been associated with reforms in other policy areas—such as active labor market policy—to the same extent as in Denmark and the Netherlands, or Austria, for that matter.

When a coalition of Sweden's four center-right parties won the election of 2006, forming the first center-right government in twelve years, this outcome was widely attributed to the failure of the Social Democrats to present convincing policies on employment and unemployment. The Social Democrats lost issue ownership in the area of employment policy for the first time since measurements began, in the sense that the employment policies of the conservative Moderate party had become more popular (Martinsson 2009, Chapter 8), and the proportion of survey respondents who said that the Social Democrats had good employment policies was the lowest ever recorded (Oscarsson and Holmberg 2008, 182). The main report from the National Election Study concludes that the Social Democrats lost the 2006 election since they "were no longer regarded as the party that offered the best solutions for employment and the economy" (Oscarsson and Holmberg 2008, 184).

Critics within the labor movement also argued that social democratic labor market policies in the 1990s and 2000s left a lot to be desired. For example, Dan Andersson, the chief economist of the main Swedish trade union confederation, LO, wrote an article in the social democratic journal *Tiden* just before he resigned in 2008. He argued that the Social Democrats had allowed labor market policies to "decline" in the 1990s and 2000s, which had created an opening for the center-right parties to run on a platform of lower benefits for the unemployed and the inactive in the election of 2006 (Andersson 2008). Mr Andersson was especially concerned with the relative decline of spending on active labor market policies after the economic crisis in the early to mid-1990s.

The absence of comprehensive reform in Sweden is not only apparent in core labor market policy areas such as unemployment insurance and active labor market policies, but also, importantly, in the sick pay system (Kenworthy 2008, 157–8). In the early 2000s, particularly around 2002–3, the large increase in the number of sick pay recipients became a matter of great concern in political circles, and it seems clear that this increase was at least partly a result of the fact that many long-term unemployed were transferred from unemployment benefit or social assistance programs to the sickness insurance system (Stensöta 2009, 14). According to the leading Swedish labor economist Bertil Holmlund (2006, 129), core labor market policies work relatively well—but the generous systems of social protection for the inactive population, Holmlund believes, may have encouraged large groups to leave the labor market.

The Politics of Labor Market Reform

The results of this analysis of labor market policies in Austria, Denmark, the Netherlands, and Sweden in the 1990s and 2000s can be summarized as follows.

1. All four countries have reduced unemployment insurance replacement rates. The biggest cuts occurred in Denmark, the Netherlands, and Sweden. The main Danish and Dutch cuts were made in the 1980s, and the main Swedish cuts were made in the 1990s. Austria had lower replacement rates to start with, and there have consequently been fewer calls for large reductions in Austria.

2. When it comes to what Eichhorst et al. (2008) term "demanding activation"—efforts to encourage the unemployed to seek and accept new jobs—Denmark and the Netherlands have made more radical policy changes than Austria and Sweden. In Denmark, the main change was a reduction in the duration of unemployment benefits from *de facto* unlimited benefits to a maximum four years. In the Netherlands, where unemployment benefits have always been of limited duration, the main changes have involved the monitoring and control of the unemployed. In Austria and Sweden, search requirements have also been increased, but both countries still have a system of unlimited benefits for the unemployed.

3. When it comes to active labor market programs—which is an example of what Eichhorst et al. (2008) call "enabling activation"— governments in Denmark and the Netherlands increased spending on such programs in the 1980s and 1990s. In Austria, there has also been a steady increase in active labor market policy spending from the early 1990s onward, although spending levels are still relatively low. In Sweden, the active component of labor market policy has declined significantly compared to the 1980s and 1990s.

4. Overall, governments in Denmark and the Netherlands have pursued larger and more coordinated reforms than Austrian and Swedish governments, in the sense that a series of policy changes across many different areas—including unemployment benefits, social assistance, active labor market policies, early retirement, disability insurance, and sickness benefits—have been motivated by the desire to encourage the reintegration of the unemployed and the inactive in the labor market. This political shift was supported, at least in principle, by parties across the political spectrum, and by the social partners.

5. All four countries reformed their public employment services at some point in the 1990s, by decentralizing administrative functions and reducing the central government's influence. In three of the cases (Sweden being the exception), these reforms involved the creation of local or regional corporatist structures. In Austria and Denmark, the systems that were established in the 1990s remain more or less intact. In the Netherlands and Sweden, there was some recentralization in the early 2000s.

In the early 2000s, Denmark and the Netherlands were regarded as the clearest examples of comprehensive labor market reform in Europe, for more or less the same reasons (Hemerijck and Schludi 2000, 218). Just as their economic policies were similar in the 1970s and 1980s, then, Danish and Dutch labor market policies were similar in the 1990s and 2000s—more so than most established theories of the welfare state would predict. The wide range of reforms that they have implemented—and the fact that these reforms have been generated through cooperation between political parties and interest organizations—distinguishes Denmark and the Netherlands from the Swedish case. The Danish and Dutch reforms also involved new kinds of trade-offs, in the sense that some political actors (notably trade unions) accepted policy changes they had previously resisted in return for desired policy changes in other areas.

My argument is that the distinctive Danish and Dutch policy trajectories can be explained by two factors: first, the fact that Denmark and the Netherlands had lived with high unemployment for a longer period of time than Austria and Sweden; second, the fact that political arrangements had changed in Denmark and the Netherlands in the course of the 1980s and early 1990s.

The Experience of Unemployment

By the early 1990s, unemployment in Denmark had been higher than the European average for almost twenty years, with the exception of a few years in the first half of the 1980s (see Figure 4.2). As the section on Denmark showed, the fact of persistent unemployment persuaded the main Danish political parties and interest organizations that something had to be done, which led to the deal between the unions and the employer organizations about unemployment insurance and active labor market policies in the early 1990s.

The Dutch experience in the 1980s and early 1990s was different, since unemployment had been declining since 1983 (with the exception of two years in the early 1990s). Yet, the long history of relatively high unemployment mattered greatly to the policies governments pursued in the 1990s, for these reforms were motivated by the fact that unemployment did not decline further, even if other economic indicators were positive. This persuaded the main Dutch political parties, and the social partners, that wage restraint was not sufficient: further reforms were required to mobilize the "silent reserves" in the labor market. In both Denmark and the Netherlands, then, there is evidence that the long history of high unemployment contributed to the big reforms of the 1990s.

In Sweden, in contrast, mass unemployment was a more recent phenomenon, and for a long period in the 1990s and early 2000s, the social democratic government appears to have assumed that unemployment would decline automatically once the crisis of the 1990s had been overcome, interest rates had come down, and the budget deficit was under control. Around 2000, this assumption seemed to be correct, since unemployment decreased rapidly in 1997–2001, but then unemployment increased again.

According to the social democratic political adviser Sten olsson (state secretary in the prime minister's office and the finance ministry in 2002–6), key policymakers realized in 2002–3 that a large proportion of those who became unemployed during the deep economic crisis of the 1990s had remained in unemployment (interview with Sten Olsson, Stockholm, September 22, 2009). The main political issue at that time, however, was the high number of sick pay recipients, which may explain why there were only relatively minor reforms in labor market policy as such in the last years before the 2006 election.

The Austrian case is again different, since Austria did not experience any periods of rapidly increasing unemployment: although unemployment increased significantly in the 1980s and 1990s, the increases were gradual and moderate, and the Austrian unemployment rate has remained lower than the European average. This probably explains why there have been no radical labor market reforms in Austria. Neither Christian democratic nor social democratic politicians appear to believe that major reforms are required. The Christian democrat Martin Bartenstein—who was Minister of Economics and Labor in 2000–8—says that politicians across the political spectrum regard Austrian labor market policies as relatively successful: "There is a common belief among stakeholders in this country that our labor market is in good shape, so we don't need any dramatic changes," Mr Bartenstein said in an interview with the author (interview with Martin Bartenstein, Vienna, February 10, 2010).

The fact that the experience of unemployment in the 1970s and 1980s mattered to labor market policies in the 1990s suggests that economic policy choices in the aftermath of the two oil crises had enduring political effects. And since these economic policy choices depended on domestic political arrangements, as I showed in Chapters 2 and 3, the manner in which the postwar political settlement changed in the 1960s, 1970s, and 1980s set Austria, Denmark, the Netherlands, and Sweden on different paths, with enduring political, economic, and social consequences.

Party Politics

When it comes to party politics, Denmark and the Netherlands developed in similar ways in the 1980s and 1990s. The center-right coalitions that were formed in 1982 remained in power until 1993 (Denmark) and 1989 (the Netherlands). In the mid to late-1990s, in contrast, these two countries were ruled by social democratic prime ministers—Poul Nyrup Rasmussen and Wim Kok—who formed new types of coalitions with center-right and liberal parties. The purple government was the first Dutch government since the Second World War that did not include the

Christian Democrats, whereas the Danish coalition between the Social Democrats and the Social Liberal Party was a change from the alternation of social democratic single-party minority governments and center-right coalition governments in the 1970s and 1980s.

In social and labor market policy, the center-right governments in the 1980s were concerned with cutting expenditure (including unemployment benefits), not with creating new programs to address the unemployment problem. As Benner and Vad (2000, 450) note, "policies aiming directly at optimizing employment were more or less absent" under the center-right governments in Denmark, and students of the Dutch case note that policies were still "passive" in the sense that governments expected wage moderation to solve the unemployment problem, while unions and employers used disability programs to shed labor—a practice that was later blamed for low labor market participation rates in the 1990s (Visser and Hemerijck 1997, 32). In other words, the reforms that did occur in Denmark and the Netherlands in the 1980s were not oriented toward increasing employment as such (although, as Robert Cox 2001, 497, notes, political developments in the austere 1980s set the stage for more comprehensive reforms in the 1990s).

The governments of the 1990s were more directly concerned with increasing employment and reducing unemployment, and it seems likely that the new political constellations that these governments represented were especially well-placed to develop the compromises between "demanding" and "enabling" activation that the Danish and Dutch reforms of the 1990s were based on. In that sense, the development of the Danish and Dutch party systems after the major changes in the 1960s and 1970s that I described in Chapter 2 also help to explain the specific character of labor market reforms in Denmark and the Netherlands in the 1990s.

Party politics developed in different ways in Austria and Sweden. As I have argued above, Austrian labor market policymaking was defined by a high level of cross-party consensus, which provided for the gradual and pragmatic reform process that I have described above. This was not the case in Sweden, where bloc politics—the competition between one group of left-wing parties and one group of right-wing parties—has remained the dominant mode of party competition and government formation. There are strong reasons to believe that this precluded the kinds of trade-offs that political parties in Denmark and the Netherlands engaged in.

176

The Revival and Crisis of Corporatism

Policy developments in Austria, Denmark, the Netherlands, and Sweden were also associated with different trends when it comes to the development of corporatist institutions. The reforms in Denmark and the Netherlands in the 1990s became possible because these two countries had reached a new political settlement after the breakdown of postwar political arrangements in the 1960s and 1970s. Unions and employers had gradually reached a new understanding regarding wage formation, which became the basis of new compromises over social and labor market policy (Visser and Hemerijck 1997; Slomp 2002; Mailand 2002).

The revival of Danish corporatism can be dated to 1987, when the Danish government, Danish LO, and the employer organization DA issued a "joint declaration" concerning their commitment to wage restraint, comparable to the "Wassenaar Agreement" in the Netherlands in 1982. This created the basis for further cooperation in other policy areas. At this time, Denmark had been ruled by a center-right government since 1982, and for the first few years, LO had pursued a confrontative strategy. However, in 1987, LO decided to seek political influence even if this involved cooperation with the government. The LO representative Finn Larsen says that 1987 was "a landmark year," since "LO clearly declared itself for a result-oriented and more pragmatic strategy. We had to accept that the conservative-liberal government would remain in office and we had to cooperate if we were to get results" (Anthonsen, Lindvall, and Schmidt Hansen 2009).

Poul Schlüter, who was prime minister in 1982–93, said in an interview with the author that he held informal meetings with the LO leadership in the mid-1980s, in order to discuss important policy issues.

When we remained in power year after year—which no one had expected— LO began to accept that we were the government and they needed to have a relationship with us. And I might just as well reveal that I had a series of secret meetings with the LO leadership. ...I have never told this to the Social Democrats. But we cooperated very well with LO (*havde et glimrende samarbejdsforhold*). At that time, LO was closely connected to the Social Democrats. They aren't really anymore. (interview with Poul Schlüter, Frederiksberg, August 26, 2005)

The former Dutch prime minister Ruud Lubbers expressed himself in similar terms in an interview with the author, when he described the formation of a Christian democratic–social democratic coalition in 1989:

177

"I knew the time had come to involve the trade unions more, and Kok [the leader of the Social Democrats] was the ideal person to do that" (interview with Ruud Lubbers, Rotterdam, March 21, 2006).

Most scholars agree that after a period of decline in the 1970s and early 1980s, Dutch corporatism resurged in the late 1980s and in the 1990s. This had important consequences for social and labor market policymaking. Marko Bos—who is director of economic affairs in the social and economic council (SER)—points out that in an advisory report from the social partners published in 1992, called *Convergence and the Consultation Economy*, the social partners made a high rate of employment one of the key objectives of social partnership. According to Mr Bos, this report "laid the foundation for a new consensus-making that typified, I think, the functioning of [the Social and Economic Council] in the 1990s" (interview with Marko Bos, The Hague, November 20, 2007). The social partners managed to agree more on how the economy works, and on effective instruments. This resulted in a high reform capacity and in a more pragmatic and innovative style of policymaking:

Gradually, step by step, we managed to build more consensus on policy orientations—how the economy is working—and then a consensus on what the effective instruments are. And that made it possible, especially during the 1990s, to have a series of reforms in the sphere of social security and the labor market. We also had reforms in the 1980s, but these were more forced by the government. (interview with Marko Bos, The Hague, November 20, 2007)

The idea of the Netherlands as a country where a consensual style of policymaking prevails—or prevailed in the 1990s—is debated among scholars and political commentators. On the one hand, the second half of the 1990s has been described as the "best of times" for social partnership in the Netherlands, since the period was defined by an "atmosphere of compromise" (Slomp 2002, 235; see also Andeweg and Irwin 2005, 144–6 and Wolinetz 2001, 262), and the Dutch "employment miracle" has often been attributed to the revival of Dutch corporatism (Visser and Hemerijck 1997). On the other hand, some scholars argue that what actually happened in the 1980s was that the unions were forced to retreat; the spirit of consensus only emerged once the crucial changes had been made (Becker 2001; Salverda 2005, 39–42).

There are also politicians on the right who question whether the trade unions were ever prepared to accept reforms that went against their interests: Gerrit Zalm, a Liberal politician who served as finance minister for long periods in the 1990s and 2000s, says that he cannot recall any reforms that led to reduced benefits, yet were supported by the trade unions. He concludes, "The idea that we had this beautiful consensus model, called the polder model, and that trade unions are willing to accept reforms—I think that is a bit of a fairy tale" (interview with Gerrit Zalm, Amsterdam, February 8, 2010).

When one compares Dutch politics in the 1990s with Dutch politics in the 1970s, however, it seems clear that the relationship between the social partners—and between the government and the social partners—improved considerably. Moreover, when comparing Denmark and the Netherlands to Sweden, it seems clear that corporatist policymaking is stronger in the former two—not only when it comes to institutional procedures but also when it comes to norms of social partnership (Anthonsen and Lindvall 2009).

The formation of a coalition between the Christian democratic ÖVP and the far right FPÖ in 2000 is often associated with a change in Austrian corporatism. For example, Emmerich (Tálos 2005*b*, 196–209) has argued that whereas Austrian corporatism remained intact through a long, difficult period of change and reform in the 1980s and 1990s, there was a break with the past in the early 2000s, when the involvement of interest organizations in policymaking became the rule rather than the exception under the new government. It is true that in some policy areas, particularly in the area of pensions, the relationship between the government and the unions became more confrontational in the early 2000s, when the unions organized anti-government demonstrations, and even strikes, in response to the government's pension reform agenda (Kelly and Hamann 2009)—a remarkable event in a country with one of the lowest strike rates in the world. Some government ministers, particularly those representing the Freedom Party, FPÖ, were also opposed to the idea of social partnership as such.

In the area of labor market policy, however, there were no significant changes in either institutions or practices of policymaking and implementation. The tripartite structure of the public employment service that had been introduced in 1994 was retained, and all of the major policy reforms in the 1990s and 2000s were negotiated with the social partners. It seems highly likely that the strength of the social partnership system—particularly in the area of labor market policy—is one part of the explanation for the Austrian reform path in unemployment insurance and active labor market policy in the late twentieth and early twenty-first centuries: beginning from a relatively less generous unemployment benefit system and a relatively low level of active labor market policy spending, Austria has made some cautious, liberal reforms in the unemployment insurance system from 1993 onward, and gradually increased its ambitions in the area of active programs, basing all these policy changes on broad agreements among interest organizations and between interest organizations and governments.

In Sweden, as I showed in Chapter 3, the corporatist policymaking model came apart in the late 1980s and early 1990s, and particularly in the area of labor market policy, there are strong disagreements between the unions and the employers, and few institutionalized negotiations that might help to reconcile these differences. Interest organizations are still influential in Sweden, but they achieve their influence through lobbying and political pressure, as in non-corporatist political systems (Svensson and Öberg 2002). Just as the Swedish tradition of "bloc politics" helps to explain the lack of quid-pro-quo agreements between the political parties over labor market policy, the absence of corporatist procedures and practices helps to explain why interest organizations have not developed a new common understanding of the problem of unemployment and the appropriate policy response.

Alternative Explanations

The argument that I have made in this chapter is that political conditions and circumstances mattered to the labor market policies that Austrian, Danish, Dutch, and Swedish governments have pursued from the 1990s onward. Politics mattered *indirectly* since the experience of unemployment from the late 1970s onward—which was arguably a consequence of political choices in the 1970s and 1980s—persuaded political parties and interest organizations in Denmark and the Netherlands that labor market reform was necessary. Politics also mattered *directly* since the Danish and Dutch labor market reforms in the 1990s were based on a new understanding between political parties and interest organizations, dating back to the 1980s.

Before concluding my analysis of unemployment compensation and active labor market policies, I will consider a few alternative explanations for the cross-country differences that this chapter has identified, specifically the role of economic circumstances, the role of political parties and trade unions, and the role of ideas and discourse.

Economic Circumstances

One possible explanation for the fact that there were fewer reforms in Austria and Sweden in the 1990s and 2000s is that the institutions and policies that were in place in these two countries by the early 1990s had fewer drawbacks than pre-reform policies in Denmark and the Netherlands. As I have already shown, key politicians in Austria appear to regard the Austrian labor market regime as relatively successful, and as many economists have pointed out, the big increase in unemployment in Sweden in the early 1990s was mainly a result of economic policy mistakes and macroeconomic shocks, not of flawed labor market policies. For example, Olivier Blanchard (2006, 25) argues that although unemployment increased in Sweden in the 1990s, the behavior of inflation in this period "suggests that this was mostly a cyclical movement—an increase in the actual unemployment rate over the natural rate." Bertil Holmlund (2006) presents a detailed analysis of the Swedish case that supports this view.

To some extent, the argument that I have presented is consistent with these observations, since I claim that the high reform intensity in Denmark and the Netherlands is at least partly a result of their long history of high unemployment, which shaped the beliefs and preferences of political parties and interest organizations. If it were shown to be the case that the problem of structural unemployment had in some sense been solved in Austria and Sweden, however, my claim that politics matters would clearly be weakened. But this would be an exaggerated claim in light of the fact that unemployment was significantly lower in Denmark and the Netherlands from the mid-1990s to the late 2000s than it was in Austria and Sweden in the same period.

Parties and Interest Organizations

I have already argued that the formation of new political coalitions helps to explain the character of labor market reform in Denmark and the Netherlands in the 1990s, and I have argued that the resurgence of corporatist policymaking made it possible for political parties and interest organizations to identify and negotiate new compromises in this policy area. Both of these arguments are systemic, however, since they hold that the *interaction* between parties and interest organizations shaped politics, not the power and influence of individual parties and organizations.

In this section, I will consider the possibility that the political balance between left and right and the political power of trade unions may explain the policy choices of governments.

As I showed in Chapter 1, many scholars expect the balance of power between left-wing parties and right-wing parties to influence labor market policy, and there is some evidence for such a claim in this chapter. For example, the largest cuts in unemployment insurance replacement rates in Denmark, the Netherlands, and Sweden occurred under center-right governments in the 1980s (Denmark and the Netherlands) and early 1990s (Sweden). Moreover, spending on active labor market policies in Denmark and the Netherlands increased under the social democratic-led governments in the mid- to late 1990s and early 2000s, but decreased under the new center-right governments that were formed in 2001 (Denmark) and 2002 (the Netherlands). However, the evidence that I have presented in this chapter also suggests that although the party composition of governments may have mattered to the particular mixes of labor market programs that different governments launched, there is no obvious correlation between the partisan composition of governments and their ability and willingness to change labor market policies in order to adjust to the fact of unemployment.

Since trade unions have obvious reasons to care about labor market policy, it is interesting to note that the development of trade union membership in Austria, Denmark, the Netherlands, and Sweden has varied greatly. As Figure 4.3 shows, trade union membership has been in more or less continuous decline in Austria and the Netherlands since the 1960s—with a particularly sharp fall in union density in the Netherlands—but in Denmark and Sweden, trade union membership reached its highest levels yet in the 1980s and 1990s; the fall in union density since the second half of the 1990s has so far merely brought these two countries back to the high level of the mid-1970s. With respect to the outcomes that concern me here, there is no obvious pattern, however: although the overall direction of labor market reform in Denmark and the Netherlands was relatively similar in the 1990s and 2000s, for instance, their union membership trends diverged.

Ideas and Discourse

An important literature on comparative European politics argues that far-reaching policy changes are only possible where governments and political parties manage to establish new ideas about the role of the state,

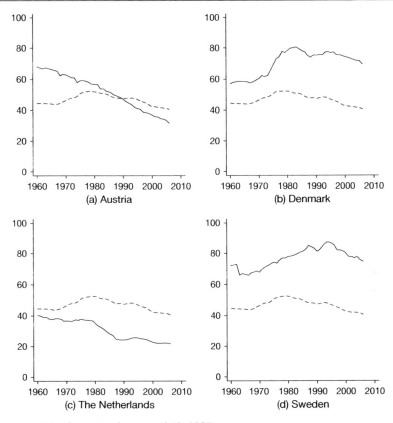

Figure 4.3 Trade union density, 1960–2007

Data source: Visser (2009). Trade union density is defined as the percentage of union members among wage and salary earners; in other words, non-employed union members (such as retired workers, students, and the unemployed) are not counted. The dotted line represents the mean union density level in the thirteen European countries that have been democracies since the Second World War, excluding countries with a population of less than 1 million.

developing a "reform discourse" that convinces key electoral groups of the need for reform. The ideas and evidence that I have presented in this chapter do not contradict this literature, but they do suggest that the variation in political discourses that scholars such as Robert Cox and Vivien Schmidt have identified in their work should be seen in the context of underlying changes in party systems, corporatist institutions, and experiences of persistent unemployment in the 1970s and 1980s.

Conclusions

The idea that unemployment insurance systems, and other forms of social protection, should be designed to encourage the unemployed to seek new jobs has become broadly accepted among experts on the labor market in the course of the 1990s and 2000s. As the economist Olivier Blanchard (2006, 45) notes in a recent survey article, there is now a "consensus" among economic experts on why some labor markets work better than others.

While there is a trade-off between efficiency and insurance, the experience of the successful European countries suggests it need not be very steep. What is important in essence is to protect workers, not jobs. This means providing unemployment insurance, generous in level, but conditional on the willingness of the unemployed to train for and accept jobs if available.

Similarly, in a recent book, the sociologist Lane Kenworthy (2008, 136) outlines a "policy package" that is intended to "provide generous bene-fits to working-age individuals and households who need them without creating excessive employment disincentives."

The package features generous transfers to those unable to work due to involuntary job loss, sickness, disability, or family responsibilities. However, benefits provided on a temporary basis should be of relatively short duration, and eligibility criteria for those provided on a permanent basis should be fairly strict. In exchange for this strictness, extensive support should be provided for those entering or returning to the work force, in the form of training, job placement, public employment, and childcare.

Finally, the political scientist Cathie Jo Martin (2004, 43) describes a new "conception of the welfare state," which combines "sticks" (stricter benefit rules and shorter benefit duration) and "carrots" (active labor market policies) in order to "reintegrate the long-term unemployed back into the core economy."

These three quotes all suggest that one of the main challenges for governments is to combine social insurance with active labor market programs in an employment-efficient manner. In this chapter, I have described and analyzed the adoption and implementation of these sorts of ideas in Austria, Denmark, the Netherlands, and Sweden. My expla-nation for the fact that governments in Denmark and the Netherlands implemented the most extensive reforms is that as a result of the polit-ical and economic developments that I described in Chapters 2 and 3,

Denmark and the Netherlands had experienced mass unemployment for a longer period of time than Austria and Sweden. Moreover, political circumstances in the 1990s had a direct effect on the policy choices that governments made, since the main Danish and Dutch reforms occurred under new forms of coalition governments, and were based on compromises and bargains between trade unions and employer organizations.

5

Conclusions

Political circumstances mattered greatly to the economic and labor market policies that governments in Austria, Denmark, the Netherlands, and Sweden pursued in response to the problem of unemployment from the early 1970s to the mid-2000s. The decision situations that politicians found themselves in were not only defined by economic shocks and structural economic changes, but also by the development of party systems and party competition, the relationship between interest organizations and the state, and the assumptions that different societies made about the purpose of political authority.

These political factors mattered in two ways. First, political events such as the emergence of new political parties or the intensification of ideological and distributional conflicts among parties and interest organizations complicated the coordination of economic and labor market decision-making within the state, and in society as a whole. Second, the breakdown of the postwar settlement—and the decline of the integrated political models that had institutionalized this historic compromise in countries such as Austria and Sweden—meant that full employment became one goal among many, rather than the overriding political imperative it had been in the past.

In this concluding chapter, I wish to offer a few more thoughts on what the theoretical ideas and empirical results that I have presented implies for comparative politics and political economy, and for broader political discussions about the ability of governments to address the problem of unemployment, which was, is, and will remain the main source of economic insecurity under capitalism.

Mass Unemployment and the State

The first part of this book identified important differences between Austrian, Danish, Dutch, and Swedish economic policies in the 1970s and 1980s. From the mid-1970s to the late 1980s, governments in Austria and Sweden, unlike governments in Denmark and the Netherlands, used macroeconomic policy to maintain full employment. Austrian governments pursued more or less expansionary fiscal policies until the mid-1980s, when they decided to give higher priority to budget consolidation. Sweden changed fiscal policies sooner, but on the other hand, Swedish governments used the devaluation instrument aggressively in the late 1970s and early 1980s, securing a competitive edge that lasted until the early 1990s.

My interpretation of these events is that politicians did not only use macroeconomic policy to achieve direct economic effects, such as price stability and low unemployment; in the Austrian and Swedish cases, they also used macroeconomic policy to shield other policies, and to protect the political models that had emerged in the first postwar decades. The political settlement assumed a full employment society. Therefore, as long as governments sought to preserve postwar political arrangements, low unemployment remained the overriding objective of economic policy. When political conditions changed—as they did everywhere, sooner or later—low unemployment became but one policy objective among others.

These dynamics of institutional change and norm-change explain why governments in Copenhagen, the Hague, Stockholm, and Vienna made such different policy choices. Major economic policy shifts were only possible where the institutions and norms that had governed politics in the first postwar decades were destabilized, and the Austrian and Swedish political models lasted longer, being more tightly coupled than the Danish and Dutch postwar models.

The second part of the book was concerned with how countries adapted their labor market policies to the fact of unemployment once unemployment had begun to increase significantly. In both Denmark and the Netherlands, governments in 1990s accomplished significant labor market reforms, seeking to address the unemployment problem directly. Social policies became more employment-oriented through a gradual "third-order" policy change, which in a certain sense mirrored the shift from full employment to low inflation as the main goal of economic policy in the 1970s and 1980s.

In Sweden, the politics of labor market policy in the 1990s and 2000s was more defensive: the Social Democrats and the trade unions were reluctant to support comprehensive labor market reforms, and many of the policy changes that were made were undertaken to cut costs, not to reduce unemployment. Austria, finally, stands out as the country where political arrangements changed the least, since the social partnership system has been relatively stable over time. This explains, I suggest, the relatively cautious and pragmatic approach to labor market reform in Austria: the unions and the employer organizations—and the main political parties—have agreed to slowly shift resources from passive to active labor market policies in the course of the 1990s and 2000s, without any major conflicts.

Coordination as a Political Problem

One implication of these results is that, at least in the four countries that I have investigated in this book, governments were able to make low unemployment a central policy objective in periods when they could develop coordinated policy responses (in either economic policy or labor market policy), and this was only possible if there were no deep disagreements among political parties and interest organizations about distributional issues, or the roles of key institutions. This condition was met in Austria and Sweden in the 1970s and 1980s, where governments could pursue full employment-oriented macroeconomic policies since Austria's and Sweden's political models were still intact and the main parties and interest organizations agreed that these models should be preserved. It was also met in Denmark and the Netherlands from the late 1980s to the 2000s, where governments were able to make social and labor market policies increasingly employment-oriented since political parties and interest organizations had reformed domestic political arrangements in the course of the 1980s and early 1990s, creating new forms of cooperation.

The policies that governments pursued in Denmark and the Netherlands in the 1990s were different from the policies that governments pursued in Austria and Sweden in the 1970s and 1980s. In the Danish and Dutch cases, governments in the 1990s adopted and implemented supply-side reforms that were directed at the unemployed individuals themselves (forcing the unemployed to look for employment while at the same time improving their chances of finding it). In the Austrian and

Swedish cases in the 1970s and 1980s, on the other hand, governments sought to control the development of the economy as a whole, maintaining high economic activity by increasing domestic or foreign demand for Austrian and Swedish goods. The underlying political mechanisms that shaped policy responses in these two periods in time also varied greatly. In 1970s and 1980s Austria and Sweden, governments were unwilling to abandon the goal of full employment since they wished to protect domestic political arrangements. In 1990s and 2000s Denmark and the Netherlands, on the contrary, it was the willingness to reform political arrangements that allowed governments and other political agents to seek novel ways of dealing with the problem of unemployment.

What these cases have in common, however, is that the coordination of policymaking among political parties and interest organizations, and within central government offices, was affected by underlying political changes. In the literature on comparative political economy, "coordination" is often conceptualized as an inherent feature of certain political economies (following Hall and Soskice 2001, for example, many scholars divide the advanced democracies into "liberal" and "coordinated" market economies on the basis of their underlying economic and institutional structures) but as Kathleen Thelen (2001, 73) has pointed out, coordination is a political process, not a permanent state of affairs; it must be created and sustained. An analysis of how Austria, Denmark, the Netherlands, and Sweden have dealt with unemployment from the 1970s to the present illustrates this important point. It also has two additional implications.

First, a political system's capacity for coordination may change greatly over time. Denmark and the Netherlands suffered from political deadlocks in the 1970s and early 1980s, when both party politics and the relationship between interest organizations and the state were characterized by uncertainty and conflict. By the 1990s, however, governments in these two countries were able to coordinate policymaking across a wide range of policy domains (as Hemerijck and Schludi 2000, 218 have noted, their "flexicurity" models depended on several mutually reinforcing strategies). Austria and Sweden, on the other hand (particularly Austria), achieved high levels of coordination in the 1970s, when they successfully fought unemployment using an array of political instruments. By the 1990s and 2000s, however, the coordination of policy in these two countries was less remarkable (especially in the Swedish case, where the corporatist policymaking model has been in decline ever since the 1980s).

The second implication follows from the first: a state's capacity for coordination cannot simply be inferred from the institutional architecture of its political economy. It depends on the dynamics of institutional change, and on the political strategies and ideas of political parties, interest organizations, and the state bureaucracy. Many comparative political economists are primarily concerned with the *functional* interconnectedness of state institutions, policies, interest groups, and firms. The results of this study suggest that more fleeting political circumstances, such as the character of political competition and the organization of policymaking within the state, matter greatly to the room for maneuver that governments have.

In the Great Recession

In 2008–9, as I noted in the Preface, the topic of unemployment acquired an urgency that I did not expect when I began this project. In the autumn of 2008, a financial crisis that had begun in 2007 generated a full-blown macroeconomic crisis with strongly negative effects on output and employment across Europe, in the United States, and beyond. Austria, Denmark, the Netherlands, and Sweden all experienced an increase in unemployment between the summer of 2008 and the winter of 2009–10, and although this increase was larger in Scandinavia than in Austria and the Netherlands (it was particularly large in Sweden), the threat of rising unemployment was a source of much concern in all four countries.

From a political perspective, one of the most interesting developments in 2008–9 was that macroeconomic policy returned to the political agenda, and not just monetary policy—which had been regarded as the main macroeconomic policy instrument from the 1980s onward—but also fiscal policy. In Chapter 4, I described a period in the 1990s and 2000s when governments increasingly treated unemployment as a microeconomic problem, and therefore as a problem that should be solved through labor market policy reforms designed to increase the likelihood that the unemployed will seek, find, and accept new jobs. The 1990s and 2000s was also a period with fewer macroeconomic shocks than in the 1970s and 1980s (with the exception of unusual cases such as Sweden in 1991–3), and both economists and politicians were content to leave macroeconomic management to central banks, who had low and stable inflation as their main goal but were also able to pay some attention to the task of minimizing fluctuations in output and employment.

In the field of macroeconomics, a convergence of Keynesian and classical ideas had developed into what Michael Woodford (2009) has called a "new neoclassical synthesis" (Carlin and Soskice 2006 prefer the label "New Keynesian" to "new neoclassical"). Both among academic macroeconomists and in international economic organizations, there was a "largely shared vision," as Olivier Blanchard, the director of the research department at the International Monetary Fund, put it in an essay in 2008. From the early or mid-1990s to the late 2000s, the basic macroeconomic frameworks were relatively stable and largely uncontested in countries such as Austria, Denmark, the Netherlands, and Sweden.

In 2008–9, however, there was a new, large macroeconomic shock, and in a matter of months, governments across the world implemented fiscal stimulus plans in a coordinated attempt to avoid another Great Depression. Just like in the 1970s (see Chapter 2), the adoption of expansionary fiscal policies was actively encouraged by international organizations such as the IMF and the OECD. Already in the autumn of 2008, the managing director of the IMF called for large fiscal stimulus packages (Spilimbergo et al. 2008, 3), and the IMF's *World Economic Outlook* in April 2009 continued to recommend "strong countercyclical policy action" (IMF 2009). In late December 2008, the International Monetary Fund released a staff position note, which said that the optimal fiscal package should be "timely, because the need for action is immediate; large, because the current and expected decrease in private demand is exceptionally large; lasting because the downturn will last for some time" (Spilimbergo et al. 2008, 2). By the end of 2008, it was also becoming clear that president-elect Barack Obama would propose significant fiscal stimulus measures when taking office in January 2009. In December, the European Union's Council of Ministers agreed to take discretionary expansionary fiscal policy measures amounting to more than 1.5 percent of GDP, and a few months later, in April 2009, the leaders of the G20 countries announced at a meeting in London that they were "undertaking an unprecedented and concerted fiscal expansion," in order to prevent a large increase in unemployment (Corsetti et al. 2010, 7).

Austria, Denmark, the Netherlands, and Sweden all implemented their own fiscal policy packages in 2008 and 2009. In Austria, the grand coalition government introduced a series of expansionary fiscal packages to support both infrastructure investments and private demand already in the autumn of 2008 (Bundesministerium für Wirtschaft, Familie und Jugend 2009, 7–8), and it continued to pursue expansionary policies in the following year. In Denmark, the center-right government agreed with the far-right Danish People's Party, on which the government depended for parliamentary support, to adopt some discretionary legislation in 2009, including a tax reform that was fully financed in the long term, but underfunded in the short term in order to produce an expansionary effect (Finansministeriet 2009, 7). The Danish budget for 2009 also included other discretionary measures, such as municipal and national infrastructure investments and subsidies to the construction sector (Finansministeriet 2009, 8–9).

In the Netherlands, the initial response of the government in the autumn of 2008 was to emphasize the need for wage restraint, true to Dutch traditions. The Netherlands was "well prepared for economic downturn," the finance minister argued (Ministerie van Financiën 2008, 1–2), and the coalition government did not envision any major changes in policy. In 2009, however, the government proposed a more active fiscal response: "The government will therefore work vigorously in 2010 on implementing a stimulus package that takes a forward-looking, structural approach to recovery in the economy and the labour market" (Ministerie van Financiën 2009, 1). In Sweden, finally, a slightly more expansionary fiscal policy was announced in the budget bill for 2009 (Prop. 2008/9: 1, 4, 20), but this bill was still dominated by the general policy agenda that the government had pursued since it came into office 2006, particularly in the areas of labor market reform and taxation. Beginning in late 2008, however, the government took a series of expansionary fiscal policy measures, including subsidies for house repairs, infrastructure investments, and education, active labor market programs, and some transfers to the municipalities in order to maintain services and prevent layoffs (Prop. 2008/9: 97).

At the time of writing, it is too early to say what the long-term consequences of the Great Recession will be, but as this book has shown, citizens and governments in Austria, Denmark, the Netherlands, and Sweden lived in the shadow of the 1970s for a period of several decades, and it seems safe to assume that European governments will continue to be affected by the Great Recession for many years to come. The experience of the 1980s, 1990s, and 2000s suggests that some of those who became unemployed during the macroeconomic crisis will find it difficult to get a new job (especially if the crisis is long-lasting). The experience of the 1970s, 1980s, 1990s, and 2000s also shows that economic crises and the way that governments respond to them have important political effects. In the 1970s and 1980s, European governments responded differently to the threat of unemployment. This later led them to respond differently to the fact of unemployment in the 1990s and 2000s. In a similar manner, the way in which European governments responded to the threat, and fact, of rapidly increasing unemployment in the Great Recession of 2008–9 is likely to have significant political repercussions.

Whatever Works

A final lesson from the Austrian, Danish, Dutch, and Swedish cases is that there are many ways to achieve low unemployment. Each of these countries was regarded as an "employment miracle" at some point in the 1970s, 1980s, 1990s, or 2000s. But each country relied on a particular mix of policies to achieve the results that met with such praise. Austrian governments in the 1970s relied on a combination of expansionary, interventionist fiscal policies, a hard currency policy, and cooperation with the social partners. Swedish governments in the 1970s and 1980s made big currency devaluations in order to reduce real wages and improve the competitiveness of the export-oriented sector of the economy. Dutch governments in the 1980s and 1990s relied on a combination of wage restraint, job incentives, the deregulation of temporary and part-time work, and employment subsidies. Danish governments in the 1990s and 2000s changed the incentive structure of unemployment benefits, established the most extensive system of active labor market policy in the developed world, and adopted expansionary fiscal policies temporarily to increase private demand. Sometimes unexpected combinations of policies and institutions work well (perhaps only unexpected combinations of policies and institutions work well).

The unemployment problem will remain one of the most important economic and social problems in Europe—in human terms, and in political terms. History will look favorably on governments who manage to do something about it. There are always options, this book suggests, but they depend on domestic political arrangements, and how those arrangements develop through time.

Bibliography

Abert, James G. 1969. *Economic Policy and Planning in the Netherlands, 1950–1965.* New Haven, CT: Yale University Press.

Allan, James P. and Lyle Scruggs. 2004. "Political Partisanship and Welfare Reform in Advanced Industrial Societies." *American Journal of Political Science* 48 (3):496–512.

Alvarez, R. Michael, Geoffrey Garrett, and Peter Lange. 1991. "Government Partisanship, Labor Organization, and Macroeconomic Performance." *American Political Science Review* 85 (2):539–56.

Andersen, Jørgen Goul and Christian Albrekt Larsen. 2004. *Magten på Borgen.* Aarhus: Aarhus Universitetsforlag.

Andersen, Torben M. 1999. "Udviklingslinier i dansk økonomi." In *Beskrivende økonomi*, edited by Torben M. Andersen, Bent Dalum, Hans Linderoth, Valdemar Smith, and Niels Westergård-Nielsen. Copenhagen: Jurist- og Økonomforbundets Forlag, 1–30.

——, Svend E. Hougaard, and Ole Risager. 1999. "Macroeconomic Perspectives on the Danish Economy." In *Macroeconomic Perspectives on the Danish Economy*, edited by Torben M. Andersen, Svend E. Hougaard, and Ole Risager. Basingstoke: Macmillan, 1–39.

Andersson, Dan. 2008. "Vilken arbetslinje väljer socialdemokratin?" *Tiden* 101 (3):6–11.

Andersson, Jenny. 2003. *Mellan tillväxt och trygghet.* Ph.D. thesis, Uppsala University.

Andeweg, Rudy B. and Galen A. Irwin. 2005. *Governance and Politics of the Netherlands.* Basingstoke: Palgrave, second ed.

——. 2009. *Governance and Politics of the Netherlands.* Basingstoke: Palgrave, third ed.

Androsch, Hannes. 1985. *Die politische Ökonomie der österreichischen Währung.* Vienna: Wirtschaftsverlag Dr. Anton Orac.

Anthonsen, Mette and Johannes Lindvall. 2009. "Party Competition and the Resilience of Corporatism." *Government and Opposition* 44 (2):167–87.

——, Johannes Lindvall, and Ulrich Schmidt Hansen. 2009. "Social Democrats, Unions, and Corporatism: Denmark and Sweden Compared." Forthcoming in *Party Politics.*

Armingeon, Klaus, Marlène Gerber, Philipp Leimgruber, and Michelle Beyeler. 2009. "Comparative Political Data Set 1960–2007." Institute of Political Science, University of Berne.

Asmussen, Balder. 2004. "Danmark i kapitalismens guldalder." *Historisk Tidsskrift* 104 (2):430–49.

——. 2007. *Drivkræfterne bag den økonomiske politik 1974–1994*. Ph.D. thesis, Aalborg University.

Auer, Peter. 2002. "Flexibility and Security: Labour Market Policy in Austria, Denmark, Ireland and the Netherlands." In *The Dynamics of Full Employment*, edited by Günther Schmid and Bernard Gazier. Cheltenham: Edward Elgar, 81–105.

Baccaro, Lucio. 2003. "What is Alive and What is Dead in the Theory of Corporatism." *British Journal of Industrial Relations* 41 (4):683–706.

Bardi, Luciano and Peter Mair. 2008. "The Parameters of Party Systems." *Party Politics* 14 (2):147–66.

Bean, Charles R. 1994. "European Unemployment: A Survey." *Journal of Economic Literature* 32 (2):573–619.

Becker, Uwe. 2001. "'Miracle' by Consensus? Consensualism and Dominance in Dutch Employment Development." *Economic and Industrial Democracy* 22 (4):453–83.

Benner, Mats. 1997. *The Politics of Growth*. Lund: Arkiv.

—— and Torben Bundgaard Vad. 2000. "Sweden and Denmark: Defending the Welfare State." In *Welfare and Work in the Open Economy, Vol. II*, edited by Fritz W. Scharpf and Vivien A. Schmidt. Oxford: Oxford University Press, 399–466.

Bergström, Hans. 1984. "Mellan dimmors frost och dun. Myterna om Haga." In *Att överskrida gränser. En vänbok till Gunnar Helén*, edited by Erik Hjalmar Linder. Stockholm: Natur och Kultur.

Berman, Sheri. 2006. *The Primacy of Politics*. Cambridge: Cambridge University Press.

Blanchard, Olivier. 2006. "European Unemployment: The Evolution of Facts and Ideas." *Economic Policy* 21 (45):7–59.

——. 2008. "The State of Macro." MIT Department of Economics Working Paper 08–17.

Bluhm, William T. 1973. *Building an Austrian Nation*. New Haven, CT: Yale University Press.

Blyth, Mark. 2001. "The Transformation of the Swedish Model." *World Politics* 54 (1):1–26.

——. 2002. *Great Transformations*. Cambridge: Cambridge University Press.

Bredgaard, Thomas, Flemming Larsen, Per Kongshøj Madsen, and Stine Rasmussen. 2009. "Flexicurity på Dansk." CARMA Research Paper 2009:2, Centre for Labour Market Research, Aalborg University.

Budgetdepartementet. Various years. *Budgetredegørelse/Finansredegørelse*. Copenhagen: Finansministeriet.

Bundesgesetzblatt für die Republik Österreich. Various years.

Bundesministerium für Arbeit, Soziales und Konsumentenschutz. 2009. *Dokumentation: Aktive Arbeitsmarktpolitik in Österreich 1994–Mitte 2009.* Vienna: Bundesministerium für Arbeit, Soziales und Konsumentenschutz.

Bundesministerium für soziale Verwaltung. Various years. *Bericht über die soziale Lage.* Vienna: Bundesministerium für soziale Verwaltung.

Bundesministerium für Wirtschaft, Familie und Jugend. 2009. *Wirtschaftsbericht.* Vienna: Bundesministerium für Wirtschaft, Familie und Jugend.

Calmfors, Lars. 1982. "Behovet av nya stabiliseringspolitiska strategier." *Ekonomisk Debatt* 10 (3):155–62.

——. 1990. "Wage Formation and Macroeconomic Policy in the Nordic Countries: A Summary." In *Wage Formation and Macroeconomic Policy in the Nordic Countries*, edited by Lars Calmfors. Stockholm: SNS Förlag.

——. 2007. "Flexicurity—An Answer or a Question?" *Sieps European Policy Analysis* (6).

——and Anders Forslund. 1990. "Wage Formation in Sweden." In *Wage Formation and Macroeconomic Policy in the Nordic Countries*, edited by Lars Calmfors. Stockholm: SNS Förlag.

Carlin, Wendy and David Soskice. 2006. *Macroeconomics.* Oxford: Oxford University Press.

Carlsson, Ingvar. 2003. *Så tänkte jag.* Stockholm: Hjalmarsson & Högberg.

Castles, Francis G. 1978. *The Social Democratic Image of Society.* London: Routledge & Kegan Paul.

Central Intelligence Agency. 2009. *World Factbook 2009.* Central Intelligence Agency.

Cooper, Richard N. 1968. *The Economics of Interdependence.* New York: McGraw-Hill.

Corsetti, Giancarlo, Michael P. Devereux, Luigi Guiso, John Hassler, Gilles Saint-Paul, Hans-Werner Sinn, Jan-Egbert Sturm, and Xavier Vives. 2010. *The EEAG Report on the European Economy 2010.* Munich: CESIfo.

Cox, Robert H. 1993. *The Development of the Dutch Welfare State.* Pittsburgh: University of Pittsburgh Press.

——. 1998. "From Safety Net to Trampoline." *Governance* 11 (4):397–414.

——. 2001. "The Social Construction of an Imperative." *World Politics* 53 (3):463–98.

Crouch, Colin. 1993. *Industrial Relations and European State Traditions.* Oxford: Oxford University Press.

Cukierman, Alex. 1994. *Central Bank Strategy, Credibility, and Independence.* Cambridge: MIT Press.

Dahlström, Carl. 2009. "The Bureaucratic Politics of Welfare-State Crisis." *Governance* 22 (2):217–38.

Davidsson, Johan. 2009. "Outsiders to Welfare." Unpublished manuscript, European University Institute, Florence.

de Klerk, R. A., H. B. M. van der Laan, and K. B. T. Thio. 1977. "Unemployment in the Netherlands: A Criticism of the den Hartog–Tjan Model." *Cambridge Journal of Economics* 1 (3):291–306.

de Mooij, R. A. 2004. "Towards Efficient Unemployment Insurance in the Netherlands." CPB Memorandum 100.

Demker, Marie. 2006. "Essor et déclin du modèle nordique à cinq partis." *Revue Internationale de Politique Comparée* 13 (3):469–82.

Den Hartog, H. and H. S. Tjan. 1976. "Investments, Wages, Prices and Demand for Labour." *De Economist* 124 (1–2):32–55.

Dennis, Bengt. 1998. *500 %*. Stockholm: Bokförlaget DN.

Denzau, Arthur T. and Douglass C. North. 1994. "Shared Mental Models." *Kyklos* 47 (1):3–31.

Det økonomiske Råd. Various years. *Dansk økonomi*. Copenhagen: Det økonomiske Råd.

Ds. 1999:58. *Kontrakt för arbete*. Stockholm: Näringsdepartementet.

Ebbinghaus, Bernhard. 2006. *Reforming Early Retirement in Europe, Japan, and the USA*. Oxford: Oxford University Press.

Eckstein, Harry. 1988. "A Culturalist Theory of Political Change." *American Political Science Review* 82 (3):789–804.

Ehnmark, Anders. 2002. "1789 års man." *Ord & Bild*.

Eichhorst, Werner and Anton Hemerijck. 2009. "Welfare and Unemployment: A European Dilemma?" In *United in Diversity?*, edited by Jens Alber and Neil Gilbert. Oxford: Oxford University Press, 201–36.

——, Otto Kaufmann, Regina Konle-Seidl, and Hans-Joachim Reinhard. 2008. "Bringing the Jobless into Work?" In *Bringing the Jobless into Work?*, edited by Werner Eichhorst, Otto Kaufmann, and Regina Konle-Seidl. Berlin: Springer, 1–16.

Einerhand, Marcel, Ingemar Eriksson, and Hans Hansen. 1993. "Unemployment Insurance in the Netherlands, Denmark and Sweden." DGSZ/FEBO Research memorandum 93/1.

Eklöf, Kurt. 1990. *Tre valutakriser 1967–1977*. Stockholm: Sveriges Riksbank.

Elklit, Jørgen. 2002. "The Politics of Electoral System Development and Change: the Danish Case." In *The Evolution of Electoral and Party Systems in the Nordic Countries*, edited by Bernard Grofman and Arend Lijphart. New York: Agathon Press, 15–66.

Elster, Jon. 1986. "Introduction." In *Rational Choice*, edited by Jon Elster. Oxford: Basil Blackwell, 1–33.

——. 1990. "When Rationality Fails." In *The Limits of Rationality*, edited by Karen S. Cook and Margaret Levi. Chicago, IL: University of Chicago Press, 19–51.

Elvander, Nils. 1988. *Den svenska modellen*. Stockholm: Allmänna förlaget.

——. 2002. "The New Swedish Regime for Collective Bargaining and Conflict Resolution." *European Journal of Industrial Relations* 8 (2):197–216.

Erixon, Lennart, editor. 2003. *Den svenska modellens ekonomiska politik*. Stockholm: Atlas.

Erlander, Tage. 1974. *1949–1954*. Stockholm: Tiden.

Esaiasson, Peter. 1990. *Svenska valkampanjer 1866–1988*. Stockholm: Allmänna förlaget.

Esping-Andersen, Gøsta. 1990. *The Three Worlds of Welfare Capitalism*. Princeton, NJ: Princeton University Press.

European Commission. 2007. *Towards Common Principles of Flexicurity: More and Better Jobs Through Flexibility and Security*. Bruxelles: European Communication COM (2007) 359.

Federal Chancellery of Austria. 2008. *Programme of the Austrian Federal Government for the 24th Legislative Period*. Vienna: Bundeskanzleramt Österreich.

Feldt, Kjell-Olof. 1991. *Alla dessa dagar*. Stockholm: Norstedts.

Finansministeriet. 2008. *Økonomisk Redegørelse*. Copenhagen: Finansministeriet.

——. 2009. "Aftale mellem regeringen og Dansk Folkeparti om forårspakke 2.0." Copenhagen: Finansministeriet.

Finer, Samuel E. 1997. *The History of Government*. Oxford: Oxford University Press, 3 Volumes.

Franzese, Jr., Robert J. 1999. "Electoral and Partisan Manipulation of Public Debt in Developed Democracies, 1956–90." Unpublished manuscript, Ann Arbor: University of Michigan.

——. 2002. "Electoral and Partisan Cycles in Economic Policies and Outcomes." *Annual Review of Political Science* 5:369–421.

Fredriksson, Peter and Bertil Holmlund. 2006. "Improving Incentives in Unemployment Insurance." *Journal of Economic Surveys* 20 (3):357–86.

Furåker, Bengt and Marianne Blomsterberg. 2002. "Arbetsmarknadspolitik." In *Arbetslivet*, edited by Lars H. Hansen and Pal Orban. Lund: Studentlitteratur, 269–96.

Garme, Cecilia. 2001. *Newcomers to Power*. Ph.D. thesis, University of Uppsala.

Gerlich, Peter and Wolfgang C. Müller. 1989. "Austria: A Crisis Resolved or a Crisis Postponed?" In *The Politics of Economic Crisis*, edited by Erik Damgaard, Peter Gerlich, and Jeremy J. Richardson. Aldershot: Avebury, 146–161.

Gilljam, Mikael and Sören Holmberg. 1990. *Väljarna inför 90-talet*. Stockholm: Norstedts Juridik.

Ginsburg, Helen. 1983. *Full Employment and Public Policy*. Lexington, Mass.: Lexington Books.

Gladdish, Ken. 1991. *Governing from the Centre*. London: Hurst.

Glyn, Andrew. 2006. *Capitalism Unleashed*. Oxford: Oxford University Press.

Gourevitch, Peter. 1986. *Politics in Hard Times*. Ithaca, NY: Cornell University Press.

Graversen, Brian Krogh and Karen Thinggard. 2005. *Loft over Ydelser*. Copenhagen: Socialforskningsinstituttet.

Green-Pedersen, Christoffer. 2002. *The Politics of Justification*. Amsterdam: Amsterdam University Press.

——. 2003. "Det danske pensionssystems endelige udformning." *Historisk Tidsskrift* 103:359–82.

——and Anders Lindbom. 2005. "Employment and Unemployment in Denmark and Sweden." In *Employment "Miracles"*, edited by Uwe Becker and Herman Schwartz. Amsterdam: Amsterdam University Press, 65–85.

——. 2006. "Politics Within Paths. Trajectories of Danish and Swedish Earnings-Related Pensions." *Journal of European Social Policy* 16:245–58.

Grillberger, Konrad. 1996. *Österreichisches Sozialrecht*. Vienna: Springer, third ed.

——. 2001. *Österreichisches Sozialrecht*. Vienna: Springer, fifth ed.

Guger, Alois. 1998. "Economic Policy and Social Democracy: The Austrian Experience." *Oxford Review of Economic Policy* 14 (1):40–58.

Gustavsson, Jakob. 1998. *The Politics of Foreign Policy Change*. Lund: Lund University Press.

Hall, Peter A. 1986. *Governing the Economy*. Cambridge: Polity Press.

——. 1989. "Conclusion." In *The Political Power of Economic Ideas*, edited by Peter A. Hall. Princeton, NJ: Princeton University Press, 361–391.

——. 1993. "Policy Paradigms, Social Learning, and the State." *Comparative Politics* 25 (3):275–96.

——. 1997. "The Role of Interests, Institutions, and Ideas in the Comparative Political Economy of the Industrialized Nations." In *Comparative Politics*, edited by Mark Irving Lichbach and Alan S. Zuckerman. Cambridge: Cambridge University Press, 174–98.

——and David Soskice. 2001. "An Introduction to Varieties of Capitalism." In *Varieties of Capitalism*, edited by Peter A. Hall and David Soskice. Oxford: Oxford University Press, 1–68.

Handler, Heinz and Eduard Hochreiter. 1998. "Austria." In *Joining Europe's Monetary Club*, edited by Erik Jones, Jeffry Frieden, and Francisco Torres. Basingstoke: Macmillan, 19–42.

Heclo, Hugh. 1974. *Modern Social Policies in Britain and Sweden*. New Haven, CT: Yale University Press.

Heinesen, Knud. 2006. *Min krønike 1932–1979*. Copenhagen: Gyldendal.

Hemerijck, Anton. 1992. *The Historical Contingencies of Dutch Corporatism*. Ph.D. thesis, University of Oxford.

——. 2002. "The Netherlands in Historical Perspective: The Rise and Fall of Dutch Policy Concertation." In *Policy Concertation and Social Partnership in Western Europe*, edited by Stefan Berger and Hugh Compston. Oxford: Berghahn Books.

——and Ive Marx. Forthcoming. "Continental Welfare at a Crossroads: The Choice Between Activation and Minimum Income Protection in Belgium and the Netherlands." In *A long good-bye to Bismarck?*, edited by Bruno Palier. Amsterdam University Press.

——and Martin Schludi. 2000. "Sequences of Policy Failures and Effective Policy Responses." In *Welfare and Work in the Open Economy, Vol. I*, edited by Fritz W. Scharpf and Vivien A. Schmidt. Oxford: Oxford University Press, 125–228.

——, Birgitte Unger, and Jelle Visser. 2000. "How Small Countries Negotiate Change." In *Welfare and Work in the Open Economy, Vol. II*, edited by Fritz W. Scharpf and Vivien A. Schmidt. Oxford: Oxford University Press, 175–263.

Hermansson, Jörgen. 1993. *Politik som intressekamp*. Stockholm: Norstedts Juridik.

——, Anna Lund, Torsten Svensson, and Per-Ola Öberg. 1999. *Avkorporatisering och lobbyism*. SOU 1999:121. Stockholm: Fritzes.

Heston, Alan, Robert Summers, and Bettina Aten. 2009. "Penn World Table, Version 6.3." Center for International Comparisons of Production, Income and Prices at the University of Pennsylvania, August 2009.

Hibbs, Douglas A. 1977. "Political Parties and Macroeconomic Policy." *American Political Science Review* 71 (4):1467–87.

——and Håkan Locking. 1996. "Wage Compression, Wage Drift and Wage Inflation in Sweden." *Labour Economics* 3 (2):109–41.

Hirschman, Albert O. 1989. "How the Keynesian Revolution Was Exported from the United States, and Other Comments." In *The Political Power of Economic Ideas*, edited by Peter A. Hall. Princeton: Princeton University Press, 347–59.

Hochreiter, Eduard and George S. Tavlas. 2004. "On the Road Again." *Journal of Policy Modeling* 26 (7):793–816.

——and Georg Winckler. 1995. "The Advantages of Tying Austria's Hands." *European Journal of Political Economy* 11 (1):83–111.

Hoffmeyer, Erik. 1993. *Pengepolitiske problemstillinger 1965–1990*. Copenhagen: Danmarks Nationalbank.

Holmlund, Bertil. 2006. "The Rise and Fall of Swedish Unemployment." In *Structural Unemployment in Western Europe*, edited by Martin Werding. Cambridge: MIT Press, 103–32.

Huber, Evelyne and John D. Stephens. 2001. *Development and Crisis of the Welfare State*. Chicago, IL: The University of Chicago Press.

Huber, Evelyne, Charles Ragin, John D. Stephens, David Brady, and Jason Beckfield. 2004. "Comparative Welfare States Data Set." Northwestern University, University of North Carolina, Duke University and Indiana University.

Huo, Jingjing, Moira Nelson, and John D. Stephens. 2008. "Decommodification and Activation in Social Democratic Policy: Resolving the Paradox." *Journal of European Social Policy* 18 (1):5–20.

ILO. 1964. "Convention Concerning Employment Policy." ILO Convention 122. Geneva: International Labour Organization.

——1982. "Resolution Concerning Statistics of the Economically Active Population, Employment, Unemployment and Underemployment." Adopted by the Thirteenth International Conference of Labour Statisticians.

IMF. 2009. *World Economic Outlook April 2009*. Washington, DC: International Monetary Fund.

Ingebritsen, Christine. 1998. *The Nordic States and European Unity*. Ithaca, NY: Cornell University Press.

Iversen, Torben. 1998. "The Choices for Scandinavian Social Democracy in Comparative Perspective." *Oxford Review of Economic Policy* 14 (1):59–75.

——. 1999. *Contested Economic Institutions*. New York: Cambridge University Press.

——and David Soskice. 2006. "New Macroeconomics and Political Science." *Annual Review of Political Science* 9:425–53.

Jahoda, Maria, Paul F. Lazarsfeld, and Hans Zeisel. 1972 [1933]. *Marienthal*. London: Tavistock Publications.

Jelavich, Barbara. 1987. *Modern Austria*. Cambridge: Cambridge University Press.

Jensen, Lotte. 2008. *Væk fra afgrunden*. Odense: Syddansk Universitetsforlag.

Johansson, Joakim. 2000. *SAF och den svenska modellen*. Ph.D. thesis, Uppsala University.

Jones, Erik. 1998. "The Netherlands." In *Joining Europe's Monetary Club*, edited by Erik Jones, Jeffry Frieden, and Francisco Torres. Basingstoke: Macmillan, 149–70.

——. 2008. *Economic Adjustment and Political Transformation in Small States*. Oxford: Oxford University Press.

Jonung, Lars. 1999. *Med backspegeln som kompass*. Stockholm: Fakta info direkt.

Junestav, Malin. 2004. *Arbetslinjer i svensk socialpolitisk debatt och lagstiftning 1930–2001*. Ph.D. thesis, Uppsala University.

Kalecki, Michal. 1943. "Political Aspects of Full Employment." *The Political Quarterly* 14 (4):322–30.

Katzenstein, Peter J. 1982. "Commentary." In *The Political Economy of Austria*, edited by Sven E. Arndt. Washington, DC: American Enterprise Institute, 150–5.

——. 1984. *Corporatism and Change*. Ithaca, NY: Cornell University Press.

——. 1985a. "Small Nations in an Open International Economy." In *Bringing the State Back In*, edited by Peter Evans, Dietrich Rueschemeyer, and Theda Skocpol. New York: Cambridge University Press, 227–51.

——. 1985b. *Small States in World Markets*. Ithaca, NY: Cornell University Press.

Kelly, John and Kerstin Hamann. 2009. "General Strikes in Western Europe 1980–2008." Paper prepared for the Labor and Employment Relations Annual Meeting, San Francisco, 3–5 January 2009.

Kenworthy, Lane. 2001a. "Wage Setting Coordination Scores." Department of Sociology, Emory University.

——. 2001b. "Wage-Setting Measures: A Survey and Assessment." *World Politics* 54 (1):57–98.

——. 2003. "Quantitative Indicators of Corporatism." *International Journal of Sociology* 33 (3):10–44.

——. 2008. *Jobs With Equality*. Oxford: Oxford University Press.

——. Forthcoming. "Labor Market Activation." In *The Oxford Handbook of Comparative Welfare States*, edited by Herbert Obinger, Christopher Pierson, Francis G. Castles, Stephen Leibfried, and Jane Lewis. Oxford: Oxford University Press.

Kienzl, Heinz. 1978. "Währungspolitik in Konjunktur und Krise." *Wirtschaft und Gesellschaft* 4 (2):175–90.

Korpi, Walter and Joakim Palme. 2003. "New Politics and Class Politics in the Context of Austerity and Globalization." *American Political Science Review* 97 (3): 425–46.

——. 2008. *The Social Citizenship Indicator Program (SCIP)*. Swedish Institute for Social Research.

Kreisky, Bruno. 1989. "Introduction." In *A Programme for Full Employment in the 1990s*. Oxford: Pergamon Press.

Kunkel, Christoph and Jonas Pontusson. 1998. "Corporatism Versus Social Democracy: Divergent Fortunes of the Austrian and Swedish Labour Movements." *West European Politics* 21 (2):1–31.

Kurzer, Paulette. 1993. *Business and Banking*. Ithaca, NY: Cornell University Press.

Kvist, Jon. 2001. "Nordic Activation in the 1990s." *Benefits* 31:5–9.

——. 2003. "A Danish Welfare-State Miracle?" *Scandinavian Journal of Public Health* 31:241–5.

Laakso, Markku and Rein Taagepera. 1979. "Effective Number of Parties: A Measure with Application to West Europe." *Comparative Political Studies* 12 (1): 3–27.

Larsen, Christian Albrekt and Jørgen Goul Andersen. 2009. "How New Economic Ideas Changed the Danish Welfare State." *Governance* 22 (2):239–61.

Larsson, Allan. 1991. *Klarspråk om Sveriges ekonomi*. Stockholm: Tiden.

Layard, Richard, Stephen Nickell, and Richard Jackman. 2005. *Unemployment*. Oxford: Oxford University Press, second ed.

Lehmbruch, Gerhard. 1967. *Proporzdemokratie*. Tübingen: J.C.B. Mohr.

——. 1977. "Liberal Corporatism and Party Government." *Comparative Political Studies* 10:91–126.

Lewin, Leif. 1967. *Planhushållningsdebatten*. Stockholm: Almqvist & Wiksell.

Lijphart, Arend. 1968. *The Politics of Accommodation*. Berkeley, CA: University of California Press.

——. 1975. *The Politics of Accommodation*. Berkeley, CA: University of California Press, second ed.

——. 1990. "The Political Consequences of Electoral Laws, 1945–85." *American Political Science Review* 84 (2):481–96.

——. 1999. *Patterns of Democracy*. New Haven, CT: Yale University Press.

Lindbeck, Assar. 1997. "The Swedish Experiment." *Journal of Economic Literature* 35 (3):1273–19.

Lindensjö, Bo and Ulf P. Lundgren. 2000. *Utbildningsreformer och politisk styrning*. Stockholm: HLS Förlag.

Lindvall, Johannes. 2004. *The Politics of Purpose*. Ph.D. thesis, University of Gothenburg.

——. 2009. "The Real But Limited Influence of Experts." *World Politics* 61 (4):703–30.

Lindvall, Johannes and Bo Rothstein. 2006. "Sweden: The Fall of the Strong State." *Scandinavian Political Studies* 29 (1):47–63.

——and Joakim Sebring. 2005. "Policy Reform and the Decline of Swedish Corporatism." *West European Politics* 28 (5):1057–74.

Lindvert, Jessica. 2006. *Ihålig arbetsmarknadspolitik*. Umeå: Boréa.

LO. 1990. *Ekonomiska utsikter hösten 1990*. Stockholm: LO.

Ludwig-Mayerhofer, Wolfgang and Angela Wroblewski. 2004. "Eppur si muove?" *European Societies* 6 (4):485–509.

Magnusson, Lars. 2002. *Sveriges ekonomiska historia*. Stockholm: Prisma.

Mailand, Mikkel. 2002. "Denmark in the 1990s." In *Policy Concertation and Social Partnership in Western Europe*, edited by Stefan Berger and Hugh Compston. Oxford: Berghahn Books, 83–95.

Mair, Peter. 1996. "Party Systems and Structures of Competition." In *Comparing Democracies*, edited by Lawrence Le Duc, Richard G. Niemi, and Pippa Norris. London: Sage, 83–106.

Malm, Stig. 1994. *13 år*. Stockholm: Utbildningsförlaget Brevskolan.

Mann, Michael. 2004. *Fascists*. Cambridge: Cambridge University Press.

Marcussen, Martin. 2000. *Ideas and Elites*. Aalborg: Aalborg University Press.

Marglin, Stephen A. 1990. "Lessons of the Golden Age." In *The Golden Age of Capitalism*, edited by Stephen A. Marglin and Juliet Schor. Oxford: Clarendon Press, 1–38.

Marterbauer, Markus. 2001. "Rehn-Meidner and Austro-Keynesianism." In *Gösta Rehn, the Swedish Model and Labour Market Policies*, edited by Henry Milner and Eskil Wadensjö. Aldershot: Ashgate, 221–41.

Martin, Cathie Jo. 2004. "Reinventing Welfare Regimes." *World Politics* 57 (1):39–69.

Martinsson, Johan. 2009. *Dissertation*. Ph.D. thesis, University of Gothenburg.

McNamara, Kathleen R. 1998. *The Currency of Ideas*. Ithaca, NY: Cornell University Press.

Mikkelsen, Richard. 1993. *Dansk pengehistorie 1960–1990*. Copenhagen: Danmarks Nationalbank.

Milward, Alan S. 1992. *The European Rescue of the Nation-State*. London: Routledge.

Ministerie van Financiën. Various years. *Budget Memorandum*. The Hague: Ministerie van Financiën.

Mjøset, Lars. 1987. "Nordic Economic Policies in the 1970s and 1980s." *International Organization* 41 (3):403–56.

Müller, Wolfgang C. 2003. "Austria." In *Delegation and Accountability in Parliamentary Democracies*, edited by Kaare Strøm, Wolfgang C. Müller, and Torbjörn Bergman. Oxford: Oxford University Press, 221–52.

Molina, Oscar and Martin Rhodes. 2002. "Corporatism: The Past, Present, and Future of a Concept." *Annual Review of Political Science* 5:305–331.

Mooslechner, Peter, Stefan W. Schmitz, and Helene Schuberth. 2007. "From Bretton Woods to the Euro." In *From Bretton Woods to the Euro*, edited by Peter

Mooslechner, Stefan W. Schmitz, and Helene Schuberth. Vienna: Österreichische Nationalbank, 21–44.

Moses, Jonathon W. 1994. "Abdication from National Policy Autonomy." *Politics & Society* 22 (2):125–48.

——. 1997. "Trojan Horses." *Review of International Political Economy* 4 (2): 382–415.

Nannestad, Peter. 1991. *Danish Design or British Disease?* Aarhus: Aarhus University Press.

——and Christoffer Green-Pedersen. 2000. "Keeping the Bumblebee Flying." Unpublished Manuscript, Department of Political Science, Aarhus University.

Nickell, Stephen. 1997. "Unemployment and Labor Market Rigidities." *Journal of Economic Perspectives* 11 (3):55–74.

——and Richard Layard. 1999. "Labor Market Institutions and Economic Performance." In *Handbook of Labor Economics*. New York: Elsevier, 3030–84.

——and Jan van Ours. 2000. "The Netherlands and the United Kingdom: a European Employment Miracle?" *Economic Policy* 15:137–80.

Notermans, Ton. 2000. *Money, Markets, and the State*. New York: Cambridge University Press.

Nycander, Svante. 2002. *Makten över arbetsmarknaden*. Stockholm: SNS Förlag.

Obinger, Herbert. 2009a. "The 'Island of the Blessed' in the Ocean of Globalisation." Unpublished manuscript, University of Bremen.

——. 2009b. "Sozialpolitische Bilanz der Großen Koalition in Österreich." In *Wohlfahrtsstaatlichkeit in entwickelten Demokratien*, edited by Herbert Obinger and Elmar Rieger. Frankfurt: Campus, 347–74.

OECD. 1973. "Memo on the effects of the oil crisis." Memorandum. In Pierre Vinde's papers, National Archives of Sweden, Stockholm. Volume 62.

——. 1988. *Why Economic Policies Change Course*. Paris: OECD.

——. 1994. *The OECD Jobs Study*. Paris: OECD.

——. 2004. *Employment Outlook*. Paris: OECD.

——. 2007. *Benefits and Wages*. Paris: OECD.

——. 2009a. *Economic Outlook 85*. Paris: OECD.

——. 2009b. *Social Expenditure Database*. Paris: OECD.

——. Various years. *Economic Survey* (of Austria, Denmark, the Netherlands, or Sweden). Paris: OECD.

Olsson, Ulf. 1991. "Planning in the Swedish Welfare State." *Studies in Political Economy* 34:147–71.

Oscarsson, Henrik and Sören Holmberg. 2008. *Regeringsskifte*. Stockholm: Norstedts Juridik.

Paulsen, Jan. 1992. *Socialpolitik*. Copenhagen: Handelshøjskolens Forlag.

Pedersen, Jesper Hartvig. 2007. "Et rids af udviklingen i det danske arbejdsløsheds-forsikringssystem fra 1907 til 2007." In *Arbejdsløshedsforsikringsloven 1907–2007*. Copenhagen: Arbejdsdirektoratet.

Pedersen, Ove K. 2006. "Corporatism and Beyond." In *National Identity and the Varieties of Capitalism*, edited by John L. Campbell, John A. Hall, and Ove K. Pedersen. Montreal: McGill-Queens University Press, 245–70.

Pekkarinen, Jukka. 1989. "Keynesianism and the Scandinavian Models of Economic Policy." In *The Political Power of Economic Ideas*, edited by Peter A. Hall. Princeton, NJ: Princeton University Press, 311–45.

Penz, Otto. 2007. "Zur ökonomischen, politischen und socialen Regulation der Ära Kreisky." In *Die Ära Kreisky und ihre Folgen*, edited by Wolfgang Marterthaner, Siegfried Mattl, Musner Lutz, and Otto Penz. Vienna: Löcker, 55–119.

Pick, Hella. 2000. *Guilty Victim*. London: I. B. Tauris.

Pontusson, Jonas. 1992. *The Limits of Social Democracy*. Ithaca, NY: Cornell University Press.

——. 2005. *Inequality and Prosperity*. Ithaca, NY: Cornell University Press.

Prop. Various years. Refers to Swedish government bills (*propositioner*), which are incorporated in Sveriges Riksdag (Various years).

Quinn, Dennis. 1997. "The Correlates of Change in International Financial Regulation." *American Political Science Review* 91 (3):531–51.

Rijksvoorlichtingsdienst. Various years. *Hoofdpunten van het regeringsbeleid*. The Hague: Staatsuitgeverij.

Rosner, Peter, Alexander Van der Bellen, and Georg Winckler. 1999. "Economic and Social Policy of the Vranitzky Era." In *The Vranitzky Era in Austria*, edited by Günther Bischof, Anton Pelinka, and Ferdinand Karlhofer. New Brunswick, NJ: Transaction Publishers, 136–64.

Rothschild, Kurt. 1994. "Austro-Keynesianism Reconsidered." In *The Kreisky Era in Austria*, edited by Günter Bischof, Anton Pelinka, and Oliver Rathkolb. New Brunswick: Transaction Publishers, 119–29.

Rothstein, Bo. 1986. *Den socialdemokratiska staten*. Lund: Arkiv.

——. 1992. *Den korporativa staten*. Stockholm: Norstedts.

——. 1996. *The Social Democratic State*. Pittsburgh: University of Pittsburgh Press.

——and Jonas Bergström. 1999. *Korporatismens fall och den svenska modellens kris*. Stockholm: SNS Förlag.

Rueda, David. 2006. "Social Democracy and Active Labour-Market Policies." *British Journal of Political Science* 36:385–406.

——. 2007. *Social Democracy Inside Out*. Oxford: Oxford University Press.

Salverda, Wiemer. 2005. "The Dutch Model." In *Employment "Miracles,"* edited by Uwe Becker and Herman Schwartz. Amsterdam University Press: Amsterdam University Press, 39–63.

Sartori, Giovanni. 1976. *Parties and Party Systems*. Cambridge: Cambridge University Press.

Åsbrink, Erik. 1982. "Big Bang, hårdvalutapolitik och consensus." Memorandum dated September 27. In Bengt Dennis's papers, the Riksbank archives, Stockholm. Volume F1A:245.

Scharpf, Fritz W. 1991. *Crisis and Choice in European Social Democracy.* Ithaca: Cornell University Press.

——. 2000. "Economic Changes, Vulnerabilities, and Institutional Capabilities." In *Welfare and Work in the Open Economy*, edited by Fritz W. Scharpf and Vivien A. Schmidt. Oxford: Oxford University Press.

—— and Vivien A. Schmidt, editors. 2000. *Welfare and Work in the Open Economy.* Oxford: Oxford University Press. 2 Vols.

Schattschneider, Elmer Eric. 1944. "Party Government and Employment Policy." *American Political Science Review* 39 (6):1147–57.

Schüllerqvist, Ulf. 1996. "Förskjutningen av svensk skolpolitisk debatt under det senaste decenniet." In *Utbildningspolitiskt systemskifte?*, edited by Tomas Englund. Stockholm: HLS Fölag.

Schmidt, Vivien A. 2002. *The Futures of European Capitalism.* Oxford: Oxford University Press.

Schmitter, Philippe C. 1974. "Still the Century of Corporatism?" *The Review of Politics* 36 (1):85–131.

Schwartz, Herman M. 2001. "The Danish 'Miracle.' Luck, Pluck, or Stuck?" *Comparative Political Studies* 34 (2):131–55.

Schweighofer, Johannes. 1995. "Labour Market and Employment Policy in Austria, 1975–1995." *inforMISEP* (50):30–43.

Scruggs, Lyle. 2004. "Welfare State Entitlements Data Set: A Comparative Institutional Analysis of Eighteen Welfare States." Version 1.1.

Seeleib-Kaiser, Martin, Silke van Dyk, and Martin Roggenkamp. 2008. *Party Politics and Social Welfare.* Cheltenham: Edward Elgar.

Seidel, Hans. 1982*a*. "The Austrian Economy: An Overview." In *The Political Economy of Austria*, edited by Sven E. Arndt. Washington, DC: American Enterprise Institute, 7–21.

——. 1982*b*. "Austro-Keynesianismus." *Wirtschaftspolitische Blätter* 29 (3):11–15.

Simon, Herbert A. 1947. *Administrative Behavior.* New York: Macmillan.

——. 1957. *Models of Man.* New York: Wiley.

Slomp, Hans. 2002. "The Netherlands in the 1990s." In *Policy Concertation and Social Partnership in Western Europe*, edited by Stefan Berger and Hugh Compston. Oxford: Berghahn Books, 235–47.

Snels, Bart. 1999. *Politics in the Dutch Economy.* Aldershot: Ashgate.

Socialdemokraterna. 1964. *Resultat och reformer.* Stockholm: Socialdemokraterna.

Sohlman, Michael. 1982*a*. "Internationella aspekter på krispolitiken." Memorandum dated September 13. In Bengt Dennis's papers, the archives of the Central Bank of Sweden, Stockholm, Vol. F1A:245.

——. 1982*b*. "PM ang. den svenska ekonomins konkurrenskraft." Memorandum, not dated. In Bengt Dennis's papers, the Riksbank archives, Stockholm, Volume F1A:245.

Sol, Els, Markus Sichert, Harm van Lieshout, and Theo Koning. 2008. "Activation as a Socio-Economic and Legal Concept: Laboratorium the Netherlands." In

Bringing the Jobless into Work?, edited by Werner Eichhorst, Otto Kaufmann, and Regina Konle-Seidl. Berlin: Springer, 161–220.

Soskice, David. 2000. "Macroeconomic Analysis and the Political Economy of Unemployment." In *Unions, Employers and Central Banks*, edited by Torben Iversen, Jonas Pontusson, and David Soskice. Cambridge: Cambridge University Press, 38–74.

SOU. 1990:44. *Demokrati och makt i Sverige*. Stockholm: Fritzes.

Spilimbergo, Antonio, Steve Symansky, Olivier Blanchard, and Carlo Cottarelli. 2008. "Fiscal Policy for the Crisis." IMF Staff Position Note, December 29 (SPN/08/01).

Stensöta, Helena. 2009. *Sjukskrivningarna och välfärdens infriare*. Stockholm: Hjalmarson & Högberg.

Österreichisches Nationalrat. Various years. *Stenographisches Protokoll*.

Stichting van de Arbeid. 1982. "General Recommendations on Aspects of an Employment Policy (The Wassenaar Agreement)." The Hague, 24 November.

Strömberg, Thord. 2001. "Bostadspolitik: En historisk parentes." In *Den nya bostadspolitiken*, edited by Anders Lindbom. Umeå: Boréa, 21–47.

Sully, Melaine A. 1990. *A Contemporary History of Austria*. London: Routledge.

Svensson, Torsten. 1996. *Novemberrevolutionen*. Stockholm: Fritzes.

——and Per-Ola Öberg. 2002. "Labour Market Organisations' Participation in Swedish Public Policy-Making." *Scandinavian Political Studies* 25 (4):295–315.

Sveriges Riksdag. Various years. *Riksdagens protokoll med bihang*.

Swedberg, Richard. 1990. *Economics and Sociology*. Princeton, NJ: Princeton University Press.

Swenson, Peter and Jonas Pontusson. 2000. "The Swedish Employer Offensive against Centralized Bargaining." In *Unions, Employers and Central Banks*, edited by Torben Iversen, Jonas Pontusson, and David Soskice. Cambridge: Cambridge University Press, 77–106.

Swidler, Ann. 2001. *Talk of Love*. Chicago, IL: University of Chicago Press.

Szász, André. 1999. *The Road to European Monetary Union*. Basingstoke: Macmillan.

Thelen, Kathleen. 2001. "Varieties of Labor Politics in the Developed Democracies." In *Varieties of Capitalism*, edited by Peter A. Hall and David Soskice. Oxford: Oxford University Press.

Therborn, Göran. 1986. *Why Some Peoples Are More Unemployed Than Others*. London: Verso.

Tichy, Gunther. 1984. "Strategy and Implementation of Employment Policy in Austria." *Kyklos* 37 (3):363–86.

Tálos, Emmerich. 1987. "Arbeitslosigkeit und Beschäftigungspolitische Steuerung." In *Arbeitslosigkeit: Österreichs Vollbeschäftigungspolitik am Ende?* Vienna: Verlag für Gesellschaftskritik, 91–166.

——. 2005a. *Vom Siegeszug zum Rückzug*. Innsbruch: Studien Verlag.

——. 2005b. "Vom Vorzeige- zum Auslaufmodell?" In *Sozialpartnerschaft*, edited by Ferdinand Karlhofer and Emmerich Tálos. Vienna: Lit, 185–216.

Toirkens, Sonja. 1988. *Schijn en werkelijkheid van het bezuinigingsbeleid 1975–1986.* Deventer: Kluwer.

Tomandl, Theodor. 2009. *Grundriss des österreichischen Sozialrechts.* Vienna: Manzsche Verlags- und Universitätsbuchhandlung, sixth ed.

Torfing, Jacob. 1999. "Workfare With Welfare." *Journal of European Social Policy* 9 (1):5–28.

———. 2004. *Det stille sporskifte i velfærdsstaten.* Aarhus: Aarhus Universitetsforlag.

Trier, Mikael. 1997. "Den økonomiske udvikling i Danmark i de 50 år." In *økonomiministeriet i 50 år 1947–1997.* Copenhagen: J. H. Schultz Information A/S, 37–55.

Truman, Edwin M. 2003. *Inflation Targeting in the World Economy.* Washington, DC: Institute for International Economics.

Ullmann-Margalit, Edna. 1986. "Opting: The Case of Big Decisions." In *Yearbook of the Institute of Advanced Study,* edited by P. Wapnewsky. Berlin, 441–54.

Unger, Brigitte. 1990. "Possibilities and Constraints for National Economic Policies in Small Countries: The Case of Austria." *German Politics and Society* 8 (21): 63–77.

———. 2001. "Österreichs Beschäftigungs- und Sozialpolitik von 1970 bis 2000." *Zeitschrift für Sozialreformen* (4):340–61.

——— and Karin Heitzmann. 2003. "The Adjustment Path of the Austrian Welfare State." *Journal of European Social Policy* 14 (4):371–387.

van Ours, Jan C. 2006. "Rising Unemployment at the Start of the Twenty-First Century: Has the Dutch Miracle Come to an End?" In *Structural Unemployment in Western Europe,* edited by Martin Werding. Cambridge: MIT Press, 133–58.

Viebrock, Elke and Jochen Clasen. 2009. "Flexicurity and Welfare Reform: A Review." *Socio-Economic Review* 7 (2):305–31.

Vifell, Åsa. 2006. *Enklaver i staten.* Ph.D. thesis, Stockholm University.

Visser, Jelle. 2002. "The First Part-Time Economy in the World." *Journal of European Social Policy* 12:23–42.

———. 2009. "The ICTWSS Database." Amsterdam: Amsterdam Institute for Advanced Labour Studies.

Visser, Jelle and Anton Hemerijck. 1997. *A Dutch Miracle.* Amsterdam: Amsterdam University Press.

Wallerstein, Michael and Miriam Golden. 1997. "The Fragmentation of the Bargaining Society." *Comparative Political Studies* 30 (6):699–731.

Walterskirchen, Ewald. 1997. "Austria's Road to Full Employment." WIFO Working Paper 89.

Ware, Alan. 1996. *Political Parties and Party Systems.* Oxford: Oxford University Press.

Weir, Margaret. 1992. *Politics and Jobs.* Princeton, NJ: Princeton University Press.

Weishaupt, Timo. 2008. *The Emergence of a New Labor Market Policy Paradigm.* Ph.D. thesis, University of Wisconsin-Madison.

Winckler, Georg. 1988. "Der Austrokeynesianismus und sein Ende." *Österreichische Zeitschrift für Politikwissenschaft* 17 (3):221–30.

Wolinetz, Steven B. 1989. "Socio-Economic Bargaining in the Netherlands." *West European Politics* 12 (1):79–98.

——. 2001. "Modell Nederland." In *Unemployment in the New Europe*, edited by Nancy Bermeo. Cambridge: Cambridge University Press, 245–67.

Woodford, Michael. 2009. "Convergence in Macroeconomics: Elements of the New Synthesis." *American Economic Journal: Macroeconomics* 1 (1):267–79.

World Bank. 2009. *World Development Indicators*. Washington, DC: World Bank.

Zalm, Gerrit. 1990. *Mythen, paradoxen en taboes in de economische politiek*. Amsterdam: De Stichting Het Vrije Universiteitsfonds.

——. 2009. *De romantische boekhouder*. Amsterdam: Balans.

Zeuthenudvalget. 1992. *Rapport fra udredningsudvalget om arbejdsmarkedets struktur-problemer*. Copenhagen.

APPENDIX A

Governments

Table A.1 Austrian governments

Period	Type of government	Parties	Prime minister
1970–1	Single-party minority	SPÖ	Kreisky
1971–83	Single-party majority	SPÖ	Kreisky
1983–6	Coalition majority	SPÖ, FPÖ	Sinowatz
1986–7	Coalition majority	SPÖ, FPÖ	Vranitzky
1987–97	Coalition majority	SPÖ, ÖVP	Vranitzky
1997–2000	Coalition majority	SPÖ, ÖVP	Klima
2000–5	Coalition majority	ÖVP, FPÖ	Schüssel
2005–7	Coalition majority	ÖVP, BZÖ	Schüssel
2007–8	Coalition majority	SPÖ, ÖVP	Gusenbauer
2008–	Coalition majority	SPÖ, ÖVP	Faymann

Note: Prime minister's party listed first. BZÖ: *Bündnis Zukunft Österreich*, far right. SPÖ: *Sozialdemokratische Partei Österreichs* (until 1991 *Sozialistische Partei Österreichs*), social democratic. ÖVP: *Österreichische Volkspartei*, Christian democratic. FPÖ: *Freiheitliche Partei Österreichs*, liberal until 1986, far right thereafter.

Table A.2 Danish governments

Period	Type of government	Parties	Prime minister
1972–3	Single-party minority	S	Jørgensen
1973–5	Single-party minority	V	Hartling
1975–8	Single-party minority	S	Jørgensen
1978–9	Coalition minority	S, V	Jørgensen
1979–82	Single-party minority	S	Jørgensen
1982–8	Coalition minority	KF, CD, KrF, V	Schlüter
1988–90	Coalition minority	KF, RV, V	Schlüter
1990–3	Coalition minority	KF, V	Schlüter
1993–4	Coalition majority	S, CD, KrF, RV	P. Rasmussen
1994–6	Coalition minority	S, CD, RV	P. Rasmussen
1996–2001	Coalition minority	S, RV	P. Rasmussen
2001–9	Coalition minority	V, KF	A. Rasmussen
2009–	Coalition minority	V, KF	L. Rasmussen

Note: Prime minister's party listed first. CD: *Centrumdemokraterne*, centrist. KF: *Det Konservative Folkeparti*, conservative. KrF: *Kristeligt Folkeparti*, Christian democratic. RV: *Det Radikale Venstre*, social liberal. S: *Socialdemokratiet*, social democratic. V: *Venstre*, liberal.

Appendix A

Table A.3 Dutch governments

Period	Type of government	Parties	Prime minister
1973–7	Coalition majority	PvdA, ARP, D66, KVP, PPR	Den Uyl
1977–81	Coalition majority	CDA, VVD	Van Agt
1981–2	Coalition majority	CDA, D66, PvdA	Van Agt
1982	Coalition majority	CDA, D66	Van Agt
1982–9	Coalition majority	CDA, VVD	Lubbers
1989–94	Coalition majority	CDA, PvdA	Lubbers
1994–2002	Coalition majority	PvdA, D66, VDD	Kok
2002–3	Coalition majority	CDA, LPF, VVD	Balkenende
2003–6	Coalition majority	CDA, D66, VDD	Balkenende
2006–7	Coalition majority	CDA, VDD	Balkenende
2007–	Coalition majority	CDA, CU, PvdA	Balkenende

Note: Prime minister's party listed first. ARP: *Anti-Revolutionaire Partij*, Christian democratic (Protestant). CDA: *Christen Democratisch Appèl*, Christian democratic (a merger of ARP, KVP, and a third Christian democratic party). CU: *ChristenUnie*, Christian democratic. D66: *Democraten 66*, social liberal. KVP: *Katholieke Volkspartij*, Christian democratic (Catholic). LPF: *Lijst Pim Fortuyn*, far right. PvdA: *Partij van de Arbeid*, social democratic. PPR: *Politieke Partij Radikalen*, left-wing. VVD: *Volkspartij voor Vrijheid en Democratie*, conservative-liberal.

Table A.4 Swedish governments

Period	Type of government	Parties	Prime minister
1969–76	Single-party minority	s	Palme
1976–8	Coalition majority	c, fp, m	Fälldin
1978–9	Single-party minority	fp	Ullsten
1979–81	Coalition majority	c, fp, m	Fälldin
1981–2	Coalition minority	c, fp	Fälldin
1982–6	Single-party minority	s	Palme
1986–91	Single-party minority	s	Carlsson
1991–4	Coalition minority	m, c, fp, kd	Bildt
1994–6	Single-party minority	s	Carlsson
1996–2006	Single-party minority	s	Persson
2006–	Coalition majority	m, c, fp, kd	Reinfeldt

Note: Prime minister's party listed first. c: *Centerpartiet*, center (agrarian). fp: *Folkpartiet liberalerna* (earlier *Folkpartiet*), liberal. kd: *Kristdemokraterna* (earlier *Kristdemokratiska samhällspartiet*), Christian democratic. m: *Moderaterna* (earlier *Moderata samlingspartiet*), conservative. s: *Sveriges socialdemokratiska arbetareparti*, social democratic.

APPENDIX B

Interviews

Austria

Androsch, Hannes. Finance Minister 1970–81. Vice-Chancellor 1975–81. Vienna, November 22, 2007.

Bartenstein, Martin. Minister of Economics and Labor 2000–8. Vienna, February 10, 2010.

Chaloupek, Günther. Economic policy adviser at the Federal Chamber of Labor 1972 to present. Director of its Department of Economic Research and Statistics since 1986. Member of the *Beirat für Wirtschafts- und Sozialfragen* since 1976. Vienna, June 8, 2006; February 11, 2010.

Farnleitner, Hannes. Employed at the Federal Economic Chamber 1964–96. Head of the Department for Economic Policy 1982–95. Minister of Economic Affairs 1996–2000. Vienna, November 22, 2007.

Hochreiter, Eduard. Held various senior research positions in the Austrian National Bank between 1975 and 2006. Vienna, June 9, 2006.

Hostasch, Eleonore (Lore). Vice president of *Österreichischer Gewerkschaftsbund* (ÖGB) 1991–5. President of the Federal Chamber of Labor 1994–7. Minister of Labor and Social Affairs 1997–2000. Vienna, February 11, 2010.

Kienzl, Heinz. Head of the Economic Policy Department of *Österreichischer Gewerkschaftsbund* (ÖGB) 1950–68. First Executive Director of the Austrian National Bank 1973–88. First Vice President of the Austrian National Bank 1988–93. Vienna, June 7, 2006.

Kopf, Johannes. Member of the cabinet of the Minister of Economics and Labor 2003–6. Member of the executive board of the *Arbeitsmarktservice* 2006 to present. Vienna, February 11, 2010.

Lacina, Ferdinand. Head of Cabinet in the Federal Chancellery 1980–2. State Secretary 1982–4. Finance Minister 1986–95. Vienna, June 6, 2006.

Seidel, Hans. Professor of Economics. State Secretary in the Finance Ministry 1981–3. Vienna, November 23, 2007.

Streissler, Erich. Professor of Economics. Vienna, June 8, 2006.

Teufelsbauer, Werner. Employed at the Federal Economic Chamber 1967–2002. Head of the Department of Economic Policy 1994–2002. Vienna, June 5, 2006.

Tichy, Gunther. Professor of Economics. Vienna, November 22, 2007.

Vranitzky, Franz. Finance Minister 1984–6. Prime Minister 1986–97. Vienna, June 7, 2006.

Walterskirchen, Ewald. Economist at the Austrian Institute of Economic Research 1970 to present. Vienna, June 6, 2006.

Denmark

Andersen, Anders. Finance Minister 1973–5. Minister of Economic Affairs 1978–9 and 1982–7. Grenå, June 20, 2005.

Andersen, Bent Rold. Professor of Economics. Member of the Council of Economic Advisers 1973–8. Chairman 1976–8. Minister of Social Affairs 1982. Næstved, March 16, 2005.

Auken, Svend. Minister of Labor 1977–82. Leader of the Social Democratic Party 1987–2002. Copenhagen, June 21, 2005.

Christophersen, Henning. Leader of the Liberal Party 1978–84. Minister of Foreign Affairs 1978–9. Finance Minister 1982–4. Letter to the author (not dated).

Hassenkam, Henrik. Civil servant in the Finance Ministry and the Ministry of Labor 1973–83. Permanent Secretary in the Ministry of Labor 1983–94. Copenhagen, March 14, 2005.

Heinesen, Knud. Budget Minister 1973. Finance Minister 1975–9 and 1981–2. Copenhagen, March 18, 2005.

Hoffmeyer, Erik. Member of the Council of Economic Advisers 1962–5. Central bank governor 1965–94. Copenhagen, March 17, 2005.

Jakobsen, Svend. Minister of Taxation 1975–7. Finance Minister 1979–81. Taastrup, March 15, 2005.

Jørgensen, Anker. Prime Minister 1972–3 and 1975–82. Copenhagen, August 25, 2005.

Lykketoft, Mogens. Head of the Economic Council of the Labour Movement 1975–81. Minister of Taxation 1981–2. Finance Minister 1993–2000. Copenhagen, March 14, 2005.

Rosted, Jørgen. Civil servant in the Finance Ministry 1976–93. Copenhagen, March 18, 2005.

Schlüter, Poul. Prime Minister 1982–93. Frederiksberg, August 26, 2005.

Simonsen, Palle. Finance Minister 1984–9. Frederiksberg, March 16, 2005.

Thomsen, Jens. Civil servant in the Economic Secretariat and the Ministry of Economic Affairs 1971–94 (except for 1973–5). Head of the Ministry of Economic Affairs 1988–94. Deputy central bank governor 1995 to present. Copenhagen, March 18, 2005.

Zeuthen, Hans. Professor of Economics. Chairman of the Council of Economic Advisers 1978–83. Copenhagen, June 21, 2005.

Østergaard, Hans Henrik. Civil servant in the Finance Ministry 1973 to present. Copenhagen, March 14, 2005.

The Netherlands

Albeda, Wil. Minister of Social Affairs 1977–81. Telephone interview, April 21, 2006.

Andriessen, Frans. Finance Minister 1977–80. The Hague, March 22, 2006.

Bos, Marko. Deputy Director of Economic Affairs at the Social and Economic Council (SER). The Hague, November 20, 2007.

Kok, Wim. Chairman of the socialist trade union NVV 1973–76. Chairman of the trade union federation FNV 1976–85. Finance Minister and Deputy Prime Minister 1989–94. Prime Minister 1994–2002. Telephone interview, March 30, 2006.

Lubbers, Ruud. Minister of Economic Affairs 1973–7. Prime Minister 1982–94. Rotterdam, March 21, 2006.

Maas, Cees. Employed at the Ministry of Finance 1977–82. Treasurer General 1986–92. Amsterdam, November 20, 2007.

Margés, Hans. Economic and financial adviser to the prime minister in 1975–83. The Hague, March 22, 2006.

Ruding, Onno. Finance Minister 1982–9. Brussels, March 21, 2006.

Szász, André. Member of the Dutch central bank's executive board 1973–94. Telephone interview, April 18, 2006.

van Paridon, Kees. Professor of Economics. Rotterdam, November 21, 2007.

Wolfson, Dirk. Professor of Economics. Rotterdam, November 21, 2007.

Zalm, Gerrit. Deputy Director of the Central Planning Bureau 1988–9. Director of the Central Planning Bureau 1989–94. Finance Minister 1994–2002 and 2003–7. Amsterdam, February 8, 2010.

Sweden

Ahlmark, Per. Leader of the Liberal Party 1975–8. Minister of Labor 1976–8. E-mail message, January 4, 2003.

Andersson, Dan. State Secretary in the Ministry of Industry, Employment and Communications 1998–2000. Chief Economist at LO 2000–8. Stockholm, November 6, 2001; telephone interview, February 1, 2010.

Bergqvist, Jan. Member of parliament (social democrat) 1969–2002. Chairman of the standing committee on finance 1994–2002. Chairman of the central bank's governing board 2002–6. Göteborg, September 17, 2001.

Bergström, Villy. Professor of Economics. Member of the central bank's executive board 1999–2005. Stockholm, April 2, 2002.

Bildt, Carl. Prime Minister 1991–4. E-mail message, January 19, 2003.

Bäckström, Urban. State Secretary in the Finance Ministry 1991–3. Central bank governor 1994–2002. Stockholm, November 5, 2001. (Not recorded.)

Calmfors, Lars. Professor of Economics. Stockholm, October 16, 2001.

Carlsson, Ingvar. Leader of the Social Democratic Party 1986–96. Prime Minister 1986–91 and 1994–6. Stockholm, January 29, 2003.

Dennis, Bengt. Central bank governor 1982–93. Stockholm, October 26, 2001.

Edin, Per-Olof. Chief economist at LO 1984–2000. Stockholm, October 23, 2001.

Eklund, Klas. Employed in various capacities at the Finance Ministry and the Prime Minister's Ministry 1982–91. Stockholm, October 26, 2001.

Feldt, Kjell-Olof. Minister of International Trade 1970–6. Finance Minister 1982–90. Chairman of the central bank's governing board 1994–8. Stockholm, October 30, 2001; telephone interview, March 31, 2003.

Franzén, Thomas. Employed in various capacities at the central bank 1976–95. Deputy governor from 1989. Stockholm, October 17, 2001.

Fälldin, Thorbjörn. Leader of the Centre Party 1971–85. Prime Minister 1976–8 and 1979–82. Ramvik, May 2, 2002.

Hamilton, Carl B. Professor of Economics. State Secretary in the Finance Ministry 1993–4. Stockholm, November 5, 2001.

Hansson, Ingemar. Professor of Economics. Director of the Finance Ministry's Economic Affairs Department 1992–9. Director of the National Institute of Economic Research 1999–2006. Stockholm, August 14, 2002.

Heikensten, Lars. Deputy governor of the central bank 1995–2002. Governor 2003–5. Previously Director of the Finance Ministry's Economic Affairs Department (until 1992). Stockholm, August 16, 2002.

Henriksson, Jens. Assistant State Secretary in the Finance Ministry 1994–2002. State Secretary 2002–6. Stockholm, October 18, 2001. Not recorded.

Herin, Jan. Chief economist at the Swedish Employers' Confederation (SAF) 1987–2001. Stockholm, April 5, 2002.

Jakobsson, Ulf. Assistant State Secretary in the Finance Ministry 1976–82. Chief economist at the Swedish Employers' Confederation (SAF) 1982–7. Stockholm, March 6, 2002.

Jonung, Lars. Professor of Economics. Economic adviser to the prime minister 1992–4. E-mail message, February 24, 2003.

Karlsson, Jan O. State Secretary in the Finance Ministry 1985–8. Economic adviser to the Social Democratic Party 1992–4. Stockholm, August 29, 2001.

Larsson, Allan. Finance Minister 1990–1. Stockholm, October 30, 2001.

Lindbeck, Assar. Professor of Economics. Stockholm, April 5, 2002.

Lindgren, Ann-Marie. Head of the Swedish labor movement's think tank, *Arbetarrörelsens tankesmedja*. Telephone interview, September 29, 2009.

Lund, Gunnar. State Secretary in the Finance Ministry 1988–91. Minister for International Economic Affairs and Financial Markets 2002–4. Stockholm, May 6, 2003.

Lundgren, Bo. Minister of Taxation and Financial Markets 1991–4. Leader of the Moderate Party 1999–2003. Göteborg, November 13, 2002.

Lundgren, Nils. Professor of Economics. Saltsjö-Duvnäs, May 7, 2003.

Löfgren, Anna-Kirsti. Economist at LO, 2002 to present. Telephone interview, October 2, 2009.

Malm, Stig. LO chairman 1983–95. Stockholm, April 3, 2002.

Mundebo, Ingemar. Budget Minister 1976–80. Stockholm, April 4, 2002.

Olsson, Sten. Political adviser in the Prime Minister's Office 1998–2002. State Secretary in the Prime Minister's Office 2002–4. State Secretary in the Finance Ministry 2004–6. Stockholm, September 22, 2009.

Pagrotsky, Leif. Employed in various capacities at the Ministry for Economic Affairs and the Finance Ministry 1977–82, 1984–7, and 1990–1; State Secretary 1994–6. Minister in the Prime Minister's Ministry 1996–7. Minister of Trade 1997–2002. Minister of Industry and Trade 2002–4. Stockholm, May 8, 2003.

Persson, Göran. Finance Minister 1994–6. Prime Minister 1996–2006. Letter forwarded by Jan Larsson, Communications Director, on November 14, 2003.

Pettersson, Bengt. Economist at the National Institute of Economic Research (*Konjunkturinstitutet*) 1949–89. Stockholm, January 28, 2003.

Rosenberg, Irma. Economic analyst at the central bank 1976–87. Member of the central bank's executive board 2003–8. Stockholm, December 11, 2002.

Rydén, Bengt. Head of the Center for Business and Policy Studies (SNS) 1974–84. Telephone interview, September 10, 2002.

Sohlman, Michael. Swedish attaché to the OECD 1977–80. Economic adviser to the Social Democratic Party 1981–2. Employed in various capacities at the Finance Ministry 1982–7. Stockholm, October 31, 2001. Telephone interview, May 30, 2002.

Söderström, Hans Tson. Economist. Head of the Center for Business and Policy Studies (SNS) 1985–2002. Stockholm, October 23, 2001.

Westerberg, Bengt. Leader of the Liberal Party 1983–95. Minister of Social Affairs 1991–4. Stockholm, November 1, 2001.

Westerberg, Sten. State Secretary in the Budget Ministry 1976–9. State Secretary in the Ministry of Economic Affairs 1979–82. Stockholm, June 3, 2002.

Wirtén Rolf. Minister of Labor 1978–80. Budget Minister 1980–2. Minister of Economic Affairs 1981–2. Linköping, May 13, 2002.

Wohlin, Lars. State Secretary in the Ministry of Economic Affairs 1976–9. Central bank governor 1979–82. Stockholm, April 3, 2002.

Wästberg, Olle. State Secretary in the Finance Ministry 1991–3. New York City, December 5, 2000.

Åberg, Carl Johan. Assistant State Secretary in the Finance Ministry 1974–7. Economic adviser to the Social Democratic Party 1977–80. Stockholm, June 3, 2002.

Åsbrink, Erik. State Secretary in the Finance Ministry 1982–90. Finance Minister 1996–9. Stockholm, October 15, 2001, and January 29, 2003.

Åsling, Nils G. Chairman of the parliament's standing committee on finance 1974–76. Minister of Industry 1976–8 and 1979–82. Stockholm, August 21, 2002.

Öberg, Svante. State Secretary in the Finance Ministry 1994–7. Telephone interview, September 4, 2003.

Index

Keynesianism 33, 138, 192
  in Austria 141–2
  in Denmark 140–1
  in the Netherlands 54–5, 139–40
  in Sweden 141–3
Kienzl, Heinz 62–3, 122
Kok, Wim 102, 104, 175, 178
Koren, Stefan 62
Kreisky, Bruno 59–61, 66, 68, 123–4

labor market policy
  instruments of 9, 146
  see also active labor market policy,
    employment protection legislation,
    unemployment benefits
Labour Party, see social democrats
  (Netherlands)
Labour Foundation (Netherlands) 20, 102–3
Lacina, Ferdinand 66, 106–8
Larsson, Allan 111–2, 114, 138
liberal parties
  in Austria, see Freedom Party
  in Denmark 18–19, 40, 42, 45–6, 82,
    96–7, 154, 177
  in the Netherlands 18–19, 40, 82, 101,
    104–5, 158–9, 175, 178
  in Sweden 18–19, 68–70, 72, 113, 125–6,
    128
LO (Landsorganisationen i Danmark), see
  unions (Denmark)
LO (Landsorganisationen i Sverige), see unions
  (Sweden)
Lubbers, Ruud 57–8, 101–4, 140, 157, 177–8
Lund, Gunnar 113
Lykketoft, Mogens 49–50, 99–100

macroeconomic policy
  instruments of 9
  emergence of 15
Margés, Hans 54, 57
Meidner, Rudolf 165
Mitterrand, François 74, 95, 142
Moderate Party, see Conservative Party
  (Sweden)
monetary policy 25–7, 117, 134–6, 191
  instruments of 9
  in Austria 61–3, 65, 67
  in Denmark 43, 47–50, 58, 97, 100–1
  in the Netherlands 54, 58, 03
  in Sweden 69–78, 109, 111–6, 133,
    142–3
  see also central banks
Mundebo, Ingemar 71–2

Nationalbanken, see central banks (Denmark)
natural gas 52, 58, 79, 88–9
Nederlandsche Bank, see central banks
  (Netherlands)
neoclassical economic ideas 33, 95, 192
  in Sweden 143
Netherlands Bureau for Economic Policy
  Analysis 139–40
norms 12, 15–17, 21–3, 83, 130,
    179, 188
  defined 22
NVV (Nederlands Verbond van
  Vakverenigingen), see unions
  (Netherlands)

OECD (Organisation for Economic
  Co-operation and Development) 40, 44,
    53, 57, 87–9, 93, 95, 145, 192
ÖGB (Österreichischer Gewerkschaftsbund), see
  unions (Austria)
oil crisis
  first 39–40
  second 95
Olsson, Sten 169, 174–5
OPEC, see oil crisis
Österreichische Nationalbank, see central
  banks (Austria)

Pacifist Socialist Party (Netherlands) 17–18
Palme, Olof 73, 130
Parity Commission for Prices and Wages
  (Austria) 20, 67, 121–2, 124
party systems 10, 12, 17–19, 79–83, 93,
    117–9, 175–6, 187
  defined 17
  in Austria 18–19, 118–9
  in Denmark 19, 81–2, 117–8, 152
  in the Netherlands 19, 82, 117–8
  in Sweden 19, 119
Persson, Göran 128–9
political arrangements 10, 16–17, 79–85,
    117–32, 175–80
political parties, role of 31–2,
    181–2
population 5–6
postwar settlement 14–15, 79, 84
productivity 39, 147, 165
PvdA, see social democrats (Netherlands)

Radical Party (Netherlands) 51
Rehn, Gösta 165–6
Rosted, Jørgen 153–4
Ruding, Onno 101–2, 104, 140

Index